The Nested Games of Brexit

This book offers a novel perspective on the UK's withdrawal from the European Union, providing insights to the ways in that domestic concerns interact with European policy to produce sometimes counter-intuitive outcomes.

The 2016 decision by the United Kingdom to withdraw from the European Union was a seminal one for both political parties in the UK. This innovative volume considers the extent to which the interrelation between the national and the European arenas produced significant opportunities for reshaping political action. The nesting of these two levels matters, firstly in allowing for the mobilisation of domestic actors around European issues and secondly, in explaining why seemingly unimportant or counter-productive actions are taken. The tensions this generated reached a critical juncture with the referendum, a rupture that highlights the extent to which a nominally second-order vote can have fundamental impacts on the first order's preferences.

Bringing together scholars from a wide range of approaches and covering various aspects of the Brexit process, this book offers a significant contribution to improving our understanding of an event that will shape British and European politics for a generation.

The chapters in this book were originally published as a special issue of the *Journal of Contemporary European Studies*.

Agnès Alexandre-Collier is Professor of British Politics at the Université de Bourgogne, France.

Pauline Schnapper is Professor of British Politics at the Sorbonne Nouvelle, Paris.

Simon Usherwood is Professor of Politics & International Relations at the Open University, United Kingdom.

The Nested Games of Brexit

Edited by
Agnès Alexandre-Collier, Pauline Schnapper and Simon Usherwood

Routledge
Taylor & Francis Group
LONDON AND NEW YORK

First published 2022
by Routledge
4 Park Square, Milton Park, Abingdon, Oxon OX14 4RN

and by Routledge
605 Third Avenue, New York, NY 10158

Routledge is an imprint of the Taylor & Francis Group, an informa business

British Library Cataloguing in Publication Data
A catalogue record for this book is available from the British Library

ISBN: 978-1-032-27200-9 (hbk)
ISBN: 978-1-032-27202-3 (pbk)
ISBN: 978-1-003-29177-0 (ebk)

DOI: 10.4324/9781003291770

Typeset in Myriad Pro
by Newgen Publishing UK

Publisher's Note
The publisher accepts responsibility for any inconsistencies that may have arisen during the conversion of this book from journal articles to book chapters, namely the inclusion of journal terminology.

Disclaimer
Every effort has been made to contact copyright holders for their permission to reprint material in this book. The publishers would be grateful to hear from any copyright holder who is not here acknowledged and will undertake to rectify any errors or omissions in future editions of this book.

Contents

Citation Information vii
Notes on Contributors ix

Introduction – The nested games of the UK's EU referendum: ruptures, reconfigurations and lessons for Europe 1
Agnès Alexandre-Collier, Pauline Schnapper and Simon Usherwood

1 Brexit and Trump: contesting new cleavage formation 9
Chris Gifford

2 Brexit, nationalism and disintegration in the European Union and the United Kingdom 22
Ben Wellings

3 Labour and the Interplay of Brexit and Electoral Politics 35
Emmanuelle Avril

4 Post-Brexit nationalism: challenging the British political tradition? 51
Emma Bell

5 Theresa May, the Brexit negotiations and the two-level game, 2017–2019 68
Pauline Schnapper

6 From UKIP to the Brexit party: the politicization of European integration and disruptive impact on national and European arenas 80
Karine Tournier-Sol

7 The post-referendum reconfigurations of conservative cleavages around black and Asian minority ethnic MPs 91
Agnès Alexandre-Collier

8 Northern Ireland and Brexit: where sovereignty and stability collide? 105
Mary C. Murphy

9 Disintegration reversed: Brexit and the cohesiveness of the EU27 119
Thierry Chopin and Christian Lequesne

Index 132

Citation Information

The chapters in this book were originally published in the *Journal of Contemporary European Studies*, volume 29, issue 3 (2021). When citing this material, please use the original page numbering for each article, as follows:

Introduction

The nested games of the UK's EU referendum: ruptures, reconfigurations and lessons for Europe
Agnès Alexandre-Collier, Pauline Schnapper and Simon Usherwood
Journal of Contemporary European Studies, volume 29, issue 3 (2021), pp. 301–308

Chapter 1

Brexit and Trump: contesting new cleavage formation
Chris Gifford
Journal of Contemporary European Studies, volume 29, issue 3 (2021), pp. 309–321

Chapter 2

Brexit, nationalism and disintegration in the European Union and the United Kingdom
Ben Wellings
Journal of Contemporary European Studies, volume 29, issue 3 (2021), pp. 322–334

Chapter 3

Labour and the Interplay of Brexit and Electoral Politics
Emmanuelle Avril
Journal of Contemporary European Studies, volume 29, issue 3 (2021), pp. 335–350

Chapter 4

Post-Brexit nationalism: challenging the British political tradition?
Emma Bell
Journal of Contemporary European Studies, volume 29, issue 3 (2021), pp. 351–367

Chapter 5

Theresa May, the Brexit negotiations and the two-level game, 2017–2019
Pauline Schnapper
Journal of Contemporary European Studies, volume 29, issue 3 (2021), pp. 368–379

Chapter 6

From UKIP to the Brexit party: the politicization of European integration and disruptive impact on national and European arenas
Karine Tournier-Sol
Journal of Contemporary European Studies, volume 29, issue 3 (2021), pp. 380–390

Chapter 7

The post-referendum reconfigurations of conservative cleavages around black and Asian minority ethnic MPs
Agnès Alexandre-Collier
Journal of Contemporary European Studies, volume 29, issue 3 (2021), pp. 391–404

Chapter 8

Northern Ireland and Brexit: where sovereignty and stability collide?
Mary C. Murphy
Journal of Contemporary European Studies, volume 29, issue 3 (2021), pp. 405–418

Chapter 9

Disintegration reversed: Brexit and the cohesiveness of the EU27
Thierry Chopin and Christian Lequesne
Journal of Contemporary European Studies, volume 29, issue 3 (2021), pp. 419–431

Notes on Contributors

Agnès Alexandre-Collier, Centre Interlangues, Texte, Image, Langage (EA 4182), Université de Bourgogne Franche-Comté, Dijon, France.

Emmanuelle Avril, Centre for Research on the English-speaking World, Université Sorbonne Nouvelle, Paris, France.

Emma Bell, LLSETI, Université De Savoie Mont-Blanc, Chambéry, France.

Thierry Chopin, Université Catholique de Lille (ESPOL), Lille, France.

Chris Gifford, University of Huddersfield, UK.

Christian Lequesne, Sciences Po - CERI, Paris, France.

Mary C. Murphy, Department of Government and Politics, University College Cork, College Road, Cork, Ireland.

Pauline Schnapper, Centre for Research on the English-speaking World, Université Sorbonne Nouvelle, Paris, France.

Karine Tournier-Sol, Département d'anglais, UFR Lettres, Université de Toulon, Toulon, France.

Simon Usherwood, Department of Politics and International Studies, Open University, Milton Keynes, UK.

Ben Wellings, Monash University, Melbourne, Australia.

Introduction

OPEN ACCESS

The nested games of the UK's EU referendum: ruptures, reconfigurations and lessons for Europe

Agnès Alexandre-Collier, Pauline Schnapper and Simon Usherwood

ABSTRACT

The 2016 decision by the United Kingdom to withdraw from the European Union was a seminal one for both parties. In this special issue, we consider the extent to which the inter-penetration of the national and the European arenas produced significant opportunities for recasting political action. The nesting of these two levels matters firstly in allowing for the politicisation and mobilisation of domestic actors around European issues and secondly in explaining why seemingly sub-optimal or counter-productive actions are taken. The tensions this generated reached a critical juncture with the referendum, a rupture that highlights the extent to which a nominally second-order vote can have fundamental impacts on the first order's structure and preferences. Bringing together scholars from a wide range of approaches and covering various aspects of the Brexit process, this special issue offers a significant contribution to improving our understanding of an event that will shape British and European politics for a generation.

Introduction

On 23 June 2016, for the first time in its history, a member-state of the European Union chose by referendum to leave the organisation, making use of Article 50 of the Lisbon Treaty, adopted in 2007. While turnout was relatively high – reflecting the intensity of public engagement and political activity in the run up to the vote – the result saw the UK split almost equally between Leave and Remain options, with the 52:48% split raising as many questions as it answered and sending shockwaves across the continent.

The June 2016 referendum on the UK's membership of the European Union (EU) was a landmark political event, far beyond its nominal decision to reverse the pattern of post-WWII British engagement in international organisations. It was a turning-point in the history of the EU, which had until then seemed to be on a never-ending process of enlargement to new countries, not the other way round. As is becoming increasingly evident since the vote, the referendum was also the occasion for many other ruptures to emerge in the polity and politics of the country whilst in turn raising longer-term questions about a possible 'spill-back' and disintegration of the EU itself (Vollaard 2014; Rosamond 2016). In Britain, the vote has led, among other things, to unprecedented (at least since 1945) strains within the two main political parties, tensions in the union between the different nations of the UK, the apparent emergence of new cleavages among voters which mainstream parties struggle to represent and more generally a feeling that the political system can no longer be defined as the stable and predictable so-called Westminster model (Evans and Menon 2017; Baldini, Bressanelli, and Massetti 2018; Curtice 2020; Mattinson 2020; Sobolewska and Ford 2020).

Crucially, these changes and ruptures are interlinked, both overtly and implicitly. The ongoing endeavour of researchers to make sense of the fundamental change in British European policy cannot do so without recognizing that all of the other tensions listed above are not simply consequences of the referendum but also explanatory factors. At the core of the analysis offered in this special issue is a shared (if variously constructed) view that political actors sit within a set of nested games (Putnam 1988; Tsebelis 1990 and more recently; Schelkle 2019), where actions in any one arena are conditioned and rationalised by incentives and objectives in another. The 2016 referendum is as much – if not indeed more – a site for advancing agendas and preferences that have little or nothing to do with European policy as it is a moment of focused political and public debate on the question of 'Europe'. But this traffic is not just one way: the scale of the rupture caused by the referendum decision has also rippled back into those other games and arenas, resulting in a wider recasting of political action and objectives in the UK and beyond.

It is with this in mind that in this special issue, we consider the long-term effects of the politicisation of European issues in the UK, which started in the early 1990s with the Maastricht Treaty and climaxed with the 2016 referendum. We also stress the importance of identity/nationalist politics and cleavages in contemporary European debates, which have been a major factor in the referendum vote. We look at the nature of the dislocation and reconfiguration of the British political order which have been both a cause and consequence of the referendum. We draw together theoretical, comparative and applied examples to consider what has changed, but also why this has happened and what it means for the future path not only of the UK but also of the European integration project as a whole.

Theoretical approaches

Although we aim to contribute to the theoretical discussion around the Brexit referendum, we have chosen not to limit our framework to a specific approach. Our goal is also to widen the scope of the British approach and provide, when the occasion arises, a more international or comparative perspective. Indeed, our contributors have adopted several, sometimes overlapping frames. At the shared core of our analysis is the notion that the referendum and its aftermath represented the creation of a substantial and consequential new arena for political contestation in the UK which illustrated the new cleavages which have emerged around European integration and globalisation (Evans 1999; Hooghe and Marks 2018). As Reif and Schmitt (1980) remarked, European affairs used to be typically second-order, with political actors involved therein making decisions on the basis of satisfying national political priorities first and foremost. This in turn leads to behaviour in the European arena that might appear sub-optimal or counter-productive. With the multiplication of levels (subnational/national/EU/global) that potential for sub-optimal action increases, along with the likelihood of perverse outcomes.

The multiplication of arenas has already been addressed by scholars to analyse political actors' decisions in the light of the rational choice theory. More precisely, Putnam's classical two-level game, and especially Tsebelis' variation of it with the idea of 'nested games', provide us with a general framework to understand the various actors' strategies. This framework can help better understand how and why actors are sometimes viewed as acting rationally in one arena and irrationally in another. Tsebelis identified cases where an actor 'confronted with a series of choices does not pick the alternative that appears to be the best' (1990, 1) and therefore appears as non-rational – such as Theresa May's attitude in the Brexit negotiations in Brussels or Jeremy Corbyn's refusal to take a clear stance on Brexit for two years. However, in his view, optimal choices can only be assessed by the observer if s/he takes into account the different levels, or games, in which the actor is simultaneously involved: 'What appears suboptimal from the perspective of only one game is in fact optimal when the whole network of games is considered' (7). The EU referendum created a new game which is to be added up to all the other arenas in which actors usually operate. It is therefore necessary to adopt a more holistic approach, which does not ignore the wider context in which actors operate in order to be able to understand their strategies. This requires the observer to go beyond the immediate political environment – such as party politics and the territorial dimension in the UK – to possibly include more structural features such as the rise of nationalism and populism in the UK and in Europe (as well as the US), the role of the media in shaping a specifically anti-European political culture, etc.

The additional explanatory value of such an approach lies in its capacity to bring together a very disparate number of elements into a more structured and integrated whole. A weakness of other models has been to look for mono-causal explanations for attitudes, intentions and actions – utilitarian self-interest, ideology or party-political advantage being just three of the more common options – whereas a nested games approach allows for the incorporation of differentiated understandings and motivations among a connected set of actors. This is not to suggest that those mono-causal models have no value, but rather that while they might work well for some participants in a wide-ranging political event, they do not work uniformly well. Seen in this light, nested games permit individual actors to follow individual logics, without having to assume that all such logics are universally held, and in so doing they cast light on why particular approaches dominate for specific actors: Brexit becomes both an amplifier of predispositions and a source of change.

If such nested games provide a shared tool in our analyses for explaining the apparently paradoxical behaviour of many political actors, then it is also important to underline that there are limits even to this rationalisation. As much as we can draw attention to the presence of nested games in operation here, we cannot – and do not – advance an overall model of what those games might be or how they are nested within each other. A recurring theme of our contributors is the subjective construction of games and relationships between them by individuals and organisations. The constructed world of someone considering the notion of an Anglosphere is not the same as that of someone working on matters of devolution, and neither might be close to the incentives felt by a party-political leader in Westminster. The consequence is that political actors are not merely playing multiple games simultaneously, but are all playing different games, with limited overlap, centred on the referendum itself. This brings us back to the notion of Reif and Schmitt (1980) that 'European' events are more means than they are ends, but builds on it with the argument that those means can also reshape those ends.

Underlying this approach to agency are the central environmental and structural factors which shape the political actors' decisions. In the Brexit context, the key concepts of integration and disintegration, whether that of Britain or of the EU, are at the heart of this environment. On the latter, there is now a burgeoning literature. Douglas Webber (2014) and Hans Vollaard (2014) underlined before the UK referendum the multi-causal nature of possible disintegration, with domestic politics one important factor. Using Stefano Bartolini's model of polity formation, Vollaard argued that 'the external consolidation of the EU has remained rather weak, first of all in terms of the permeability of its boundaries. Entry of new Member States has been a common feature in the EU's history, while the Lisbon treaty even includes an exit clause' (9). He added that populations dissatisfied with the allocation of resources and welfare 'resist European integration and urge the closure of national borders to restore the congruence of participation, social sharing and cultural homogeneity within national states' (10). This relates to the post-functionalist approach which defines the conditions under which European issues become politicised and escape the control of mainstream parties (Hooghe and Marks 2009; Schimmelfennig 2014, 2018) and can provide explanations for the conditions under which disintegration might happen. Ben Rosamond (2016) identified shortly after the referendum the risk of the EU incrementally disintegrating as a possible effect of Brexit. In his perspective, disintegration would be a process leading to an unspecified outcome rather than an immediate outcome. Yet since the referendum the EU has proved more resilient than anticipated, with public opinion becoming more, not less, positive about the EU and governments maintaining a united front in the negotiation with the UK government. However, Leruth, Gänzle, and

Trondal (2019) argue that the dynamics of disintegration are more deeply seated than might be apparent from this seeming recovery, not least because Brexit is only one of the number of deep challenges faced by the EU at present, each going to the core of its efforts to provide effective outputs and affective belonging.

Similarly, in the UK there have also been a number of authors in the last few decades drawing attention to the fragile state of the union between the different constituting nations, which the differentiated results in the different parts of the United Kingdom have exacerbated. Tom Nairn's *The Break-Up of Britain* (1977) and *After* Britain as well as Linda Colley's *Britons: Forging the Nation* (1994), for instance, stressed the relative contingency of the union and the risk of its dislocation. The rise of Scottish (and to a lesser extent Welsh) nationalism was at first the main reason for it, but with the EU referendum the question of Ireland and its possible reunification has resurfaced as well (Greer 2018). The relative contingency of the union and the re-emergence of the English question are some of the most fascinating issues raised by the outcome of the referendum, not least because of the centrality of Englishness in the narrative of the Leave campaign (Henderson et al. 2017). In part, this comes back to the logic of the referendum itself, where a simple, UK-wide majority was the sole condition for success (in voting terms) and the relative size of England within the Union made it a much more consequential focus than had been the case in the logic of the devolution debate where the rights of the smaller nations had been paramount.

A critical juncture

The various works included here therefore raise the idea that rather than simply being a second-order game, the referendum was sufficiently important to create marked effects on the first-order game of national politics in the UK, not only in terms of political strategies and mobilisation but also through frames and narratives. It might well be that the referendum acted as a critical juncture, opening up new opportunities and incentives (Capoccia and Kelemen 2007; Soifer 2012; Meyer and Minkoff 2004). Thus, while British politicians (especially then Prime Minister David Cameron) and activists might have initially approached the referendum as a means to secure their previous objectives, the scale and scope of the decision has instead provided a point of rupture that changes what those objectives might be and how they might be achieved, as well as modifying the shape of domestic arenas and incentives in other EU member states. The referendum in effect reconfigures the national game that created it, as well as the European game in which it is embedded, even if the Brexit referendum has not led to an immediate unravelling of the EU.

At one level, this should not be a contentious idea: implicit in the notion of nested games is that there are iterated sequences of decisions in one or another arena that necessarily shape action and preferences in another. In its most Machiavellian conceptualisation, political actors use precisely such dynamics to force opponents into otherwise unwanted action by changing situations and facts on the ground: the Suez crisis of 1956 might serve as an example of how problematic this can be, from a nested perspective (cf. Richardson 1992). Such moves find their echoes in the accusations thrown about that several of the leading campaigners for Leave were motivated not by any ideological incentive, but rather by the sensing of an opportunity to advance themselves politically (see Shipman 2016, 2017 for the most insightful take on this). While Boris Johnson might have profited from that calculation, ultimately rising to become Prime Minister in 2019 and installing many of his erstwhile colleagues from Vote Leave around the Cabinet table, it is also clear that his time in office will be profoundly and unavoidably conditioned by the withdrawal process. That this can be written even as the UK, along with the rest of world, is working through the consequences of the COVID-19 pandemic and its enormous social, economic and political effects, sure merely underlines the case being made here: the knock-on effects of the referendum decision have now been compounded by the political choices that Johnson has made about the shape of the future UK–EU relationship.

And such effects are not limited to the UK. As much as the EU's attentions in the period since the referendum have been focused elsewhere – the migration crisis, the persistent weakness of the eurozone architecture and, more recently, coronavirus – the creation of a new pathway of action in withdrawal has evidently reshaped debate, not least with regard to populist parties and forces across the continent. Brexit may well be a cautionary tale, but ultimately, it speaks both to the compromises of membership and to the option to exit. Indeed, precisely because Brexit has been so difficult for British politicians to operationalise, space is left to eurosceptics elsewhere to argue that they would be able to avoid all the bear traps that the UK has fallen into, resulting in an exit with all the gains and none of the costs. That such a narrative has not yet emerged in other member states says more about the extent of British delay than it does about any effort by the EU to resolve the underlining conditions that facilitated the UK's decision in the first place.

One of the issues raised is whether these effects were already there and merely exposed by the referendum or whether the latter created them. In David Cameron's words (Oliver 2016), did the referendum mean 'unleashing demons', whose number and impact are only progressively becoming clear and therefore opened a new cycle in both European and British politics? Or did it reveal underlying trends which had been masked or neglected previously? What was structural and what was contingent in the process? As mentioned earlier, all of this also raises a question of agency: who shapes events and who is carried along by more powerful forces? To answer these questions, this special issue will try and disaggregate 'Brexit' – again thinking about the relation of structural and contingent factors – and recognise how its various elements operate within a series of interconnected and nested games.

Articles in the special issue

We bring together articles which look at the ruptures and reconfigurations triggered or revealed by the referendum from three main angles. The first four articles examine the political mobilisation and party dynamics that the referendum created in Britain.

Emmanuelle Avril looks at the case of the Labour Party post-2016 and shows how electoral politics found itself nested in the Brexit game, with Jeremy Corbyn trying not entirely unsuccessfully to straddle the two horses of accepting the referendum result and opposing the deal achieved by the May government. This enabled him to please – to a certain extent – his two constituencies of remainer MPs and leave voters, especially in the north of England.

In her article on the fate of UKIP, Karine Tournier-Sol starts from a post-functionalist perspective to identify the specific role played by the party as agent and producer of the politicisation of European issues in Britain. UKIP embodies the interaction between the national and European arenas, between first and second-order games. She then in turn shows how the Brexit vote impacted the party, which turned out to be a victim of the ruptures it had triggered, with a drop in its membership and standing in the polls and Nigel Farage's creation of a new Brexit Party, which again had a disruptive impact on the 2019 European and on the radicalization of the Conservative Party's stance on Brexit.

Agnès Alexandre-Collier's case study of the Conservative Party uses the lens of the ethnic minority MPs. This article thus takes a specific interest in Conservative Black and Asian Minority Ethnic (BAME) MPs who turned out to be more active on the 'leave' side of the referendum campaign. While it may have seemed illogical that so many Conservative BAME MPs made the suboptimal decision to support the 'leave' campaign and run the risk of losing supporters within their immigrant community, this decision actually makes sense, following Tsebelis' theory (1990) when one understands that BAME Conservative MPs, who are involved in 'nested games', have actually favoured other arenas (their party, their constituency), which, they believed, would deliver higher electoral payoffs.

Pauline Schnapper starts from the two-level game model developed by Putnam to understand Theresa May's apparently irrational 'red lines' in her negotiation with the EU between 2017 and 2019, to which she adds a discursive institutionalist approach. She stresses the constraints of domestic politics and the difficulty that she met when she attempted to follow two lines of negotiation in Brussels and London in parallel with a 'communicative' and a 'coordinative' discourse, to use Vivien Schmidt's typology. This could not, she argues, converge into a single successful outcome.

The second set of articles broadens the 'games' to include analyses of the external context in which British actors navigate. Chris Gifford compares the Brexit voters in the UK and Trump voters in the US. He qualifies the widespread but simplistic idea that a new social and political cleavage has appeared between nationalists/populists and cosmopolitans/liberals, also framed as losers and winners of globalisation in these two electorates. He shows that in political cultures that have been fragmented by globalisation, political identities are more fluid than what cleavage theory would suggest and that populists *create* more than they *reflect* these social/cultural differences, in particular the narrative of white working-class disadvantage.

Emma Bell compares the types of nationalism that have emerged during and since the referendum campaign among the Conservative and Labour parties. She contrasts the neo-liberal centralist British brand of nationalism now dominant among the Conservatives, heir to an older imperial one, to the economic community-based form of nationalism promoted under Jeremy Corbyn's leadership of the Labour Party. Yet the landslide victory of Boris Johnson's Conservative Party on 12 December 2019 followed by the election of Keir Starmer as the new leader of the Labour Party on 4 April 2020 have signalled ideological shifts which the COVID-19 pandemic crisis seems to have radicalised. The impact of external factors is therefore likely to be even stronger than expected.

The final group of articles further explores this structural dimension through the lens of contingency by covering the debate about integration and disintegration, both at the UK and EU levels. Mary Murphy, looking at the debate about Europe in Northern Ireland and the role played by the Irish border question in the negotiation with the EU, shows how the EU has become politicised in Northern Ireland, to an extent which was unimaginable before 2016. She underlines the frailty of the peace process and the dangers to peace posed by the referendum outcome and the challenge it represents to the place of Northern Ireland in the UK.

Ben Wellings argues that Brexit calls us to account for nationalist politics as an independent variable in the historic construction and deconstruction of the European Union. Nationalism, which European integration was meant to limit or even suppress, has grown and forces us to rethink the processes of EU dis/integration. This reconsideration is not without its problems, though, as the tropes of nationalism and of mythic communities across borders are forced to confront the harsh realities of global interconnection and interdependence. Ideas such as the Anglosphere might have been successful in mobilising Leave voters at the time of the referendum, but their ability to provide a course of political action that is either viable or even desired by all involved will become ever more critical in the coming years of the evolution of British foreign policy.

Finally, in their analysis of the post-2016 EU, Thierry Chopin and Christian Lequesne question the EU disintegration theory. Using the concept of cohesiveness, they stress the paradoxical cohesive effect of Brexit on the EU-27, including those whose preferences had aligned closely with those of Britain until then. This has led to less, not more, euroscepticism across the EU, as documented by opinion polls, and a united EU-27 front in the negotiations with the UK.

Taken together, the articles set out a vista across the multiple spaces and games that have characterised the Brexit process in its critical phase, and suggests a number of paths to be explored as it moves into the next stage of building a new EU–UK relationship. First and foremost, there is the question of the tension between choices made in favour of some option and those made in opposition. Much of the referendum campaign was informed by generic feelings of disempowerment ('taking back control') and disillusionment with how politics had become (especially from the 'left behinds' identified by Ford and Goodwin 2014). But rejection of the status quo is a far cry from an acceptance of any given alternative: the structural openness of the Leave proposition in the referendum, where campaigners would happily take any justification for voters to join them, has now had to move towards a crystallisation of a replacement policy. This special issue suggests that the viability of pre-existing narratives to succeed in such an environment is likely to be very variable and there consequently exists both a potential for new frames to arise and a possibility that none of them comes to provide adequate utility in addressing the public's concerns.

In any outcome, the changing operation of party politics, the devolution settlement, economic organisation and the EU–UK relationship itself will all produce a new environment for political actors that may in turn generate further instability. The ripples that the referendum produced in the water have already started to return back to recast and reshape incentives and preferences for all involved. With a timescale of several years before anything approaching a stable EU–UK relationship can emerge, our collective analysis points to a need for a long-term evaluation of the impact of Brexit on the British state and society, not to mention the EU itself, taking into account the mutating positions and characteristics of all involved. What we can say at this moment in time is that the future remains open to various paths, and the importance of engagement with this, as researchers and as citizens, is as strong as it ever has been.

Disclosure statement

No potential conflict of interest was reported by the author(s).

References

Baldini, G., E. Bressanelli, and E. Massetti. 2018. ""Who Is in Control? Brexit and the Westminster Model." *The Political Quarterly* 89 (4): 537–544. doi:10.1111/1467-923X.12596.

Capoccia, G., and R. D. Kelemen. "The study of critical junctures: Theory, narrative, and counterfactuals in historical institutionalism." *World politics* 59, no. 3 (2007): 341–369.

Colley, L. 1994. *Britons: Forging the Nation 1707-1837*. New Haven: Yale University Press.

Curtice, J. (2020), *Has Brexit Gone Off the Boil? Or Are the Embers of Brexit Still Glowing?* NatCen Social Research, disponible sur https://whatukthinks.org/eu/analysis/has-brexit-gone-off-the-boil-or-are-the-embers-of-brexit-still-glowing/

Evans, G., ed. *The end of class politics?:class voting in comparative context*. Oxford University Press, 1999.

Evans, G., and A. Menon. 2017. *Brexit and British Politics*. Cambridge: Polity Press.

Ford, R., and M. Goodwin. 2014. *Revolt on the Right: Explaining Support for the Radical Right in Britain*. Basingstoke: Routledge.

Greer, A. 2018. "Brexit and Devolution." *Political Quarterly* 89 (1): 134–138. doi:10.1111/1467-923X.12442.

Henderson, A., C. Jeffery, D. Wincott, and R. W. Jones. 2017. "How Brexit Was Made in England." *The British Journal of Politics and International Relations* 19 (4): 631–646. doi:10.1177/1369148117730542.

Hooghe, L., and G. Marks. "A postfunctionalist theory of European integration: From permissive consensus to constraining." British journal of political science (2009): 1–23.

Hooghe, L., and G. Marks. "Cleavage theory meets Europe's crises: Lipset, Rokkan, and the transnational cleavage." *Journal of European Public Policy* 25, no. 1 (2018): 109–135.

Leruth, B., S. Gänzle, and J. Trondal. 2019. "Exploring Differentiated Disintegration in a Post-Brexit European Union." *Journal of Common Market Studies* 57 (5): 1013–1030. doi:10.1111/jcms.12869.

Mattinson, D. 2020. *Beyond the Red Wall: Why Labour Lost, How the Conservatives Won and What Will Happen Next*. London: Biteback Publishing.

Nairn, T. 1977. *The Break-Up of Britain*. London: NLB.

Oliver, C. 2016. *Unleashing the Demons. The inside Story of Brexit*. London: Hodder & Stoughton.

Putnam, R. 1988. "Diplomacy and Domestic Politics: The Logic of Two-level Games." *International Organization* 42 (3): 427–460. doi:10.1017/S0020818300027697.

Reif, K., and H. Schmitt. "Nine second-order national elections–a conceptual framework for the analysis of European Election results." *European journal of political research* 8, no. 1 (1980): 3–44.

Richardson, L. 1992. "Avoiding and Incurring Losses: Decision-making in the Suez Crisis." *International Journal: Canada's Journal of Global Policy Analysis* 47 (2): 370–401. doi:10.1177/002070209204700207.

Rosamond, B. 2016. "Brexit and the Problem of European Disintegration." *Journal of Contemporary European Research* 12 (4): 864–871.

Schelkle, W. 2019. "Integration and Disintegration: Two-level Games in the EU." In *Diverging Capitalisms: Britain, the City of London and Europe*, edited by C. Hay and D. Bailey, 125–147. Basingstoke: Palgrave Macmillan.

Schimmelfennig, F. "European integration in the euro crisis: The limits of postfunctionalism." *Journal of European Integration* 36, no. 3 (2014): 321–337.

Schimmelfennig, F. 2018. "Brexit: Differentiated Disintegration in the European Union." *Journal of European Public Policy* 25 (8): 1154–1173. doi:10.1080/13501763.2018.1467954.

Shipman, T. 2016. *All Out War: The Full Story of How Brexit Sank Britain's Political Class*. London: HarperCollins UK.

Shipman, T. 2017. *Fall Out: A Year of Political Mayhem*. London: HarperCollins UK.
Sobolewska, M., and R. Ford. 2020. *Brexitland*. Cambridge: Cambridge University Press.
Soifer, H. "The causal logic of critical junctures." *Comparative political studies* 45, no. 12 (2012): 1572–1597.
Tsebelis, G. 1990. *Nested Games: Rational Choice in Comparative Politics*. Berkeley: University of California Press.
Vollaard, H. 2014. "Explaining European Disintegration." *Journal of Common Market Studies* 2014 (1): 1–18.
Webber, D. "How likely is it that the European Union will dis integrate? A critical analysis of competing theoretical perspectives." *European Journal of International Relations* 20, no. 2 (2014): 341–365.
Meyer, D., and D. Minkoff. "Conceptualizing political opportunity." *Social forces* 82, no. 4 (2004): 1457–1492.

Brexit and Trump: contesting new cleavage formation

Chris Gifford

ABSTRACT
The 2016 referendum on the UK's membership of the EU and the election of Donald Trump in the US are seen to have exposed fundamental social divisions and acute political antagonisms. While each reflected the idiosyncrasies of their domestic political scenes, these events pointed to transnational trends and developments that were shared across and beyond Anglo-America. In the Brexit and Trump votes, the anger and frustrations of being 'left behind' was considered to have translated into a politics of social conservatism, exclusive nationalism and populist anti-elitism. The forces of globalisation seemed to have split national communities into two distinct social worlds with irreconcilable interests and values. This article examines whether these significant political events can be explained in terms of cleavage formation. The evidence from the Brexit referendum and Trump election points to a complex picture of voting in which social groups express multiple and intersecting identities and experiences. The article emphasises the universalising processes of individualisation and fragmentation in globalised societies underlying new forms of political conflict. Finally, the article assesses the role of racism in generating political divides in contexts where identities are fractured and uncertain and a new politics of exclusion has taken hold.

The Brexit and Trump votes have been viewed as the clearest and most dramatic expression of new cleavages that are shaping social and political landscapes across globalised societies. The hallmark of this is seen to be social division and political polarisation that is challenging the fabric and cohesion of national communities. It is a divide believed to be rooted in the inequalities generated by economic globalisation but transcending traditional class relations and their left/right articulation to encompass divisions over values and cultural identities (Delanty 2017; Crouch 2017; Calhoun 2017; Inglehart and Norris 2017; Hooghe and Marks 2018). Characteristic of this is the rise amongst significant sections of society in support for populist, nationalist and xenophobic movements, parties and politicians, which direct their opposition to the perceived dominance of liberal elites and a cosmopolitan ethos. On this view, the forms of populist political mobilisation seen with the Brexit referendum and the election of Trump have their roots in the realities of people's lived experiences, their changing material conditions and their increasingly threatened identities.

A considerable amount of research and analysis has been brought to bear on the 2016 votes in the UK and US, much of which speaks to new cleavage formation. In their aftermath, academic analysis and informed media commentary turned its attention to groups considered to have been 'left behind' by the forces of economic globalisation; those who have seen their jobs gone overseas, their living standards eroded and their communities fractured by immigration (Goodwin and Heath 2016a, 2016b; Hobolt 2016b, McKenzie 2017). On this reading, the Brexit and Trump votes were a backlash and an attack on mainstream political parties and a metropolitan establishment that no longer represented, or even considered, their interests and concerns. Such explanations have been supported by the socio-demographic evidence from UK and the US that pointed to the relationship between being older, less qualified and on a lower income and supporting Trump or Brexit (British Election Study Team 2016; Goodwin and Heath 2016a; Turney et al. 2017). A key dividing line that received considerable attention both in the UK and the US was between graduates and non-graduates and how this plays out geographically in the divide between the metropolitan centres and post-industrial and rural 'backwaters' (Jennings and Stoker 2016; Pew Research Center 2016, McGill 2016). Both academic analyses and public commentary sought to present the factors underpinning the votes in terms of social binaries, which aligned with the polarised choices on offer to voters in both elections. In this sense, political polarisation was seen to mirror social polarisation.

Two works in particular seem to capture the Brexit and Trump zeitgeist. In the UK, political journalist and commentator, David Goodhart's (2017) *The Road to Somewhere* made a distinction between the 'citizens of anywhere' and 'citizens of somewhere', as the central divide characterising modern Britain. On the one side were the affluent cosmopolitan 'anywheres', comfortable with the dynamism and diversity of the modern world. They were mobile, having moved from they were brought up to go to university, and they valued autonomy and self-realisation over community and tradition. On the other side were the national 'somewheres' who experienced jobs going overseas, their living standards eroded and their communities fractured by immigration. They were less mobile and rooted to the towns and suburbs in which they had often grown up. They were nostalgic for a world that had been lost and regretted the passing of more traditional ways of life. As they witnessed globalisation and multiculturalism directly threaten their moral order, they became more intolerant and authoritarian in their views.

Meanwhile, across the Atlantic, following five years of ethnographic work in Louisiana, the sociologist Arlie Hochschild (2016a) appeared to capture a similar mindset amongst the typical Trump supporter. She spoke metaphorically of how those 'waiting in line' for the security and prosperity promised by the American dream had become resentful of those they considered as 'the line cutters'. Not only had they experienced long hours, redundancies, poor working conditions and reduced pensions but they now saw others, careerist women, immigrants, blacks, 'cutting in' front of them, whilst the federal government denied them the same opportunities. While published before the US Hochschild (2016b); Hochschild (2016c)) subsequently asserted that her work provided an in-depth explanation of the appeal of Trump amongst a white working class. Goodhart and Hochschild are examples of academics and public intellectuals who have received considerable media recognition as experts able to offer in depth explanations of Brexit and Trump (for example, Badger 2018; Wolf 2019). Such analyses have fitted with a widespread media framing that accepts the proposition that large sections of Western societies hold common and justifiable grievances that have been ignored by mainstream political elites.[1]

The Brexit result and the Trump election have been used to confirm both in academic and wider media commentary that societies are facing a critical juncture in which new political cleavages have taken hold. Cleavage theory (Lipset and Rokkan 1967; Bartolini and Mair 1990) traditionally understands party competition as the expression of underlying social divisions associated with the formation of closed groups defined in opposition to others. In modern societies, while such divisions have included religious affiliations, urban/rural conflicts, they have been dominated by a class cleavage. However, political scientists have also pointed to the declining role of these traditional social divisions in structuring individual choices and increased volatility in the relationship between social groups and political preferences. For some, this has coincided with the emergence of a new value based cleavage in the West, particularly associated with the expansion of education and expressed in an opposition between post-materialist and materialist values (Inglehart 1997). The Brexit and Trump votes can therefore be located within this longstanding debate over how political cleavages are constituted and being transformed. Moreover, as we have seen, both votes have specifically contributed to the growing appreciation of the autonomous role of globalization in cleavage formation, as Zürn and de Wilde note:

> Where the class cleavage resulted from the industrial revolution as political entrepreneurs employed liberal and socialist ideologies to successfully mobilize significant parts of society, globalization as the next 'societal revolution' could generate its own cleavage if—again—political entrepreneurs mobilize both winners and losers. (Zürn and de Wilde 2016, 281)

Globalisation takes on a significance in relation to cleavage formation because it erodes the national protections of social classes directly transforming their material interests, whilst simultaneously reconfiguring values by uprooting and challenging traditional cultural systems (Giddens 2003). In particular it is the rise of populist politics that signals a transformation in cleavage formation as these parties 'articulate a new *structural conflict* that opposes globalisation "losers" to globalisation "winners " ', which can takes the form of opposition to economic and cultural and political processes of denationalization (Kriesi 2014, 369). While growing economic inequality and dislocation is a key driver, it is the value dimension that arguably has been fundamental to formation of new political cleavages. Inglehart and Norris (2017, 446) for instance locate the immediate causes of the rise of Trump and populist parties in terms of a cultural backlash and value orientations that can cut across economic lines and draws people together in opposition to immigration.

Taken together with the general rise of populist parties, the Brexit and Trump votes seem to confirm the reemergence of cleavage politics in Western societies reversing the trend towards social fragmentation and the erosion of the cleavages that were typical of industrial society. From such a perspective, deep structural divisions were at work in the Brexit referendum and Trump election that transcended context specific political orientations. Nevertheless, to be consistent with cleavage theory, it is important to recognise that 'the translation of social conflict into political and party alternatives – turns out to be quite fraught and complex' (Mair 2005, 371). Mair's (2005) influential theory of cleavage formation points to three distinct components that are necessary before we can speak of a new cleavage. A clear social division needs to exist that is then normatively reproduced in terms of specific values and identities, which in turn is politically organized in the form of a political party or movement. Mair's (2005, 373) criteria for cleavage formation are appropriately demanding including a shared social experience, a collective sense of identity and a common value system.

The Trump/Brexit votes raise key questions about the relationship between social structure and collective identity formation and political outcomes. The mounting evidence of a value divide in contemporary politics, documented for some time, has not shown conclusively that this is the expression of coherent social groups with distinct cultural identities. Bornschier (2009, 6–7) notes that value differences are still relatively young and we do not know whether they will have the same persistence as class and religious cleavages. Drawing on Blühdorn and Butzlaff's (2019) rethinking of populism, a central proposition of this article is that coherent collective identity formation remains inconsistent with processes of differentiation and fragmentation that characterises contemporary social change. From this perspective, the Brexit and Trump votes occurred in a context where processes of globalized modernisation render individual and collective values and interests increasingly inconsistent and volatile and their articulation and organization profoundly challenging (Blühdorn and Butzlaff 2019, 200). Global capitalism demands flexible, self-responsible and disciplined workers who in turn expect to pursue consumption based projects of self-realisation, as they are freed from the constraints, and security, of traditional settings (Blühdorn and Butzlaff 2019, 201–2). The rise of the populist right is fueled by the core dilemma of late modernity, which is the continued expectation of consumer-based lifestyles and forms of self-realisation in contexts where access to the necessary organizational and material resources are increasingly restricted. As such right wing populist movements are not rejecting the achievements of modernization but are primarily concerned about not being able to sustain their historically privileged access to them. In so doing they look to re-appropriate democracy for their particular ends by organizing 'societal inclusion into the politics of exclusion; they secure the democratization of exclusion and thus help to maintain – for those included – our freedom, our values and our lifestyles' (ibid: 204).

On this view, the attempts to locate the Brexit/Trump votes in broad social groups with distinct values and interests – somewhere/nowhere, nationalists/cosmopolitans, winners/losers – is problematic in political cultures that have been fragmented and individualised by globalisation. The article therefore proceeds by examining the Brexit/Trump votes in terms of intersecting identities, diverse status conflicts and fluid political identities that do not lend themselves to the kinds of coherent collective identities that historically gave rise to consistent political cleavages. Populism is perfectly suited to this individualized politics because it provides 'empty signifiers' such as 'the people' and 'the nation', which can be filled with any array of phenomena depending on the specifics of a political context as long as they effectively trigger individual concerns and grievances. In this regard, the article examines the crucial role of race and immigration in mobilizing support for Brexit and Trump.

Brexit, Trump and social divisions in late modern societies

In the immediate aftermath of both the US election and UK referendum, survey analysis seemed to confirm the idea that on both sides of the Atlantic, each side of the divide shared common social characteristics. Typically, the Clinton/Remain voter was considered to be younger and better educated in contrast to the older, white, low skilled Trump/Leave supporter (Ashcroft 2016; British Election Study Team 2016; Pew Research Center 2016). The dominant explanations therefore looked to socio-economic position, based on education and occupation, but intersected with other factors such as age. Nevertheless, such explanations have not stood up to close scrutiny. In the case of Trump, exit polls showed his supporters had a median income of 72,000 USD significantly above the US figure, and that he won the majority amongst the white college educated (CNN 2016). Metzgar (2016) pointed out that college educated whites made up 30% of the white population but 40% of Trump supporters. In the UK, drawing on a mix of high quality data sources, Swales (2016) claimed that while the largest percentage group voting for Brexit were indeed those who are economically deprived, the second largest group making up almost double the percentage of the population (23% to 12%) were affluent Eurosceptics with an average age of 47. Antonucci et al. (2017, 225) found no association between identifying as working class and voting leave and that many intermediate groups were as likely to vote leave as those on lower incomes. Swales' conclusion is that the coalition that delivered Brexit was far broader than that of the 'left behind'. Dorling and Tomlinson (2019) present a strong case that the Leave result was decided by the large numbers of middle-class voters in the South and Midlands of the England.

The intersection of socio-economic position with age and education has also been central to the analysis of the votes. Lord Ashcroft (2016) polls based on surveys on referendum day showed disproportionate support for Remain from the young and educated including 81% of those in full time education, whereas a large majority of those whose education ended at secondary school voted to leave. However, Antonucci et al. (2017) argued that the relationship between higher levels of education and the lower likelihood of voting leave in the UK's referendum was not linear, as those with higher grades at GCSE and A-levels were more likely to vote leave. Moreover, the criteria for being classed as 'educated' has changed over time considering that older groups who left school at 18 with 'A' levels would have done so in a context when going to university was the privilege of a small minority (less than 15% up until 1990). The simple divide between those with and without degrees masks the considerable educational differences within groups without degrees as well as amongst degree holders. Evidence of young graduates in low-skilled occupations in the UK (Jennings and Stoker 2017, 363), carrying considerable debt burdens, points to precarious economic circumstances and opportunities for a significant number in the UK. In the US, growing evidence points to the relative disadvantage of recent generations compared to previous ones as a result of the considerable increase in the student debt burden, where the consequences are delayed homeownership, marriage and parenting (Mezza, Ringo, Sherlund and Sommer 2016). Neither is the association between age and values conclusive. For example, analyses of long-term trends in the UK do not support the idea that young people are becoming more socially liberal than previous generations (Grasso et al. 2019). Being younger remains a considerable source of disadvantage in both the UK and US, particularly when it intersects with factors such as race and class, and the positioning of younger age groups on the side of globalisation's 'winners' is problematic to say the least. Younger people are by far the least likely to vote and often face systemic barriers to their registration.

The social categories such as class, age and education used to explain both the Brexit and Trump vote are particularly sensitive to the complexity of place. Graduates in 'low skilled communities' were more likely to vote for Brexit and those with A' levels had similar voting patterns to the low skilled (Goodwin and Heath 2016a). Much has been made of the divide in the UK between university cities and towns and the rest the country, however this is only the case for those cities that can be described as highly metropolitan. Savage (2015) argues that it is the specific university attended and the geographical location that sustains elitism within higher education, as it is 'the elite institutions which hold the glittering prizes' Savage (2015, 257). World-class institutions in affluent cosmopolitan towns and cities operate as hubs for the attainment of cultural capital and the reproduction of privilege but are far from typical of mass higher education in both the UK and the US.

The national framing of the social demographics of the Trump/Brexit votes, even if the nation is understood as divided regionally,[2] cannot address this specificity of place (Evans 2017). Walley (2017) notes how Hochschild's participants' views were refracted through their Cajun ethnic identities and their opposition to what they saw as the corrupt Louisiana government. Hochschild's participants turned enthusiastically to Trump, consistent with their deep conservatism and history of white supremacism, which contrasted with Walley's own study of the working class in the Calumet 'rust belt' region of Southeast Chicago and northeast Indiana. She found little evidence of support for Trump during the primaries. Clinton's victory in the popular vote reflected continued working class support, but declining voter turnout also suggested that significant numbers were not motivated to turn out to support her, enabling Trump to succeed in areas previously held by the Democrats. In the referendum, just over a quarter (28%) did not vote, not much lower than in general elections, and this was particularly the case in areas where Remain support was stronger (Dorling and Tomlinson 2019, 536).

From a closer reading of Hochschild's ethnography, the sharp divide between the college educated appeared less clear-cut than it at first appeared. Walley (2017, 333) noted that 'tellingly' half of those in Hochschild's study were college educated with some sharing liberal concerns over corporate responsibility and environmental degradation. Walley pointed to 'a demographic reductionism that distracted attention from other competing factors at play and from the multiple ways that class is constituted' (2017, 235). In certain respects, one would expect this to be challenged by ethnographic studies that look to address the deeper causes of Brexit and Trump such as those identified by Hochschild in the US and Evans (2017) and Mckenzie (2017a, 2017b) in the UK. Yet while providing rich and often fascinating insights into people's lived experience, the use of the category of class, particularly working class, is arguably over-generalised to the point of reproducing simplistic binaries. For example, Mckenzie informs us that, 'since June 2016 and the referendum result elites in the political classes as well as middle-class "cosmopolitans" appear to have no grasp or awareness in acknowledging working-class experience, or to have any reflexivity of their own historical or present politically privileged positions' (2017b: 268). The white working-class marginalization thesis seems therefore to point to a self-conscious group with a shared experience and common grievances. Yet the category of 'white working class' renders invisible how these experiences are intersected by other identities and positions to do with factors such as age, gender and disability.

The fragmentation of social classes, and their communities, and the intensification of intersectional differentiation have resulted in 'a categorical transformation and radicalisation of social inequalities' (Beck 2007, 686). Standing (2016) for example has pointed to the precarity of contemporary work, which cuts across traditional occupation hierarchies. The rise of the precariat illustrate how globalization has disorganized work and the economy, undermining social institutions that provided security and belonging, whilst simultaneously exhorting individuals to self-actualize as fully autonomous beings. In his examination of Brexit's 'left behind' constituency, Watson points to the neo-liberal redrawing of the social contract 'moralises enhanced personal autonomy rather than social inclusion' 'reminding people of their responsibility to remake themselves in the image of the ideal economic subject if they expect to be able to activate their rights as citizens' (Watson 2018, 22). Responsibility for the economy has been contracted out to individuals while global capitalism has been systematically deskilling or automating jobs, polarising workforces and producing dramatic increases in income inequality alongside wage stagnation. It is not that people have been left and excluded from globalization but that they have actively participated in the reconstitution of 'their' national economies in line with its demanding imperatives 'only to find that that the rewards of the new social contract are entirely illusory' (ibid: 28). This particularly relates to those amorphous groups who have collectively been referred to as the 'squeezed middle'. Antonucci et al. (2017, 225) found that what was typical of leave voters was a 'specific negative feeling – *the feeling of being worthless* – that could be interpreted as a failure in managing risks of globalization' (ibid). In this respect, people's perception of their economic insecurity and worth takes on a significance that may not necessarily reflect their material realities but is meaningful nonetheless. In the US despite a strong economic recovery since the Great Recession, Republican voters remained pessimistic about the economy and believed their own financial position had worsened under Obama (Sides, Tesler, and Vavreck 2019, 590).

By definition the Brexit referendum and the Trump elections offered citizens binary choices and exemplified continued political polarisation within both countries. However, both events have also pointed to the complex relationship between political palorisation and social structure that does not lead to any straightforward conclusions regarding the relationship between social division, collective identity, political expression and organization. There remains something about both the Trump and Brexit votes that makes them difficult to read. Dorling and Tomlinson (2019, 536) noted that it was remarkable how little was known about what actually happened years after the referendum. The 'freezing' of cleavages such as class and religion in the twentieth century implied a coherence in the relationship between social and the political, which under the conditions of late modernity has significantly fractured. In contexts of social dislocation and fragmentation, the politicization of race and immigration, with its polarizing effect on electorates, took on a particular importance during both UK referendum and the US election.

Racism and political polarisation

A significant framing of the votes that has proved especially controversial is race and immigration. Both academic and media accounts of the votes focused on the relationship between experiences of socio-economic disadvantage and opposition to immigration. Hochschild's Southern Americans and Goodhart's UK 'somewheres' experience their own loss of status and opportunity in direct relation to the perceived advantages that they believe have accrued to minorities and migrants as a consequence of policies such as affirmative action and multiculturalism. Eatwell and Goodwin (2018) have argued that the growth of national populism reflects legitimate concerns held by people whose identities continue to be rooted in the nation as an ethical community. They argue that 'we need to appreciate how people feel' considering they are 'intensely anxious about recent high levels of immigration and ethnic change, which they see as damaging the nation' Eatwell and Goodwin (2018, 281). The focus on white marginalisation as the explanation is problematic considering that ethnic minorities experience far greater disadvantage in the UK and US. As Bhambra points out:

> The difference between minorities and majorities expressing group sentiments is that the sentiments of the former arise in the context of a wish for inclusion and equality, while those of the latter are a consequence of a wish to exclude and dominate Bhambra (2017a, 220)

Bhambra (2017a) argues that a 'methodological whiteness' has distorted accounts of the votes, legitimating demands for the 'restoration' and defence of privileged forms of material and cultural belonging.

Nevertheless, to place race at the centre of explanations of the Brexit and Trump votes risks simply overlaying explanations of social and political binaries with the categories of race and ethnicity. As such new cleavage formation is racialised: open, progressive cosmopolitans are pitied against anti-immigrant, exclusive nationalists. On this reading, voters who turned out for Trump did so because of their latent sympathies with white supremacy (Coates 2017), while Brexit was motivated by a deep-rooted colonial racism (Virdee and McGeever 2018: 8). Yet explanations in terms of structural racism has to be aligned with the complex evidence on issues of race and immigration that characterised both votes. When considering the Trump election, al Gharbi (2018, 4) argues that there 'is a powerful *a priori* case for doubting deterministic narratives about the role of race and racism' because of a general methodological unreliability. In the case of Trump' victory, al-Gharbi argues that there has been a systemic representation of Trumps' supporters as white supremacists that is not supported by the evidence. Countervailing evidence includes the stagnant turnout and lower vote share amongst whites compared to Mitt Romney in 2012, which meant Trump's success depended on a larger share of votes from Asians, Hispanics and African Americans (Al Gharbi 2018, 8). Moreover, many of the electorate who voted for Trump had voted for Obama in 2008 and 2012 whose popularity on leaving office was the highest it had been in his second term. Al Gharbi notes that while race was undoubtedly a critical factor in the election, it is very difficult to make 'sweeping generalizations about white people on the basis of these votes' (al-Gharbi 2018: 6). In the case of Brexit, a significant majority of UK citizens reported being in favour of EU migrants staying in the UK, including those who had voted to leave (Katwala, Rutter and Ballinger 2016). A British Future report, based on citizens panels held across the UK, concluded that people had 'moderate and constructive views and see both the pressures and gains of migration' (Rutter and Carter 2018). While immigration seemed to dominate the Brexit campaign and its immediate aftermath, the issue subsequently faded as the negotiation process progressed.

The framing of the UK and US as racist societies can assume the institutional reproduction of homogenous and exclusive ethnic identities. Yet, when looked at comparatively, the US and the UK have lacked the cultural homogeneity and traditions of exclusive ethnic citizenship that was typical of European models of nation-state building. In the case of the US, white majority rule was not rooted in a shared culture. As Danielle Allen notes, the moves to end segregation between 1954 and 1967 not only dissolved the idea of a distinct and inferior 'durable minority' but in so doing disbanded the idea of a 'durable majority', 'which had long erased differences among a variety of Eastern Europeans, as well as other "white", ethnicities in opposition to "black"' Allen (2004, 163). Consequently, Allen reframes the problem of American citizenship more broadly than race as one of corrosive mistrust, insecurity and self-interest, which can only be healed by cultivating the confidence and agency to claim one's political majority by 'talking to strangers' Allen (2004, 168). The extensive diversity of US society means that understandings of national citizenship rooted in notions of one people are fundamentally unstable in their failure to address difference.

The post-segregation experience of citizenship in the US has parallels with a post-imperial UK. As Bhambra points out 'British citizenship emerged in – was configured by – the multiracial and ethnolinguistically plural context of empire and Commonwealth' (2017b, 96). The UK was not and never has been a nation-state. It was an Empire, and Commonwealth, and a multi-national state consisting of four separate nations. The UK, colonies and Dominions operated a de facto common citizenship (formally subjecthood) until after the Second World War, when attempts began to restrict citizenship in terms of British nationality. The 1948 British Nationality Act limited citizenship to the UK and the colonies but allowed for extensive rights for Commonwealth citizens to migrate to the UK. In effect, Britain as a global power operated a policy of free movement for colonial and Commonwealth citizens. However, growing concerns about 'coloured immigration' in the 1960s saw restrictions introduced under the Commonwealth Immigrants Acts of 1962 and 1968. The process of defining national citizenship in the UK has been an *ad hoc* process that increasingly placed restrictions on black and Asian immigration from the New Commonwealth countries. It was not associated with nation building but a gradual reversal of a policy of Empire and Commonwealth free movement without any coherent conception of national citizenship. As Brubaker noted 'while other countries were debating the citizenship status of immigrants, Britain was debating the immigration status of citizens Brubaker (1989, 11). The problem in UK has been the difficulty of institutionalizing and constituting an exclusive national community in contexts of diversity and differentiation as a consequence of the legacy of a multi-cultural, multi-national empire.

The claims of a recent upsurge of English nationalism should be viewed in this context (Calhoun 2016, 2017; Jennings and Stoker 2016; Virdee and McGeever 2017). In a number of explanations Brexit has been viewed as a turning point at which the historical absence of a strong sense of English nationhood and national identity (Kumar 2006) has been challenged. Henderson et al. (2016) claim to have identified a strong link between Euroscepticism and an exclusive Englishness and concluded that the referendum campaign was creating a politicised English national identity. Calhoun argued those who had supported leave were not simply voting against the European Union but 'for English nationalism' (2017 loc 1601). Virdee and McGeever saw Englishness to be the 'invisible driver of Brexit' (2017: 3). This English nationalism is considered to be profoundly reactionary, rooted in the past and nostalgia for Empire (Calhoun 2017, Virdee and McGeever 2017), and to have particularly taken hold amongst disadvantaged 'backwater areas' amongst those who were 'socially conservative and fear change, immigration and global dynamics' (Jennings and Stoker 2016, 381). Nevertheless, the search for new cleavage formation in English nationalism is problematic. There remains no distinct English movement or political party that has proved able to garner popular support (Mycock 2013). High levels of economic inequality, ethnic diversity and regional differentiation characterise England and provide little basis to mobilise a common identity rooted in shared notions of the national community. Indeed, for large sections of the English population in cosmopolitan cities, it has very little meaning or is viewed as threatening because of its racist overtones, as in the case of those who identify as British Asian and Black British. In sum, Brexit has not ushered in a newly confident and coherent English nationalism.

The challenge in the Brexit/Trump era is to understand the politics of difference *within* dominant identities that have been mobilised in terms of their 'oneness' in opposition to 'others'. Racism is a case in point as it articulates in complex ways in formally democratic societies where civic integration can lead to complex and changing conceptions of an individual's social worth and citizenship status (Lockwood 1996). Soysal for example points to the de-nationalisation of immigration policy in European states:

> Integration, as conveyed by these national- and European-level frameworks, is not a nation-centered project. It is not posed as a process of confirming or furthering national collectivity and identity. Instead, the thrust is on the individual immigrants' capacities and efforts to take part productively in the rights and institutions offered in the system. (2012, 11)

In individualised, neo-liberal societies in which direct discrimination is legally prohibited, everyday racism and discrimination more readily takes the form of judgements of social worth with reference to factors such as language skills, welfare claiming and criminality. The more direct and explicit expressions of racist nationalism during the Trump and Brexit campaigns could be seen as a reversal of this trend, but this is to misunderstand its specificity. In both the US and the UK, the mainstream right has experienced a declining share of the national vote, ideological divisions with the main parties and the rise of parties that threaten to split its vote, such as the United Kingdom Independence Party (and now the Brexit Party) in the UK.

What was notable about the election of Trump as Presidential candidate was his willingness to reverse the Republican leaderships and exploit negative attitudes to immigration amongst white Republicans. In particular, he targeted Muslims and Mexicans in order to mobilise longstanding racist attitudes within the party base, which moderate party leaders had chosen to ignore (Sides, Tesler, and Vavreck 2019). He particularly capitalised on the polarising effect of the Obama Presidency in which for certain sections of US society economic outcomes under a black President were understood in racialised terms, so that their experience of disadvantage was expressed in relation to the perceived government assisted advantages accruing to ethnic minorities. Trump's willingness to repeat Birtherist conspiracy theories was significant in this respect. The claim that Obama's presidency was ineligible because he was born outside of the US and was in fact a secret Muslim intent on undermining America from within became powerful in mobilising the Conservative right during the Obama years. It symbolised the extent to which power and privilege was accruing to those who were not true American citizens.

What was distinctive about the Trump strategy and the nature of the 2016 campaign was the extent to which exclusive identities and racist sentiments were mobilised. It was not the case that these identities and attitudes had changed much in aggregate but that they were made to matter more than they had in previous elections (Sides, Tesler, and Vavreck 2019, 6–7). People were made to feel that their racism was valid and that issues such as Mexican immigration were of fundamental national importance. This was not without risks as it potentially alienated white voters who did not want to be seen as racist. In this regard the often very vocal support of groups such as 'Blacks for Trump' and 'Latinos for Trump' took on a symbolic significance in countering accusations of racism. Hence, despite its low vote share amongst non-whites, the Trump campaign actively pursued sections of the black and Latino communities. His courting of Kanye West was similarly played out in front of the media helping to challenge accusations of white supremacist sympathies.

Similarly, in the UK there was no evidence that people had become more racist by the time of the referendum. A recent British Social Attitudes (Harding 2017, 9) Report concluded that 'although attitudes towards immigration may have polarised, it is not clear that people have become more concerned about immigration' and that between 2002 and 2014 attitudes towards immigration had become more positive.[3] As in the case of the US, it was the activation and mobilisation of racist attitudes and anti-immigrant sentiment by key political actors that proved decisive. Crucial to this was the politicisation by United Kingdom Independence Party of the free movement of EU citizens that significantly contributed to their topping the national vote in the 2014 European elections. UKIP activated racist and anti-immigration sentiments against other white Europeans bringing to the fore, an issue that had barely registered amongst voters in the past. Moreover, its rise destabilised David Cameron's attempt to pivot the Conservative party to the centre ground and emboldened hardline ideological Eurosceptics and pressurised Cameron into supporting a referendum on UK membership of the EU. The ability of UKIP to influence the Conservative party highlighted the historical symbiotic relationship between the mainstream and extreme right in the UK. The eclipsing of the National Front by the early 1980s was a direct consequence of the decision of the Conservative party under Margaret Thatcher to use race for electoral purposes and went on to introduce the 1981 British Nationality Act that made it harder for non-white ethnic minorities to secure British citizenship. Uniting the right of the Conservative party with the extreme right has been the ideological legacy of Enoch Powell, who despite his ostracism by the Conservative leadership, successfully placed anti-immigration and Euroscepticism at the centre of right-wing nationalism in the UK. Powellism offered an ideological legitimacy to the Conservative right and has been strategically deployed in the face of threats from far-right parties to its electoral base. Attempts to move the party to the centre ground have consequently resulted in Powellite rebellions within the party and provided opportunities for extreme right parties and movements. The re-positioning of the Conservative party as a hard Brexit party, firmly opposed to free movement and any relationship with the EU, was a shift in a Powellite direction, which had the desired effect of eclipsing UKIP.

The political constitution of an ethnic majority within the UK has been a mode of domination to position non-white minorities and more recently other white Europeans as inferior and other. Nevertheless, as a form of representation it is inherently unstable and has been politically constituted for specific purposes. This exposes the more fundamental conceptual problem with interpretations of the Trump/Brexit votes as the manifestation of 'real' common identities that have in some ways been silenced by a liberal consensus. The assumption of a coherent majority national culture is problematic in contexts of globalised societies that experience high levels of internal differentiation and fragmentation. Within contexts of super-diversity, racism has to be perpetuated in amorphous and subtle ways, drawing and redrawing hierarchies of citizens and non-citizens in terms of oppositions such as good and bad migrants, established versus new minorities. Hence while populists will perpetuate an essentialist ethno-nationalist racism, they also subvert these discourses and resist accusations of racism to broaden their appeal. Eatwell and Goodwin (2018, 76–77) point to UKIP's opposition to European migration, while Nigel Farage would appear on stage 'flanked by ethnic minority supporters' and praise the contributions of immigrants from the Commonwealth. This played to a longstanding Eurosceptic idea that the UK's turn to Europe had been a betrayal of its Commonwealth citizens. Many leave voting areas had significant South Asian populations who arguably were attracted by the pro-Commonwealth rhetoric and considered Leave's anti-immigrant stance as not directed at them but at East Europeans (Ehsan 2017).

As affluent societies face significant challenges to their economic, ecological and cultural sustainability questions over who has and has not access to resources, demands for the resumption of lost privileges and protection of existing ones has become paramount. A key feature of this late modern politics of privilege is that it is individualistic and moralistic. In the both the UK and US, economic anxiety was translated into what Sides, Tesler, and Vavreck (2019, 318) refer to as 'racialised economics' which was highly moralised. On this view a raft of different ethnic groups could be seen to be accruing privileges and advantages that are undeserved such as access to welfare, jobs and the country itself, and if they were poor and marginalised this was not the result of discrimination but viewed as a failure to integrate or work hard. Contra the cultural backlash thesis, this politics of racial exclusion allows individuals, privileged and underprivileged, to reaffirm their commitment and adherence to the norms and values of 'self-realisation, self-expression and political self-determination' (Blühdorn and Butzlaff 2018: 205).

However, it is also indicative of the how the politics of exclusion is not reducible to issues of race and constitutes dividing lines such as that between an underserving, corrupt elite and 'the people' that speak to a myriad of intersectional identities. In certain respects, the Trump and Leave campaigns purposely sought to appeal beyond white majorities.

Conclusion

In looking for the causes of the divisions opened up by the Brexit and Trump votes, attention amongst academics and political commentators has focused on the social conditions and concomitant collective identities underlying them. Deep polarising forces stemming from globalisation and political alienation are seen to have manifested themselves as profound challenges to political establishments. This has been substantiated by reference to the social characteristics of those who voted for leave or for Trump and the attitudes they express and values they defend. Yet in this article it has been proposed that the evidence for the social and normative base for a new political cleavage remains ambiguous. Moreover, social categories such as age, class, education and ethnicity cannot be understood without considering how social and cultural identities are formed and expressed historically and in contexts of advanced globalisation. On this reading, political grievances reflect highly differentiated and individualised experiences of living in conditions of precarity and risk.

Furthermore, it is essential to grasp how the concepts and categories we use to understand these divisions have significant normative implications. The highlighting of the complexity of categories such as 'class', 'educated', 'white' is necessary in order to resist the populist claims to *reflect* and *represent* 'real' fears and concerns of the 'majority'. The dominant Brexit/Trump narrative of white working class disadvantage has been used to constitute a new political subject. This involves processes of attributing certain characteristics to groups and producing narratives of homogenous identities to be defended and communities needing to be restored. In diverse and cosmopolitan contexts in which the minority/majority division has become difficult to fix and determine, populists have become adept at re-imagining 'otherness' and constituting it in ways that appeal to people's indeterminate and individualised grievances. The UK leave vote and the election of Donald Trump demonstrate how powerful political actors considered aberrational have become adept at symbolically redrawing the political community along highly exclusionary lines co-opted the immense power of party machines and the state. If we are to apply cleavage theory to the Brexit and Trump votes then it has to be from the vantage of late modernity and the liquidity of communal identities, which 'derive power not from their expected duration, but, paradoxically, from their precariousness and uncertain future, from the vigilance and emotional investment which their brittle existence vociferously demands' (Bauman 2000, 199–200). In the political spectacles of Trump and Brexit the frozen cleavages of modern societies give way to their liquid counterparts.

Notes

1. Similarly, Eatwell and Goodwin (2018) examination of national populism as the legitimate expression of values ignored and held in contempt by liberals, received considerable media attention as it aligned with the dominant media framing, despite claims to challenge conventional orthodoxy.
2. Regional divisions are presented as simple binaries between East/West coast and the Deep/South, Mid-West in the US and the North and South of England in the UK.
3. http://www.bsa.natcen.ac.uk/latest-report/british-social-attitudes-34/immigration.aspx

Disclosure statement

No potential conflict of interest was reported by the author.

References

Al Gharbi, M. 2018. "Race and the Race for the White House: On Social Research in the Age of Trump." *The American Sociologist* 49 (4): 496–519. Advanced online publication. doi:10.1007/s12108-018-9373-5.

Allen, D. 2004. *Talking to Strangers: Anxieties of Citizenship since Brown V. Board of Education*. Chicago: University of Chicago Publishing.

Antonucci, L., L. Horvath, Y. Kutiyski, and A. Krouwel. 2017. "The Malaise of the Squeezed Middle: Challenging the Narrative of the 'Left Behind' Brexiter." *Competition & Change* 21 (3): 211–229. doi:10.1177/1024529417704135.

Ashcroft, M. 2016. "How the UK Voted on Thursday … and Why?" 24th June. Accessed 16th April 2018. https://lordashcroftpolls.com/2016/06/how-the-united-kingdom-voted-and-why/

Badger, E. 2018. "Estranged in Their Land: Both Sides Feel Lost and Left Out". *The New York Times*, October 4th

Bartolini, S., and P. Mair. 1990. "Policy Competition, Spatial Distance and Electoral Instability." *West European Politics* 13 (4): 1–16. doi:10.1080/01402389008424816.

Bauman, Z. 2000. *Liquid Modernity*. Cambridge: Polity Press.

Beck, U. 2007. "Beyond Class and Nation: Reframing Social Inequalities in a Globalizing World." *The British Journal of Sociology* 58 (4): 679–705. doi:10.1111/j.1468-4446.2007.00171.x.

Bhambra, G. K. 2017a. "Brexit, Trump, and 'Methodological Whiteness': On the Misrecognition of Race and Class." *The British Journal of Sociology* 68 (51): 214–232. doi:10.1111/1468-4446.12317.

Bhambra, G. K. 2017b. "Locating Brexit in the Pragmatics of Race, Citizenship and Empire." In *Brexit: Sociological Responses*, edited by W. Outhwaite, 91–100. London: Anthem Press.

Blühdorn, I., and F. Butzlaff. 2019. "Rethinking Populism: Peak Democracy, Liquid Identity and the Performance of Sovereignty." *European Journal of Social Theory* 22 (2): 191–211. doi:10.1177/1368431017754057.

Bornschier, S. 2009. "Cleavage Politics in Old and New Democracies." *Living Reviews in Democracy*, 1, Accessed 3 December 2020. https://ethz.ch/content/dam/ethz/special-interest/gess/cis/cis-dam/CIS_DAM_2015/WorkingPapers/Living_Reviews_Democracy/Bornschier.pdf

British Election Study Team. 2016. "Brexit Britain: British Election Study Insights from the post-EU Referendum Wave of the BES Internet Panel." Accessed 19 January 2017. https://www.britishelectionstudy.com/bes-resources/brexit-britain-british-election-study-insights-from-the-post-eu-referendum-wave-of-the-bes-internet-panel/#.XO0Y0SOZPOQ

Brubaker, W. R. 1989. *Immigration and the Politics of Citizenship in Europe and North America*. Lanham, Maryland: Rowman and Littlefield.

Calhoun, C. 2016. "Brexit Is a Mutiny against the Cosmopolitan Elite." *New Perspectives Quarterly* 33 (3): 50–58.

Calhoun, C. 2017. "Populism, Nationalism and Brexit." In *Brexit:Sociological Responses*, edited by W. Outhwaite, 56–76. London: Anthem Press.

CNN. 2016. "Election 2016: Exit Polls." November 23rd. https://edition.cnn.com/election/2016/results/exit-polls

Coates, T.-N. 2017. *We Were Eight Years in Power: An American Tragedy*. New York: One World.

Crouch, C. 2017. "Globalization, Nationalism and the Changing Axes of Political Identity." In *Brexit: Sociological Responses*, edited by W. Outhwaite, 101–109. London: Anthem Press.

Delanty, G. 2017. "A Divided Nation in A Divided Europe: Emerging Cleavages and the Crisis of European Integration." In *Brexit: Sociological Responses*, edited by W. Outhwaite, 111–124. London: Anthem Press.

Dorling, D., and S. Tomlinson. 2019. *Rule Britannia: Brexit and the End of Empire*. London: Biteback Publishing.

Eatwell, R., and M. Goodwin. 2018. *National Populism: The Revolt Against Liberal Democracy*. London: Pelican Books.

Ehsan, R. 2017. "The British Asian Vote for Brexit Contains a Few Surprises." *LSE Blog*. Accessed 29th October 2020. https://blogs.lse.ac.uk/brexit/2017/02/20/the-british-asian-vote-for-brexit-contains-a-few-surprises/

Evans, G. 2017. "Brexit Britain: Why We are All Postindustrial Now." *American Ethnologist* 44 (2): 215–219. doi:10.1111/amet.12470.

Giddens, A. 2003. *Runaway World: How Globalization Is Reshaping Our Lives*. New York: Routledge.

Goodhart, D. 2017. *The Road to Somewhere: The Populist Revolt and the Future of Politics*. Oxford: Oxford University Press.

Goodwin, M. J., and O. Heath. 2016a. "The 2016 Referendum, Brexit and the Left Behind: An Aggregate-level Analysis of the Result." *The Political Quarterly* 87 (3): 323–332. doi:10.1111/1467-923X.12285.

Goodwin, M. J., and O. Heath 2016b. "Brexit Vote Explained: Poverty, Low Skills and Lack of Opportunities." York: Joseph Rowntree Foundation. Accessed 23rd April 2018. https://www.jrf.org.uk/report/brexit-vote-explained-poverty-low-skills-and-lack-opportunities

Grasso, M. T., S. Farrall, E. Gray, C. Hay, and W. Jennings. 2019. "Thatcher's Children, Blair's Babies, Political Socialization and Trickle-down Value Change: An Age, Period and Cohort Analysis." *British Journal of Political Science* 49 (1): 17–36. doi:10.1017/S0007123416000375.

Harding, R. 2017. "Key Findings: A Kind-hearted but Not Soft-hearted Country." *British Social Attitudes: the 34th report*, London: NatCen Social Research. Accessed 30th June 2017. http://www.bsa.natcen.ac.uk/latest-report/british-social-attitudes-34/key-findings/context.aspx

Henderson, A., C. Jeffery, R. Liñeira, R. Scully, D. Wincott, and R. Wyn Jones. 2016. "England, Englishness and Brexit." *The Political Quarterly* 87 (2): 187–199. doi:10.1111/1467-923X.12262.

Hobolt, S. B. 2016. "The Brexit Vote: A Divided Nation, a Divided Continent." *Journal of European Public Policy* 23 (9): 1259–1277. doi:10.1080/13501763.2016.1225785.

Hochschild, A. 2016c. "The Ecstatic Edge of Politics: Sociology and Donald Trump." *Contemporary Sociology: A Journal of Reviews* 45 (6): 683–689. doi:10.1177/0094306116671947.

Hochschild, A. R. 2016a. *Strangers in Their Own Land. A Journey to the Heart of Our Political Divide*. New York: New York Press.

Hochschild, A. R. 2016b. "How the 'Great Paradox' of American Politics Holds the Secret to Trump's Success." *The Guardian*, 7th September. Accessed 23rd April 2018. https://www.theguardian.com/us-news/2016/sep/07/how-great-paradox-american-politics-holds-secret-trumps-success

Hooghe, L., and G. Marks. 2018. "Cleavage Theory Meets Europe's Crises: Lipset, Rokkan, and the Transnational Cleavage." *Journal of European Public Policy* 25 (1): 109–135. doi:10.1080/13501763.2017.1310279.

Inglehart, R. F. 1997. *Modernization and Postmodernization. Cultural, Economic, and Political Change in 43 Societies*. Princeton, NJ: Princeton University Press.

Inglehart, R. F., and P. Norris. 2017. "Trump and the Populist Authoritarian Parties: The Silent Revolution in Reverse." *Perspectives on Politics* 15 (2): 443–454. doi:10.1017/S1537592717000111.

Jennings, W., and G. Stoker. 2016. "The Bifurcation of Politics: Two Englands." *The Political Quarterly* 87 (3): 372–382. doi:10.1111/1467-923X.12228.

Jennings, W., and G. Stoker. 2017. "Tilting Towards the Cosmopolitan Axis? Political Change in England and the 2017 General Election." *The Political Quarterly* 88 (3): 359–369. doi:10.1111/1467-923X.12403.

Katwaller, S., J. Rutter, and S. Ballinger 2016. "Disbanding the Tribes: What the Referendum Told Us about Britain." British Future, Accessed 13th September 2018. http://www.britishfuture.org/publication/disbanding-the-tribes-what-the-referendum-told-us-about-britain-and-what-it-didnt/

Kaufman, E. 2017. *Racial Self-Interest Is Not Racism: Ethno-demographic Interests and the Immigration Debate*. London: Policy Exchange.

Kriesi, H. 2014. "The Populist Challenge." *West European Politics* 37 (2): 361–378. doi:10.1080/01402382.2014.887879.

Kumar, K. 2006. "English and French National Identity: Comparisons and Contrasts." *Nations and Nationalism* 12 (3): 413–432. doi:10.1111/j.1469-8129.2006.00247.x.

Lipset, S. M., and S. Rokkan, Eds.. 1967. *Party Systems and Voter Alignments: Cross-National Perspectives*. Vol. 7. New York: Free press.

Lockwood, D. 1996. "Civic Integration and Class Formation." *The British Journal of Sociology* 47 (3): 531–550. doi:10.2307/591369.

Mair, P. 2005. "Cleavages." In *Handbook of Party Politics*, edited by R. S. Katz, 371–375. London: Sage.

McGill, A. 2016. "America's Educational Divide Put Trump in the Whitehouse"." *The Atlantic*, November 27th.

Mckenzie, L. 2017a. "'It's Not Ideal': Reconsidering 'Anger'and 'Apathy'in the Brexit Vote among an Invisible Working Class." *Competition & Change* 21 (3): 199–210. doi:10.1177/1024529417704134.

Mckenzie, L. 2017b. "The Class Politics of Prejudice: Brexit and the Land of No-hope and Glory." *The British Journal of Sociology* 68 (51): 265–280.

Metzgar, J. 2016. "Misrepresting the White Working Class: What the Narrating of Class Gets Wrong." https://workingclassstudies.wordpress.com/2016/03/14/misrepresenting-the-white-working-class-what-the-narrating-class-gets-wrong/

Mezza, A. A., D. R. Ringo, S. M. Sherlund, and K. Sommer. 2016. "Student Loans and Homeownership." *Finance and Economics Discussion Series 2016–010*. Washington: Board of Governors of the Federal Reserve System. doi:10.17016/FEDS.2016.010r.

Mycock, A. 2013. "Understanding the post-British English Nation State." In *Literature of an Independent England*, edited by M. Gardiner and C. Westall, 15–30. London: Palgrave Macmillan.

Pew Research Center. 2016. "A Wider Educational Gap between More and Less Educated Adults." https://www.people-press.org/2016/04/26/a-wider-ideological-gap-between-more-and-less-educated-adults/

Rutter, J., and R. Carter. 2018. *National Conversation on Immigration: Final Report to the Home Affairs Committee*. London: British Future and Hope not Hate.
Savage, M. 2015. *Social Class in the 21st Century*. London: Pelican Books.
Sides, J., M. Tesler, and L. Vavreck. 2019. *Identity Crisis: The 2016 Presidential Campaign and the Battle for the Meaning of America*. Kindle ed. Princeton and Oxford: Princeton University Press.
Soysal, Y. N. 2012. "Citizenship, Immigration, and the European Social Project: Rights and Obligations of Individuality." *The British Journal of Sociology* 63 (1): 1–21. doi:10.1111/j.1468-4446.2011.01404.x.
Standing, G. 2016. *The Precariat: The New Dangerous Classes*. London: Bloomsbury.
Swales, K. 2016. *Understanding the Leave Vote*. London: NatCen Social Research. https://whatukthinks.org/eu/analysis/understanding-the-leave-vote/
Turney, S., F. Levy, J. Citrin, and N. O'Brian. 2017. "Waiting for Trump: The Move to the Right of White Working-Class Men, 1968–2016." *The California Journal of Politics and Policy* Available as UC Berkeley Working Paper at. http://escholarship.ucop.edu/uc/item/1cq9k81z
Virdee, S., and B. McGeever. 2018. "Racism, Crisis, Brexit." *Ethnic and Racial Studies* 41 (10): 1802–1819. doi:10.1080/01419870.2017.1361544.
Walley, C. J. 2017. "Trump's Election and the "White Working Class": What We Missed." *American Ethnologist* 44 (2): 231–236. doi:10.1111/amet.12473.
Watson, M. 2018. "Brexit, the Left behind and the Let Down: The Political Abstraction of 'The Economy' and the UK's EU Referendum." *British Politics* 13 (1): 17–30. doi:10.1057/s41293-017-0062-8.
Wolf, M. 2019. "Britain Is once Again the Sick Man of Europe" *The Financial Times*, April 18th.
Zürn, M., and P. de Wilde. 2016. "Debating Globalization: Cosmopolitanism and Communitarianism as Political Ideologies." *Journal of Political Ideologies* 21 (3): 280–301. doi:10.1080/13569317.2016.1207741.

Brexit, nationalism and disintegration in the European Union and the United Kingdom

Ben Wellings

ABSTRACT

Brexit calls us to account for nationalist politics as an independent variable in the historic construction and disintegration of the European Union. By examining the nationalist politics animating the campaigns to leave the European Union throughout the United Kingdom and the politics of keeping the UK united as the 'games' of the Brexit negotiations played out, this article argues for the centrality of nationalism in any further understandings of the inter-related process and politics of Brexit and European disintegration. Moreover, the Brexit referendum opened up contestation between executive, parliamentary, national and popular sovereignties in the differing nations of the United Kingdom and had a noticeable effect on *British*, as well as European, disintegration. Such inter-related drivers of disintegration must alert scholars to treat member-states as internally variegated and driven by imperatives to maintain state sovereignty in the face of challenges from sub-state, EU and global levels. European integration generates nationalism and creates polity contestation within the member-state as well as against the EU.

Introduction

Various explanations for the United Kingdom's vote to leave the European Union have been advanced since the 2016 referendum. For the most part, these explanations have focused on the implications of inequality brought about by the political economies of globalisation and European integration. Analyses of the withdrawal negotiations have focused on leadership and parliamentary politics. But Brexit was more than just the 2016 referendum and the subsequent politics of a negotiated withdrawal. It was the most salient part of a wider politics of nationalist mobilisation *within* the United Kingdom in the 10 years pre-dating the attempt to leave the European Union. It involved contestation between competing locations and ideas of sovereignty: executive, parliamentary, national and popular. It was underpinned by newly-politicised national identities within the United Kingdom, notably England's, where European integration generated a nationalist reaction. Therefore, Brexit calls us to account for nationalist politics as an independent variable in the historic integration and disintegration of the European Union. By examining the nationalist politics animating the campaigns to leave the European Union throughout the United Kingdom, and the politics of keeping the UK united as the Brexit negotiations played out, this article argues for the centrality of nationalism in any further understandings of the process and politics of European disintegration.

By contextualising Brexit as part of a wider analysis of nationalist mobilisation, this article sits apart from existing analyses of Brexit. Building on research published over the past decade that was increasingly concerned with challenges to established ways of theorising the drivers of European integration, this article is principally an engagement with Douglas Webber's recent work on European disintegration (Webber 2017, 2019). However, it augments this new perspective by adding nationalist and territorial politics as an explanatory variable to Webber's emphasis on hegemonic stability theory. The article has two broad sections: the first on the inter-relationship between nationalism, Brexit and *European* disintegration; and the second examining the inter-relationship between nationalism, Brexit and *British* disintegration. By placing contestations over national sovereignty at the heart of its analysis, this article suggests a clear direction for further research on European disintegration.

Nationalism, Brexit and European disintegration

The 'quadruple crisis' of the 2010 s provided ample evidence for those interested in the processes of European integration and disintegration. Surveying the politics of the Eurozone crisis in 2015, Claus Offe felt safe to conclude that the EU depended on 'receiving more loyalty and support from its citizens than it receives' (Offe 2015, 72). Offe's analysis suggested political immobility and an end to assumptions about the 'halting but irreversible' trajectory of European integration towards ever closer union (Offe 2015, 56).

Similarly, Jan Zielonka argued that the EU had fallen into a 'technocrat-populist trap' (Zielonka 2014, 45). This trap had significant political consequences on the future prospects for European unity because when 'technocrats dominate policy-making while populists dominate politics … interdependence no longer generates integration but instead prompts distinetegation' (Zielonka 2014, 47). This prognosis went further than Offe's, suggesting a *reversal* of the historic process of European integration. This was a development that was seriously under-theorised – and hence under-anticipated and poorly understood – amongst analysts and practitioners straddling the liberal centre of European politics. Even by 2018, when the Eurozone crisis had been compounded by the crisis in Ukraine, the migration crisis of 2015 and Brexit, Zielonka noted that there were many theories of European integration, but practically none of European disintegration (Zielonka 2018, 28).

But 'practically none' was not none at all (Vollard, 2014). Developments in European integration theory had anticipated the possibility of *dis*integration beyond a fluctuation of the primacy of member-states or European institutions as the drivers of integration. Asserting the importance – indeed primacy – of domestic politics as a variable in the process of integration and disintegration, 'post-functionalists' set themselves against the automaticity of neofunctionalists and liberal intergovernmentalists (Hooghe and Marks, 2009). Early theorisation of the processes of European integration that became known as 'neofunctionalism' anticipated that political loyalties would be shifted from member-states to European institutions when the logic of integrating nation-states into larger polities became apparent (Haas, [1958]). Post-functionalist theorising also differed from liberal intergovernmentalism in according a greater primacy to political agency than this approach, or neofunctionalism before it. In the lead up to the Brexit referendum of 2016, Andrew Moravscik, the leading exponent of liberal intergovernmentalism, stressed that the EU was so economically integrated that dis-integration was all but impossible and therefore political agency was futile (Moravscik 2016).

Against such conceptualisations of European integration that stressed its practically irreversible trajectory, some theorising had taken place that sought to account for the possibility of disintegration. Analysts in and of the UK were attuned to this possibility. Paul Taylor suggested that in order to outline an emerging theory of *dis*integration we should turn our attention to the means by which European integration originated and the ways those origins were theorised. According to Taylor, 'an integration theory needed two elements: a sense of a system defined with regard to stated criteria which was different from the current system; and a sense of dynamic processes in the current system for creating that different system' (Taylor 2008, 92). This opens up the possibility that both the existing system and existing theories contain within them the genesis of future systems and theories.

This means that an adaption of existing theories of European integration may shed light on the process of European disintegration, thus far under-theorised in the literature.

Similarly, Hagen Schulz-Forberg and Bo Stråth sought to outline 'a new historical underpinning of the European integration process' that would inform political understandings of the process and politics of European integration. Importantly, they sought 'a non-teleological approach' that emphasised political contingency and sensitised analysts and practitioners to 'the risks, setbacks and possible collapse of European integration' (Schulz-Forberg and Stråth 2010: xi). During the Eurozone crisis Kenneth Dyson noted the 'spillover' of the Eurozone crisis from the realm of technocratic management to that of politics and politicised cultures more broadly:

> Paradoxically, the very attempt of the ECB and the European Council to strengthen their leadership role served to increase criticism of the way in which the eurozone crisis was deepening the legitimacy crisis, defined as the "democratic deficit" in the EU, creating a crisis of identity ... The issue was not simply economic, it was also cultural and political (Dyson 2017, 53).

The types of politicisation and mobilisation associated with the EU's quadruple crisis of the 2010 s permitted and necessitated a shift in the understanding of resistance to further – or any – European integration. From the margins of (continental) European politics, what was now widely known as 'Euroscepticism' was re-conceptualised as an 'embedded and persistent' (Startin and Usherwood 2013, 13) element of the EU's political system. At the same time, Hans-Jörg Trenz noted a shift from *policy* to *polity* contestation amongst Eurosceptic parties and movements within the EU (Trenz 2018, 293). Trenz argued that 'Euroscepticism is best understood as a delegitimizing practice that unfolds through normative assessment and cognitive framing of the legitimacy of the EU polity' (Trenz 2018, 302). European disintegration could thus be seen as an intended consequence of such de-legitimisation.

The most sustained attempt to understand the drivers of disintegration in the wake of the 'quadruple crisis' in the EU was outlined by Douglas Webber (Webber 2019). Webber defined European disintegration as a reduction of the range of issue areas in which the EU exercises policy-making competences and, within specific areas, a reduction of the scope of common policies (Webber 2019, 13). He divided disintegration into separate categories: sectoral, vertical and horizontal disintegration. Sectoral disintegration concerned the reduction in scope of EU competencies, of which the suspension of the Schengen Agreements in the wake of the migration crisis and terrorist attacks of 2015 were an example. Vertical disintegration concerns the relative strength of the EU's supranational institutions vis-à-vis its members-states, of which the intensive transgovernmentalism of the Eurozone crisis was the most salient example (Webber 2019, 14). Brexit was understood as an instance of horizontal disintegration, which effectively amounted to the first secession of a member-state from the EU and its predecessors, Greenland and the formerly French departments of Algeria notwithstanding (Webber 2019, 180). In addition to Zielonka's emphasis on the unfulfilled political promises from centrist parties that represented the true engines of disintegration (Zielonka 2014, 31), Webber added a more structural approach. For Webber, it was above all the absence of deliberate and strategic German stabilising hegemony, that posed the greatest risk of disintegration within the European Union (Webber 2019, 208).

On the importance of Brexit to emerging understandings of European disintegration, Webber argued that of the four crises affecting the EU in the 2010s Brexit testified 'most powerfully to the impact on European integration of domestic politics, of mass politicization and political polarization around EU issues in the member-states ... that emphasize the ultimate primacy of politics over economics' (Webber 2019, 202). Although he qualified this by noting that postfunctionalism was better at explaining the onset of the crisis rather than its limited and contained outcomes (Webber 2019, 39), the importance of the politics of Brexit for European integration was not in dispute. Yet Christian Lequesne went further than Webber and argued that Brexit represented an 'epistemological breach' in the theorising of European integration and disintegration. For Lequesne, 'Brexit shows forcefully that there is no other choice for EU scholars than going back to a detailed study of national polities and politics if they have the ambition to renew EU theories' (Lequesne, 2018: 290); an argument echoed by Ben Leruth, Stefan Gänzle and Jarle Trondal (Leruth et al. 2019, 1013).

European disintegration and nationalist politics

Lequesne's focus was on the political consequences of social cleavages that arose in the post-Maastricht period of European integration. Similarly, Frank Schimmelfennig highlighted the importance of various integration effects, including immigration, ideas about self-determination, the rise of Eurosceptic parties, and the availability of a referendum as explanatory variables (Schimmelfennig 2018, 1154). But Brexit can push consideration of the independent variable in European disintegration further than national politics alone. Brexit calls us to account for *nationalist politics* as a variable in the historic construction and deconstruction of the European Union. Even if the motives for uniting Europe were at times driven as much by the needs of US strategy and big business as by ideals for peace (Berend 2016, 1), European integration also had at its origins a desire to overcome inter-state conflict by containing nationalism. Nationalism and European integration were conjoined concepts, even before the post-1945 era of integration. Therefore, bringing an understanding of nationalism and nationalist politics back into theories of European integration opens up a neglected but important area of analysis and one which the nationalist politics underpinning Brexit forces us to consider anew.

In the case of the United Kingdom, the decisive shift from 'policy contestation' (Euroscepticism) to 'polity contestation' (secessionism in the guise of Brexit) in the context of the wider EU crises led to major instance of 'horizontal' (and therefore implicitly 'sectoral') disintegration (Webber 2019, 180). The link between nationalism, British disintegration and Brexit requires analysis at the intersection of politicised national identities and calls for European disintegration (Wellings 2019). The quadruple crisis in the EU politicised national identities whilst at the same time implying or creating closer forms of integration and political management to address those crises (Fligstein, Polyakova, and Sandholtz 2012, 120). Developing Webber's technique that existing theories of European integration might, if inverted, provide insights into European disintegration, and by placing not just national politics but nationalist politics at the centre of analysis, we can begin to comprehend the relationship between nationalism, European integration and disintegration. Therefore, such nested games of Brexit require us to attend to the domestic drivers of disintegration. This includes not only European disintegration, but British disintegration too.

Despite the salience of (US) federalism as a template for early theories of integration, some of the notable early theorisation of European integration came out of attempts to understand previous instances of multi-national polities, in Karl Deutsch's case the Austro-Hungarian Empire. The 'transactional' approach associated with Deutsch, suggested that 'a perpetual dynamic process of mutual attention, communication, perception of needs and responsiveness in the process of decision-making' would drive actors towards what could become peaceable 'security communities' where war had been eliminated as a social institution (Deutsch cited in Eilstrup-Sangiovanni 2006; [1957], 76). Similarly, neofunctionalism anticipated that what Ernest Haas called a 'new nationalism' should form as a result of new levels of governance across Western Europe (Haas 1968 [1958], 13–14). But identity formation was not a major concern in neofunctionalist theorising. Rather, it was (or should have been) a rational by-product of a new scale of political organisation in Europe.

Politics, however, is not as rational as assumed in neofunctionalist theorising; nor is the product of increased transnational communication as assuredly uni-directional as the functioning of security communities like the EU might suggest. Craig Parsons showed the importance of ideas in shaping the politics of early European integration, particularly in a direction that suited successive French governments (even anti-European ones from 1958–69) whilst simultaneously allowing the establishment of permanent European institutions. Basing his conclusions on the argument 'not only that ideas cause actors to make certain choices, but that the institutionalization of certain ideas gradually reconstructs the interests of powerful actors', Parsons concluded that:

> Europe's institutions do not reflect a simple aggregation of structurally determined interests. Nor are they merely an incremental institutional evolution from their founders' intentions. They are the product of a supremely political project that has bound all Europeans into a certain ideological agenda (Parsons 2003, 7-8).

Thus, if Europe is a supremely political project, it can be wound back by supremely political efforts, even if the weight of institutions makes this a difficult task. Brexit represents such a supremely political effort in which ideas and identities appear to trump economic considerations. Constructivist theorising asserts that ideas and identity formation are important for guiding actions. Importantly such identity formation does not have to be in a pro-European direction, as the intensification of Eurosceptic attitudes in the UK and across the EU attests. This position challenged the teleology of the early (implicitly) pro-European theories and (explicitly) pro-European histories of European integration (Varsori 2010: 22; Kaiser 2010, 45). When allied with the postfunctionalist emphasis on mass politicisation and mobilisation, the links and tensions between national and European identities become an important element in the legitimisation of the European project. As Furio Cerutti has argued, 'only when people come to find that staying united is at the same time convenient for their well-being and relevant to their image of collective life can a new polity reach the critical point of acceptance' (Cerutti and Lucarelli 2008, 13): a point that has been under political challenge in the EU and UK during the 2010s. Yet as has been noted, the process of European identity formation was notably weak compared to national identities and 'no general subjective consciousness accompanied the process' of European integration (Anderson, 2009, 475). Furthermore, the 'critical point of acceptance' was one that needed to be constantly renegotiated and rearticulated, particularly in the context of the quadruple crisis. This crisis challenged the legitimacy of the EU and European integration that 'erodes exactly those attitudes and motivations that matter as prerequisites for its solution': a shared sense of community and affinity within the EU (Offe 2015, 77).

The link between identity and legitimacy was not made strongly prior to the crises of the 2010s (Cerutti and Lucarelli 2008, 218). Where it was, it tended to be made in generally positive terms, with nested national and European identities informing and supporting each other in the goal of legitimising European integration (Cram 2009, 110). Such findings tended to point towards a 'Europeanisation' of national identities. But as Jeffery Checkel and Peter Katzenstein noted, 'identities simply do not nest in the positive-sum way seen by all too many EU scholars ... Identities can be sharply conflictual rather than complementary' (Checkel and Katzenstein 2009, 8), meaning that with its emphasis on institutions and the state, the literature on Europeanisation often missed 'the politics and conflict that accompany transformational dynamics' (Checkel and Katzenstein 2009, 10). The transformational dynamics of the EU crises meant that identity formation proceeded in an anti-integration direction. As FitzGibbon, Leruth and Startin demonstrated, from chaotic origins Euroscepticism emerged as a pan-European and transnational phenomenon during the 2010 s and as such constituted a new sphere of opposition within the EU (FitzGibbon, Leruth, and Startin 2017, 11), thus challenging the assumption that integration would lead to a stronger European identity. The politics of nationalism in the Brexit referendum suggested that European integration had – certainly in the case of England and Wales – resulted in a heightened salience of nationalist politics rather than its containment and complementarity.

Thus, what began as an historic attempt to contain nationalism, ended up generating it. The links between nationalism and Euroscepticism are complex: FitzGibbon, Leruth and Startin also note that Eurosceptic transnational organisation helps Eurosceptics avoid the appearance of nationalism as much as mobilise it within their own polities (FitzGibbon, Leruth, and Startin 2017, 10). Furthermore, Euroscepticism is also a phenomenon on the green-left of politics as well as on the right. Nevertheless, popular support for right-wing and populist Eurosceptic parties rested on exclusive understandings of national identity even before the crises of the 2010s (Leconte 2010, 185). Such a connection permitted some scholars to examine this link, asking 'When and to what extent has European integration has been a catalyst for nationalist developments, and when and to what extent has it been a damper on nationalism in European nation-states?' (Karolewski and Suszycki 2007, 3).

Much of the answer to this question depends on the definition of nationalism employed. Most conceptualisation of nationalism has been undertaken by historical sociologists. Whilst not denying its exclusivity, most analysts have approached nationalism as a mode of integration, seeking out the symbols and discourses that unite disparate individuals and groups into a historically contingent entity that came to be known as the nation (Anderson 1991, 6). Whilst disagreeing on the historic origins of this phenomenon – meaning that it is unclear whether 'Europe' can be said to have pre-dated the emergence of nationalism or was tied up with it – almost all scholars agree that nationalism was a historic product of accelerated change, even if nationalists themselves spoke in language that stressed continuity with the past. In this analysis, nationalism was not an atavistic throwback to a golden age but was instead a rational, ontological response to changing economic, social and political conditions. For Tom Nairn, the figure most associated with an analysis of *British* disintegration.

> ... it is through nationalism that societies try to propel themselves forward to certain kinds of goals (industrialisation, prosperity, equality with other peoples etc.) *by a certain sort of regression* – by looking inwards, drawing more deeply upon their indigenous resources, resurrecting past folk heroes and myths about themselves and so on (Nairn, 2003 [1977]: 336) [emphasis in the original].

From this perspective, the EU crises, nested in a longer terms process of globalisation since the end of the Cold War, operated as another historical instance of accelerating change, the like of which produced nationalism in the past. The weakening appeal of common narratives of integration in an enlarged EU were notable before the onset of the crises, but were accelerated by them (Manners and Murray 2016). But it is not just the case that the changes and insecurity associated with the crises weakened the sense of commonality and affinity required to legitimise the EU; rather it is that European integration generated nationalism, a process accelerated by the way the various crises were framed, interpreted and exploited by political entrepreneurs (Dines, Nicola, and Vacchelli 2018). Against a decade of increasingly politicised identities within the UK, the Brexit referendum permitted just such a mobilisation of nationalist politics. In this way, Brexit became a critical juncture in both British and EU politics that had a profound impact on how we understand European integration and disintegration.

Nationalism, Brexit and British disintegration

The UK's decision to leave the European Union stands as the most significant example of what Webber describes as 'horizontal' disintegration in the history of the EU. But what began in 2016 as another crisis of European integration, became a crisis of *British* disintegration as the politics of negotiating a withdrawal developed thereafter. This development suggests two inter-related drivers of disintegration: national politics that 'spill-up' from the member-state to affect the speed and direction of European integration and nationalist politics within the member-state that propel its government towards policies and politics that generate *European* disintegration. Thus, European politics should not be treated as second-order politics as far as the member-states are concerned, but about polity contestation *within* member-states as well as contestation directed towards the EU.

Like the EU, the UK is a multi-national polity. In considering the relative weakness of European solidarity in the first years of the twenty-first century Paul Taylor thought that a comparison with the historical process of British integration might prove a useful comparator for the EU. Noting that there was a high degree of social and commercial solidarity amongst elites from the eighteenth century, and the important part played by common institutions, not least the military, Taylor suggested that social solidarity was far more important than political solidarity in creating the conditions for a strong sense of European identification: 'Increasing social intermixing, including intermarriage, among French and Germans, would be a powerful indicator of integration, as Karl Deutsch suggested in the 1960 s – probably more important than comitology!' (Taylor 2008, 107–108).

Yet the decade after the publication of Taylor's work, the UK seemed far from the model of unity and integration than had been supposed in Taylor's comparison. Whereas the EU had been widening and deepening since the 1990 s integrating new states into its forms for governance, the UK had been on a different trajectory. Central government responded to territorial politics and nationalist challenges by decentralising government to Scotland, Wales and Northern Ireland and returning civic government to London and – in the 2010s – other metropolitan areas. Thus, the multi-national composition of the UK had been institutionalised in the two decades prior to the Brexit referendum through these major constitutional reforms in the first term of the New Labour government, 1997–2001. Furthermore, the intention that this measure of devolution would negate the political rise of secessionist nationalism proved illusory. Using the new political terrain of devolved government in Scotland to prove its abilities to promote the 'Scottish interest' and thereby gaining a majority in the Scottish Parliament in 2011, the secessionist Scottish National Party (SNP) held a referendum in 2014 in which a significant minority of 45% of the Scottish electorate voted to leave the UK, particularly those self-described as exclusively Scottish, middle class, left-leaning and young (Mann and Fenton 2017, 159–164). Yet both the campaigns to take Scotland out of the UK and to keep Scotland in it, used the EU for different ends. The policy of 'independence in Europe', developed by the SNP in the early 1990s with analogous ideas feeding into secessionist nationalisms in Wales (and Catalonia) sought to keep Scotland in the EU as a way to bolster the economic viability of an independent Scotland of five million people. Given the EU's support for the territorial integrity of its member-states, the campaign to keep Scotland in the UK argued (ironically as it turned out) that only by staying in the UK could Scots guarantee remaining in the EU.

What the politics of nationalism showed in this period was that *polity* contestation noted by Trenz above was not just directed at the EU by Eurosceptics, but also by secessionist nationalists at its member-states; even if these secessionist parties like the Scottish National Party (SNP) tended to be (officially) pro-EU. But if European disintegration theory had been only sketched out, this was also true for theories of British integration, with such theories being decidedly marginal in the fields of Politics and International Relations and usually left to historians (Colley 2014). Taken together, devolution and the national distinctiveness of the Brexit vote could have acted as a phenomenon forcing an examination of 'British integration and disintegration theory'. However, Political Science was slow to catch up and still tended to treat the United Kingdom as England writ large, resulting in what Ailsa Henderson et al. (2017) called a 'triple effacement' that marginalised Northern Ireland, pushed Scotland and Wales to the edges of research, whilst at the same time effacing England. The effect of which was that 'we end up analysing the United Kingdom as a fictive country: Anglo-Britain' (Henderson et al. 2017, 632). The theoretical point to make here is that contestation over European integration and British integration are inter-related concepts, as shown by the referendums on Scottish independence in 2014, the Brexit referendum in 2016 and the UK General Elections of 2017 and 2019. Therefore, the assumed unity of Eurosceptic attitudes within a multi-national member-state vis-à-vis the EU needs to be augmented with an analysis of the dynamics of nationalism within that member-state and the place of European integration in generating such nationalist responses.

In this light, the famed awkwardness of the UK's relationship with the EU (George 1998) can be seen as a product of the UK's own internal awkwardness. Brexit – understood as an ongoing politics of nationalist mobilisation since 2010 - rather than just the referendum, negotiations and 2017 and 2019 elections alone – is not only a form of horizontal European disintegration (*à la* Webber) but is also the product of multiple competing sovereignties within the UK, including national sovereignties (Bickerton 2019). The Brexit referendum itself was a product of these nationalist mobilisations, in particular in England, where a decade-old politicised sense of anti-establishment nationhood (Kenny 2014) found an outlet for expression in the vote to leave the EU. These contestations and mobilisations pre-date the 2016 referendum but their political expression was facilitated and exacerbated by that event. In this sense, Brexit represented a moment that had been building as a result of nationalist mobilisations within the UK, where key actors sought to 'take back control', not only from the EU but from each other too.

Contested sovereignties and disintegration

Referendums assume that there is a settled political community whose will can be expressed via some sort of majority vote (either simple or qualified). Yet the politics of nationalist mobilisation in the years ahead of the Brexit vote suggested that this was not the case in the United Kingdom. The 2016 referendum and 2019 election revealed a variable political geometry within the UK which contrasted England and Wales with Scotland and Northern Ireland (the latter being divided amongst nationalist and loyalist communities). Furthermore, these results represented a series of contested sovereignties: one in which the English electorate sought to take back control from the EU; one in which the Scottish National Party sought to take back control from the UK by retaining membership of the EU; and one in which the UK and Republic of Ireland (supported by the EU) sought to share control of the Northern Irish border. All of this suggested that the idea that the United Kingdom could, should or would leave the EU as one people because 'Britons' had voted as one people was open to serious question.

Brexit provided a UK-wide vehicle for nationalist contestation within the UK. It did so precisely because the UK is not a federal polity, but a devolved one where – notionally – the UK government could rescind the powers of any devolved parliament or assembly as it had in the case of Northern Ireland – although at great political cost were it to do so elsewhere and short of actually disestablishing Parliaments and assemblies, as the *Wales Act* (2017) established. Because the UK is a quasi-federation negotiating its exit from an emerging confederation, these moving parts opened up political opportunities for actors within these institutions and re-emerging polities. Three of these contestations played out and constituted what was called 'Brexit' but formed three distinct parts of the Brexit process: contestation between popular sovereignty and parliamentary sovereignty during the referendum; contestation between executive sovereignty and parliamentary sovereignty during the negotiations with the EU; and contestation between Westminster and the devolved administrations during and after the negotiations. All of these contests fed into different visions of national sovereignty throughout the United Kingdom.

Thus, the idea of nested and two-level games in negotiations between the UK and the EU needs to be supported by an awareness of the three forms of contestation happening domestically within the UK. The first of these contestations was between parliamentary sovereignty – the idea that the Westminster parliament is the ultimate source of authority in the UK and cannot be bound by any successor – and popular sovereignty. Popular sovereignty, the idea that the ultimate source of political authority within a polity is 'the People' constituted a single body, clearly has some part in the British constitution through General Elections. However, the incremental and inexplicit nature that was venerated as the genius of the British system, combined with a mixture of Tory paternalism, Labour welfare-ism and steering from Whitehall that added up to a 'government knows best' attitude, had eroded since the 1980s. This trend was accelerated by the Global Financial Crisis and the resulting decade-long austerity after 2008. Referendums were a relative novelty in the British Political Tradition and sat uncomfortably within it. New Labour used referendums as *post facto* endorsements of decisions already taken by Parliament. Designed originally to help citizens reconnect with politics and politicians after the 'expenses scandal' of 2009, referendums, initially focused on the *EU Act (2011)* (Wellings and Vines 2016) and ultimately including the Brexit referendum, placed 'the British people' at the centre of politics at a moment when the sense of identity underpinning this collectivity had never been more openly diverse and meant different things in different parts of the UK.

The *EU Act* of 2011 was overtaken by the events of 2016. But it was indicative of the way that popular sovereignty expressed via referendums was invoked as a means to underpin Parliamentary sovereignty, yet at the same time undermined it. It was also an example of what Chris Gifford described as the 'structural susceptibility to populist politics' embedded in post-War British politics that contained a significant Eurosceptic dimension (Gifford, 2014: 6). The national-populist mobilisations during the Brexit campaign were notable. In a speech to the European Parliament 28 June 2016, Nigel Farage stated that the result of the 2016 referendum:

> ... was a remarkable result, it was indeed a seismic result, not just for British politics, for European politics but perhaps even for global politics too because what the little people did, what the ordinary people did, what the people who have been oppressed over the last few years and see their living standards go down – they rejected the multinationals, they rejected the merchant banks, they rejected big politics and they said, actually, we want our country back, we want our fishing waters back, we want our borders back, we want to be an independent self-governing, normal nation and that is what we have done and that is what must happen (BBC News 2016).

The invocation that 'that is what must happen' illustrated the tension between direct and representative versions of democracy and the way that the referendum was framed as the *sine qua non* of democracy and therefore trumped other expressions of the general will of the British people(s) via the various parliaments and assemblies in the UK. This challenge came not only from the pro-Brexit camp but from the increasingly mobilised and emboldened Remainers too. An example of this 'progressive-populism' came from Caroline Lucas, the Green Party co-leader. Lucas told attendees at the People's Vote event held in Camden on 15 April 2018 that Brexit was 'not inevitable', adding: 'We'll do everything we can in Parliament for a people's vote. This issue is far too important to leave to the politicians' (cited in BBC News Politics 2018). Neither Farage nor Lucas addressed the issue of which people's will was being evoked. In this way, the referendum tended to highlight national divisions rather than reinforce a British *demos*.

The importance of the referendum as a device for restraining, halting or reversing European integration in the UK, meant that Westminster was at risk of being 'left behind' by the politics of European disintegration. But popular sovereignty was not the only challenge to Parliament's authority. The second contestation was between parliamentary and executive sovereignty. In the wake of the vote, the UK government initially planned to use Royal Prerogative (a measure usually associated with treaty negotiations or declarations of war) to leave the EU without the politically risky measure of consulting Parliament or the devolved legislatures, particularly Scotland that had voted 62–38% to Remain in the EU. Until January 2017, it appeared as if the executive, in alliance with 'the People' (or their tribunes), had between them taken joint control over the process of leaving the EU at the expense of Parliament. However, this changed with the UK High and Supreme Court rulings of 2016 and 2017 that upheld Westminster's right for a 'meaningful vote', but simultaneously dismissed the rights of the Scottish parliament and devolved assemblies for a similar vote. These developments allowed Westminster parliament the opportunity to take back control from the executive, which it did in 2017–19 through Parliamentary manoeuvring. But the High and Supreme Court decisions turned the Anglo-Welsh majority vote to leave into an expression of the general will across the UK. This was an interpretation that the results of 2016 suggested no longer existed on the question of the UK's membership of the EU.

These decisions also effectively elevated the Westminster parliament as a representative, deliberative body above the idea of 'the People' as embodied in the vote of 23 June 2016. That 'the People' were the losers in these legal decisions was illustrated by the opprobrium directed at the judges in the *R (Miller) v. Secretary for Exiting the European Union* case of 2016–17, whom the (unelected) *Daily Mail* described as the 'enemies of the people' for their decision (Slack 2016). However, the elevation of the People above that of parliaments had an unintended consequence: it opened up the question that if 'the People' were sovereign, then who exactly were 'the People'? The insertion of popular sovereignty via device of a referendum, and its differentiated outcome across the nations of the UK in 2016, raised questions about which people or poeples were being represented in this political contest. This is where the nationalist mobilisations of the Brexit period are important to consider alongside the socio-economic resentments that the referendum highlighted (Hobolt 2016, 1260).

Like weakening 'European' narratives during the crises of the 2010 s, 'British' narratives were also weakening, for related but distinct reasons. This was not because of a decline in Britishness *per se* (Mann and Fenton 2017, 69), but rather that Britishness began to mean different things in different parts of the UK. With regard to attitudes towards the EU, self-identifying 'British' people in England were pro-EU; in Scotland, Wales and Northern Ireland they were anti-EU (Henderson et al. 2017). However, the variance within British identity was little visible in the way it was rhetorically invoked from the centre of British politics after June 2016. Updating Richard Rose's idea of Westminster as 'the fifth nation' of the United Kingdom, Arthur Aughey argued that whereas post-devolution Britishness was usually spoken of as 'the *collective* values and interests which it is the job of Westminster to express (the fifth nation)', it was now perhaps 'better to speak of it in terms of the *collected* values and interests of a multi-national association which it is the job of Westminster to secure (a fifth nation)' (Aughey 2010, 282). Ironically, this disaggregated world view in Westminster rested heavily on a powerful integrating myth of a unitary state (and hence nationhood) that survived devolution – at least in English consciousness (Paun 2018, 50–52). The narratives of 'Global Britain' coming from the 'fifth nation' at Westminster after 2016, represented another attempt at taking back control: this time by the Unionist parliamentary Conservative and Labour parties to contain a politicised and mobilised *Englishness* that had played such an important part in the result of the Brexit referendum.

Nevertheless, the adherence to Theresa May's 'precious union' (May 2016) amongst Conservative grassroots party activists and the electorate can be questioned. The second deal negotiated between the UK and the EU in October 2019 underscored the implicit Englishness of the Johnson government, by weakening Northern Ireland's ties to the rest of the UK. This suggested that the significant elements of the pre-2016 English resentment that were directed at the governance of the UK as well as the EU (Ford and Sobolewska 2018, 160), also found their way into government policy after Johnson became Prime Minister. Although much of the initial analysis of the socio-economic drivers of the leave vote focused on age and education, it became clear that it was England – minus London – that had delivered the vote to leave (Hennig and Dorling 2016). Admittedly, the Englishness of the 2016 referendum campaign was masked by the British framing of the rhetoric: the remain campaign in England was called 'Britain Better in Europe'; whereas in other parts of the UK the national element was highlighted, as in 'Scotland Better in Europe'. This implicit Englishness became apparent during the Brexit negotiations when it was clear that the impact of Brexit on Scotland and, especially, Northern Ireland had been given very little consideration by the Brexiteers during the campaign. Data collected by the Centre on Constitutional Change revealed the fragility of English loyalty towards the Union during the Brexit negotiations. This research showed that clear majorities of English Conservatives would support Scottish independence or the collapse of the Northern Irish peace process as a price for leaving the EU (Centre on Constitutional Change 2018). This result replicated in a YouGov poll conducted in mid-2019 which found the same attitudes (YouGov 2019). All of this was consistent with the merged nature of English and political British identification, of which UKIP's ostensible Unionism, but implicit Englishness, was emblematic (Hayton 2016, 408). Thus, what we can call English nationalism – directed ostensibly at the EU but more subtly at the UK – was a key driver of the rupture of Brexit. More than this, *nationalist* politics – as much as national (member-state) politics – reconfigured the political terrain on which the games of Brexit played out.

This Englishness matters because, in Webber's terms, England is the UK's hegemon. Devolution (British disintegration) was a necessary but not sufficient condition for the politicisation of English nationhood and thus the contemporary manifestation of English nationalism (Kenny 2014, 27). Euroscepticism, as much as resentment towards Scotland, was a driver of politicised Englishness (Wyn Jones et al. 2012; Wyn Jones et al. 2013). Thus, if a hegemonic nation within a multi-national polity turns towards policies of European disintegration as the English did in the years before the Brexit referendum, it creates the potential to incline the whole member-state in a political direction that anticipates further European disintegration. This political turn is a result not only of polity contestation directed at the EU itself, but of the politics of national integration within the member-state too.

If this is correct, it suggests to analysts of European disintegration to attend to the drivers and content of specific national traditions through which support for European integration will be framed. This implies a re-evaluation of the drivers of Eurosceptic attitudes. Hans-Jörg Trenz argues that 'the strength of Euroscepticism is not in its argumentative power that convinces people but its vagueness and ideological indeterminacy that draws on people's unarticulated feelings and emotions' (Trenz 2018, 297). Thus, as a 'thin' ideology (if it can be called such), Euroscepticism requires filling. Although it is usually nationalism that is described as a 'thin' ideology, in the case of Euroscepticism it is nationalism that can fill this void. But when Trenz states that 'there is no coherent narrative thread that adherents can follow, take up and continue' (Trenz 2018, 297) this was not the case with elite Brexiteers who linked their de-legitimising narratives very closely to English politico-historical narratives allowing them to frame the rupture of Brexit within the continuity of the national past (Wellings 2019, 132). It was rhetorical claims such as Boris Johnson's that 'We used to run the biggest empire the world has ever seen and with a much smaller domestic population and a relatively tiny Civil Service. Are we really unable to do trade deals?' (Johnson 2016), that gave the leave campaign its nostalgic air and shifted the game from two (EU-member-state) to four (national-member-state-EU-global) levels. Although generally dismissed as unrealistic nostalgic fantasy this is better understood as the recurrence of a political tradition dating back to the mid-nineteenth century, that informs and particular Anglo-British world view in times of crisis (Kenny and Pearce 2018, 161).

Conclusions

Brexit may well turn out to be an isolated and unrepresentative phenomenon, not only because of British exceptionalism or due to the costs of leaving the EU, but because it is the only place where a hegemonic nation within a multinational polity became politicised over membership of the EU. It may be that Brexit provides another $n = 1$ problem in theorising European integration based on comparative analyses. But there are other member-states where the conditions for such politicisation exists at the time of writing: Flanders in Belgium and the northern parts of Italy. The politics of independence in Catalonia were similar to those in Scotland, even if the idea of the EU facilitating independence were much more greatly circumscribed in 2017 than they were even in 2014. The theoretical point to make here is that contestation over European integration and British integration are related concepts and therefore the assumed unity of the member-state vis-à-vis the European Union needs to be augmented with an analysis of the dynamics of nationalism *within* that member-state. Adapting Webber, a shift from pro- to anti-integration sentiment within hegemonic nations will have consequences for both European integration and the integration of the member-state in question.

This article has argued for sensitivity towards nationalist and intra-state politics in emerging theories of European disintegration. The inter-related phenomena of European and British disintegration must alert scholars not to see member-state politics towards European integration as solely a process of rational interest formation. Instead theorists of European disintegration should treat member-states as internally variegated and driven by imperatives to maintain state sovereignty in the face of challenges from sub-state, EU and global levels. Such politics of nationalist mobilisation and contestations over sovereignty are far from 'second order'. In the case of the UK in the period dominated by the politics of Brexit (2010–19), European integration generated a variable nationalist response – pro-EU in Scotland; anti-EU in England – that created the conditions of nationalist mobilisation that brought the UK to the referendum of 2016 and the subsequent politics of withdrawal from the EU. The period of negotiations from 2017 to 2019 were marked by inter- and intra-party divisions, but this was a political terrain complicated by the significance of nationalist and loyalist representation at Westminster and the existence of devolved legislatures. In particular, it was the nationalist mobilisation of anti-EU sentiment in England – the UK's hegemonic nation – that created the rupture of Brexit for both the European Union and the United Kingdom.

Disclosure statement

No potential conflict of interest was reported by the author.

ORCID

Ben Wellings http://orcid.org/0000-0003-4621-2431

References

Anderson, B. 1991. *Imagined Communities. Reflections on the Origins and Spread of Nationalism*. London: Verso.
Anderson, P. 2009. *The New Old World*. London: Verso.
Aughey, A. 2010. "Fifth Nation: The United Kingdom between Definite and Indefinite Articles." *British Politics* 5 (3): 265–285. doi:10.1057/bp.2010.8.
BBC News EU Referendum. 2016. "Brexit Vote: bitter exchanges in EU Parliament debate." accessed 29 June 2016. http://www.bbc.com/news/uk-politics-eu-referendum-36648664
BBC News Politics. 2018. "Brexit: "People's Vote" Campaign Group Launched", BBC News Politics, 15 April 2018, accessed 16 April 2018. http://www.bbc.com/news/uk-43774200
Berend, I. 2016. *The History of European Integration. A New Perspective*. Abingdon: Routledge.
Bickerton, C. 2019. "Parliamentary, Popular and Pooled: Conflicts of Sovereignty in the United Kingdom's Exit from the European Union." *Journal of European Integration*. doi:10.1080/07036337.2019.1670172.
Centre on Constitutional Change. 2018. "'May's "Precious Union" Has Little Support in Brexit Britain". accessed 9 May 2019. https://www.centreonconstitutionalchange.ac.uk/news/press-release-may's-'precious-union'-has-little-support-brexit-britain
Cerutti, F. 2008. "Why Political Identity and Legitimacy Matter in the European Union." In *The Search for a European Identity. Values, Policies and Legitimacy of the European Union*, edited by F. Cerutti and S. Lucarelli. Abingdon: Routledge.
Cerutti, F., and S. Lucarelli, eds. 2008. *The Search for a European Identity. Values, Policies and Legitimacy of the European Union*. Abingdon: Routledge.
Checkel, J., and P. Katzenstein. 2009. "The Politicisation of European Identity." In *European Identity*, edited by J. Checkel and P. Katzenstein. Cambridge: Cambridge University Press.
Colley, L. 2014. *Acts of Union and Disunion. What Has Held the UK Together – And What Is Dividing It?* London: Profile Books.
Cram, L. 2009. "Identity and European Integration: Diversity as a Source of Integration." *Nations and Nationalism* 15 (1): 109–128. doi:10.1111/j.1469-8129.2009.00367.x.
Deutsch, K. 1953. *Nationalism and Social Communication*. Cambridge MA: MIT Press.
Deutsch, K. W., S. A. Burrell, R. A. Kann, M. Lee Jr., M. Lichterman, R. E. Lindgren, F. L. Loewenheim, and R. W. Van Wagenen. 1957. *Political Community and the North Atlantic Area: International Organization in the Light of Historical Experience*. Princeton: Princeton University Press.
Dines, N., N. Montagna, and E. Vacchelli. 2018. "Beyond Crisis Talk. Interrogating Migration and Crisis in Europe." *Sociology* 52 (3): 439–477. doi:10.1177/0038038518767372.
Dyson, K. 2017. "Playing for High Stakes: The Eurozone Crisis." In *The European Union in Crisis*, edited by D. Dinan, N. Nugent, and Patterson. Basingstoke: Palgrave Macmillan.
Eilstrup-Sangiovanni, M. 2006. *Debates on European Integration. A Reader*. Basingstoke: Palgrave Macmillan.
FitzGibbon, J., B. Leruth, and N. Startin. 2017. *Euroscepticism as a Transnational and Pan-European Phenomenon. The Emergence of a New Sphere of Opposition*. Abingdon: Routledge.
Fligstein, N., A. Polyakova, and W. Sandholtz. 2012. "European Integration, Nationalism and European Identity." *Journal of Common Market Studies* 50 (S1): 106–122. doi:10.1111/j.1468-5965.2011.02230.x.
Ford, R., and Sobolewska. 2018. "UKIP, Brexit and the Disruptive Political Potential of English National Identity." In *Governing England. English Identity and Institutions in a Changing United Kingdom*, edited by M. Kenny, I. McLean, and A. Paun. Oxford: Oxford University Press.
Gellner, E. 1983. *Nations and Nationalism*. Oxford: Blackwell.
George, S. 1998. *An Awkward Partner. Britain in the European Community 3e*. Oxford: Oxford University Press.
Haas, E. 1968 [1958]. *The Uniting of Europe*. Standord CA: Stanford University Press.
Hayton, R. 2016. "The UK Independence Party and the Politics of Englishness." *Political Studies Review* 14 (3): 400–410. doi:10.1177/1478929916649612.
Henderson, A., C. Jeffery, R. Scully, D. Wincott, and R. WynJones. 2017. "How Brexit Was Made in England." *British Journal of Politics and International Relations* 19 (4): 631–646. doi:10.1177/1369148117730542.
Hennig, B., and D. Dorling. 2016. "In Focus: The EU Referendum." *Political Insight*. September 2016 20–21.
Hobolt, S. 2016. "The Brexit Vote: A Divided Nation, a Divided Continent." *Journal of European Public Policy* 23 (9): 1259–1277. doi:10.1080/13501763.2016.1225785.
Johnson, B. 2016. "There Is Only One Way to Get the Change We Want – Vote to Leave the EU", *The Telegraph*, 21 February 2016, accessed 22 February 2016. http://www.telegraph.co.uk/news/newstopics/eureferendum/12167643/Boris-Johnson-there-is-only-one-way-to-get-the-change-we-want-vote-to-leave-the-EU.html

Kaiser, W. 2010. "From Isolation to Centrality: Contemporary History Meets European Studies." In *European Union History, Themes and Debates*, edited by W. Kaiser and A. Varsori. Basingstoke: Palgrave Macmillan.

Karolewski, I. P., and A. Suszycki, A. (eds.) 2007. *Nationalism and European Integration. The Need for New Theoretical and Empirical Insights*. Continuum Books: New York.

Kenny, M. 2014. *The Politics of English Nationhood*. Oxford: Oxford University Press.

Kenny, M., I. McLean, and A. Paun. eds. 2018. *Governing England. English Identity and Institutions in a Changing United Kingdom*. Oxford: Oxford University Press.

Kenny, M., and N. Pearce. 2018. *Shadows of Empire: The Anglosphere in British Politics*. Cambridge: Polity Press.

Leconte, C. 2010. *Understanding Euroscepticism*. Basingstoke: Palgrave Macmillan.

Leruth, B., S. Gänzle, and J. Trondal. 2019. "Exploring Differentiated Disintegration in a Post-Brexit European Union." *Journal of Common Market Studies* 57 (5): 1013–1030. doi:10.1111/jcms.12869.

Lequesne, C. 2018. "Brexit and the Future of EU Theory." In *The Routledge Handbook of the Politics of Brexit*, edited by P. Diamond, P. Nedergaard and B. Rosamond. Abingdon: Routledge.

Mann, R., and S. Fenton. 2017. *Nation, Class and Resentment. The Politics of National Identity in England, Scotland and Wales*. Basingstoke: Palgrave Macmillan.

Manners, I., and P. Murray. 2016. "The end of a noble narrative? European integration narratives after the Nobel Peace Prize." *Journal of common market studies* 54 (1): 185–202.

May, T. 2016. "Statement from the New Prime Minister Theresa May, 13 July 2016." accessed 18 September 2016. https://www.gov.uk/government/speeches/statement-from-the-new-prime-minister-theresa-may

Moravscik, A. 2016. "The Great Brexit Kabuki – A Masterclass in Political Theatre." *Financial Times* 8 (April): 2016.

Nairn, T. 2003 [1977]. *The Break-up of Britain. Crisis and Neo-nationalism*. London: Verso.

Offe, C. 2015. *Europe Entrapped*. Cambridge: Polity Press.

Parsons, C. 2003. *A Certain Idea of Europe*. Ithaca, NY: Cornell University Press.

Paun, A. 2018. "Sovereignty, Evolution and the English Constitution." In *Governing England. English Identity and Institutions in a Changing United Kingdom*, edited by M. Kenny, I. McLean, and A. Paun. Oxford: Oxford University Press.

Schimmelfennig, F. 2018. "Brexit: Differentiated Disintegration in the European Union." *Journal of European Public Policy* 25 (8): 1154–1173. doi:10.1080/13501763.2018.1467954.

Schulz-Forberg, H., and B. Stråth. 2010. *The Political History of European Integration. The Hypocrisy of Democracy Through Market*. Abingdon: Routledge.

Slack, J. 2016. "Enemies of the People: Fury over "Out of Touch" Judges Who Have "Declared War on Democracy" by Defying 17.4m Brexit Voters and Who Could Trigger a Constitutional Crisis". *Daily Mail*, 3 November 2016, accessed 17 July 2017. http://www.dailymail.co.uk/news/article-3903436/Enemies-people-Fury-touch-judges-defied-17-4m-Brexit-voters-trigger-constitutional-crisis.html

Startin, N., and S. Usherwood. 2013. "Euroscepticism as a Persistent Phenomenon." *Journal of Common Market Studies* 51 (1): 1–16. doi: 10.1111/j.1468-5965.2012.02297.x.

Taylor, P. 2008. *The End of European Integration: Anti-Europeanism Explained*. Abingdon: Routledge.

Trenz, H.-J. 2018. "Euroscepticism as Polity Contestation." In *The Routledge Handbook of Euroscepticism*. Abingdon: Routledge.

Varsori, A. 2010. "From Normative Impetus to Professionalization: Origins and Operations of Research Networks." In *European Union History, Themes and Debates*, edited by W. Kaiser and A. Varsori. Basingstoke: Palgrave Macmillan.

Vollard, H. 2014. "Explaining European Disintegration." *Journal of Common Market Studies* 52 (2): 1142–1159. doi:10.1111/jcms.12132.

Webber, D. 2017. "Can the EU Survive?" In *The European Union in Crisis*, edited by D. Dinan, N. Nugent, and W. Paterson. Basingstoke: Palgrave Macmillan.

Webber, D. 2019. *European Disintegration. The Politics of Crisis in the European Union*. Basingstoke: Palgrave Macmillan.

Wellings, B. 2019. *English Nationalism, Brexit and the Anglosphere. Wider Still and Wider*. Manchester: Manchester University Press.

Wellings, B., and E. Vines. 2016. "'Populism and Sovereignty: The EU Act and the In-Out Referendum, 2010-15'." *Parliamentary Affairs* 69 (2): 309–326. doi:10.1093/pa/gsv045.

Wyn Jones, R., G. Lodge, C. Jeffery, G. Gottfried, R. Scully, A. Henderson and D. Wincott. 2013. *England and Its Two Unions: Anatomy of a Nation and Its Discontents*. London: Institute for Public Policy Research.

Wyn Jones, R., G. Lodge, A. Henderson, and D. Wincott. 2012. *The Dog that Finally Barked. England as an Emerging Political Community*. London: Institute for Public Policy Research.

YouGov. 2019. "Most Conservative Members Would See Party Destroyed to Achive Brexit." 18 June 2019. accessed 19 December 2019. https://yougov.co.uk/topics/politics/articles-reports/2019/06/18/most-conservative-members-would-see-party-destroye

Zielonka, J. 2014. *Is the EU Doomed?* Cambridge: Polity Press.

Zielonka, J. 2018. *Counter-revolution. Liberal Europe in Retreat*.

Labour and the Interplay of Brexit and Electoral Politics

Emmanuelle Avril

ABSTRACT

This article analyses the interplay of Brexit as an issue *per se* and as a game of electoral politics between Labour and the Conservatives, from the time of the 2016 EU referendum to the December 2019 election. It seeks to provide a nuanced and multidimensional understanding of Labour's strategic choices in relation to Brexit which goes beyond one-dimensional accounts of Jeremy Corbyn's failure of leadership. This is achieved through a game theory approach whereby the game of electoral politics is conceived of as 'nested' inside the Brexit game in a way which makes the two arenas interdependent, also taking into account the level of intra-party politics and the tensions within Labour itself. Thus the first section of the article unpicks the strategic dilemmas Labour was facing, while the second section examines Labour's ambivalent response to these challenges. The final section explores the dynamic balance of contradictory forces at play, tracking the evolution of Labour's position in the electoral game from 2016 to 2019 through an analysis of the main strengths and weaknesses of the party at various points during the period.

Introduction

Academic and media analyses of the Labour Party's handling of Brexit have tended to focus almost exclusively on the performance of the leadership, and more specifically that of Jeremy Corbyn, the party leader, who was almost universally viewed as inept if not deliberately obstructive, a sentiment seemingly confirmed by Labour's dismal results in the December 2019 general election in which the party lost 60 seats. The common assumption among pro-EU advocates is that, throughout the Brexit debate, Labour held the key to the outcome but failed to deliver, in effect facilitating Brexit, while those who favoured exit from the EU resented his equivocations on honouring the referendum result. Corbyn's ambivalent stance over Brexit is an obvious place to start when trying to understand Labour's predicament. Yet a more interesting line of analysis lies not so much in assessing how ineffectual the party leadership was on the matter of Brexit, but in examining the new dynamic resulting from the interaction between the EU arena and the UK electoral arena. Indeed, the puzzlement felt by observers as well as members of the Labour Party since the referendum calls for an approach able to identify the combination of structural and contingent factors accounting for the party's position in the Brexit debate.

This article therefore proposes to analyse the interplay of Brexit as an issue *per se* and of Brexit as a game of electoral politics – also taking into account the level of intra-party politics and the tensions within Labour itself – from the referendum campaign of 2016 to the December 2019 general election. It assesses Labour's responses through the lens of rational-choice theory, calling more specifically on the theory of nested games which frames this special issue, in which the game of electoral politics and the Brexit game are embedded – nested – in each other. The nested games theoretical framework is useful on two main levels. First, it conceptualises the notion that, when games are embedded, the analysis of one the games in isolation from the others may lead to puzzles, and that only the study of the whole network of games will explain an actor's behaviour (Tsebelis 1990, 5). The analysis of Labour's behaviour over Brexit therefore needs to take into account the various moving parts within all the layers of games simultaneously. Secondly, the nested games approach helps understand that seemingly irrational behaviour is in fact frequently the reflection of a 'disagreement between the actor and observer' (1990: 6–7) and that what can be regarded as an (sub)optimal choice in one arena may not be so in another. If a choice appears as suboptimal, it may be because the observer's perspective is incomplete, possibly because there are more options than the observer believes, or because the player may be actually in the process of trying to change the rules of the game so as to increase his strategy space. Therefore one key aspect of nested games, as in the case of Brexit and electoral politics, is that they pose a challenge for both the players and the observers of the game. For the players, 'the challenge [...] is to understand just what game they are playing in', as all players may not be playing the same game. For the observer, the challenge is to 'analyse [the games] in a way that minimizes the misunderstanding' (McCain 2014, 316).

This article tracks the evolution of Labour's position on Brexit, from the referendum to the December 2019 general election, paying attention to all the moving parts in all layers of game, so as to assess the complex impact of Brexit on the game of electoral politics and on Labour. Thus the first section of the article unpicks the manifold strategic dilemmas Labour was faced with, while the second section examines Labour's ambivalent responses to those challenges. The third and final section explores the dynamic balance of contradictory forces at play, tracking the evolution of Labour's position in the electoral game from 2016 to 2019 through an analysis of the main strengths and weaknesses of the party at various points during the period and within the multiple nested games it operated in.

1. Brexit and Labour's Strategic Dilemmas

One of the main ironies of the 2016 EU referendum campaign is that Labour should have been in a strong position to make the case for Remain since the once dividing issue of Europe had been pacified in the late 1980s (Evans 2000; Hooghe, Marks, and Wilson 2002). There were indeed only a handful of prominent Eurosceptic Labour MPs (Kate Hoey and Gisela Stuart were among the most vocal) and in total, on the eve of the vote, only 10 Labour MPs had declared they would vote Leave (BBC News 2016a), while all the key figures in the party supported Remain. In addition, a poll conducted in June 2016 showed that 90% of Labour Party members had voted to Remain (YouGov2016b). Therefore the Labour Party as an organisation looked unambiguously pro-Remain.

Yet there were several caveats to this apparent consensus. First, it was widely believed that Jeremy Corbyn – a traditional left-wing critic of the EU – had only reluctantly agreed to toe the party line: documents leaked from the leader's office purported to show that Corbyn had 'sabotaged' the Remain campaign (BBC News2016b). In the BBC documentary *Brexit: Battle for Britain* broadcast on 8 August 2016, Lord Mandelson also accused Corbyn of having deliberately sabotaged the campaign to keep Britain in the EU. This reflected a view among Remainers that not only that Corbyn was to blame for the referendum result but that, having failed to play his expected role during the campaign, he should then have placed the party's dominant Pro-EU sentiment ahead of the voters'. Secondly, a major weakness lay with the lack of passion that the European issue then inspired at grassroots level (as opposed to the heartfelt pro-EU sentiment displayed by most Labour MPs). A measure of this indifference is the fact that at the 2016 annual conference, Brexit was not picked as one of the eight topics deserving of a debate by either the Constituency Labour Party or trade union delegates (although this may have simply been a result of conference agenda management by the leadership to avoid a public expression of rifts on the topic). Finally, polls showed that Labour voters were divided on the issue, with about a third harbouring anti-EU sentiment (YouGov 2016a). For all these reasons, regardless of his own lack of enthusiasm, Corbyn's task, which was to mobilise campaigners for Remain and bring the anti-EU voters over to the Remain side, was by any measure a very challenging one.

Following the EU referendum vote, Labour's tactics over Brexit were based on often contradictory analyses of Labour voters' behaviour in the referendum, in the June 2017 general election and in the May 2019 European Elections, as well as their voting intentions as expressed in opinion polls throughout the period, making it difficult to devise an overall strategy. Because of the majoritarian First-Past-The-Post system used in general elections, particularly crucial in this triangulation exercise was analysis of the vote in the Leave constituencies in the North of England and the Midlands – 59.3% voted to leave in the West Midlands; 58% in the North East (Electoral Commission 2020) – which made up a large part of the party's 'heartlands' and became known in the media during the December 2019 election campaign as Labour's 'Red Wall'. Therefore, even though overall the Labour referendum vote had gone 2 to 1 in favour of Remain, there was a perception that the UK's electoral system has created 'an almost impossible electoral quandary [. . .], for around 70% of Labour voters supported Remain, but 70% of Labour constituencies were majority Leave' (Harrop 2017b: 4). The task of designing Labour's best electoral strategy was rendered all the more complex that not only was the Labour vote polarised between two seemingly antagonistic categories of voters, but the Leave vote, and, within this, the Labour Leave vote, was itself fragmented: the pro-democracy public opinion research company Datapraxis identified five different types of Labour Leave voters, labelled 'blue-collar working households', 'legacy older council estate', those 'struggling to make ends meet', the 'totally disaffected', and a younger group termed 'transient terraces' (Datapraxis 2019: 24). In the circumstances campaigns were not succeeding in reversing Eurosceptic sentiment among several sections of the Labour vote.

Another key factor was differential turnout – which measures how different groups within society turnout for elections – since turnout among Labour voters was the lowest of the main parties: only 73% of those who had voted Labour in 2015 turned out to vote in the referendum, compared to 80% of those of who had voted Liberal Democrat, 83% of those who had voted Conservative, and 86% of those who had voted UKIP (Ipsos MORI 2016). This has indeed been a chronic problem for Labour as voters from lower social grades as well as Black, Asian, and minority ethnic (BAME) voters tend to vote less: 69% of BAME voters voted to Remain but only 58% of those who were registered to vote actually did so.

Therefore, there was a perception among Labour strategists, such as campaign coordinators John McDonnell and Karie Murphy, as well as Corbyn's director of communications and strategy Seumas Milne, that Labour found itself trapped in a bind as it needed to find a way to recapture the lost Labour voters without alienating the urban middle-class pro-EU voters (a category of voters routinely labelled the 'cosmopolitan' vote). This required building 'the electoral alliance between the "haves" and "have nots" that is required to win greater numbers of marginal seats' (Diamond and Cadywould 2017: 26). The weight of the Leave vote in party strongholds in the North and the Midlands is one reason why the Labour leadership and some MPs vowed to 'accept' the referendum result and were wary of proclaiming a pro-European stance. But closer analysis of the results and of what the polls meant for Labour showed that, in Leave constituencies, a clear majority (58%) of Labour voters across in the North and the Midlands had voted to Remain (Curtice 2017). One study conducted by the pro-Remain group *Best for Britain* corroborated the idea that fear of Brexit Labour voters had been overestimated, since it found numerous examples of Labour-held constituencies where Remain supporters in fact outnumbered the MP's majority (Crerar 2018). Focus groups also suggested Labour Leave voters would vote for a Labour government even if its position on Brexit changed, as they were also concerned about other issues such as the NHS and the railways (Curtice 2017). In the 2017 general election, Labour's support mainly consisted of Remain voters, with Labour successfully uniting urban Britain, from the young and economically precarious to the liberal professional classes. But Labour also won the support of sufficient Leave voters to hold on to most of its Eurosceptic heartlands, partly because Brexit was now considered a 'done deal' (Harrop 2017b: 4). In addition, with the Conservatives favouring a 'hard' Brexit and Labour a much 'softer' one, many Remainers felt comfortable voting Labour. Data collected by the *British Election Study* in the run-up to the December 2019 election also indicated that the optimal strategy for Labour would be to make a clear pitch to Remainers (Fieldhouse 2019). All these elements show that the perception that Labour needed to hold on to its Leave vote – a notion Ford described in a tweet on 14 January 2019 as 'one of the most damaging zombie beliefs in the whole politics of Brexit debate' – was essentially fallacious and that there would in fact be an electoral dividend for Labour in many seats if they moved position and opposed Brexit.

At the same time, most surveys showed little change in people's general attitude to Brexit (e.g. Hobolt, Leeper and Tilley 2017: 18), as people's identities as Remainers and Leavers became more and more entrenched over time. The intractable character of the Leave vote was demonstrated in the May 2019 local elections, in which Labour fared unexpectedly poorly in the working-class and Leave-leaning constituencies the party would need to win in order to secure a majority in the Commons (the Labour vote fell by an average of two points in northern seats). The disappointing results were interpreted by the Labour leadership as a sign that Labour Leavers were getting impatient with the prevarications and just wanted to see 'Brexit done' (Stewart 2019b), an analysis which the Boris Johnson-led Conservative party shared and successfully seized upon. Although poll tracking since June 2017 showed that the Corbyn anti-austerity project still had purchase among large sections of the voters in Leave constituencies (YouGov 2019), the 2019 local election results were interpreted by the leadership as a warning against the party drifting too far towards a Remain position.

In addition, the Brexit issue now seemed to trump all others. According to research carried out by Goodwin and Heath (2017), in the 2017 general election, 'most voters ranked Brexit as the top issue facing Britain, with 57% identifying "leaving the EU" as among the most important issues, well ahead of health (40%), immigration (36%) and the economy (27%)'. As the successive Brexit deadlines drew closer, prominence of the issue among the membership was also increasing: a YouGov survey conducted in September 2018 showed 86% of party members calling for a second referendum (Helm, 2018). Given these elements, Labour understandably sought to downplay Brexit as an issue – a strategy reflected by the lack of prominence given to Brexit on the party's website, where it stood as one element of policy as any other, on a par with the economy, education, or housing. In the foreword to the 2019 election Manifesto, Corbyn reiterated this line: 'Some people say this is the Brexit election. But it's also the climate election, the investment election, the NHS election, the living standards election, the education election, the poverty election, the fair taxes election' (Labour Party 2019).

Beyond aspects of electoral politics, Brexit also blatantly exposed the potential interferences between a direct democracy mechanism such as a referendum and the rules of representative democracy (de Vreese 2006; Hobolt 2006, 2009; Leemann and Wasserfallen 2016). In the bipolar adversarial UK parliamentary system, characterised by a high level of stability because of the (usually) strong majorities commanded by the winning party, a key function of political parties is to aggregate often diverse interests, thus providing some degree of consensus among the various groups each represents. But the direct democracy mechanism of the referendum resulted in the confrontation of two antagonistic positions, polarising public opinion around a new pro- and anti-Brexit line of cleavage. The forces at play in the Brexit debate eroded even further an already weakened two-party system (Schleiter and Belu 2016). While the mechanism of the majoritarian First-Past-The-Post system may hinder the emergence of new parties (attempts to build a new Macron-style centrist party collapsed after a few months), the centrifugal forces of Brexit have been shattering the broad church, catch-all party model, pushing both mainstream parties further and further into a corner of having to position themselves on this polarising issue. In accepting the result of the vote and giving no sign that it would push for a reversal of the decision, the Labour party leadership signalled that it has decided to prioritise talking to the Leave voters in a bid to reconnect the party with its working-class vote (Ainsley 2018; Berry 2018; Evans and Tilley 2000). As the terms of the debate shifted to what kind of Brexit should be favoured, not whether to stay in or come out, with the Labour leadership pitching itself as the champion of the 'softer Brexit' option, the two-party system seemed at first to have reasserted itself (Heath and Goodwin 2017). Paradoxically, for a time, it was the parties which had adopted a clear stance on Brexit (UKIP and the Liberal Democrats) which were destabilised the most. Yet the radicalisation and continuing tensions within the conservative party under Boris Johnson and Labour's dismal results in December 2019 also show that the broad church party model has been stretched to breaking point. Whatever recomposition follows, both within the Labour Party and the party system as a whole, it will demonstrate that the EU referendum has reconfigured the national game that created it.

Another aspect of Labour's strategic dilemmas flowed from the unusual feature of a referendum result which failed to obtain 'loser's consent' from the 48% who had voted against Brexit (van der Eijk 2017). The reasons for this lack of consent include the closeness of the result (Nigel Farage, expecting the results to go the other way by a similarly small margin had warned that he would not accept the result and demand a second referendum), the conduct of the campaign (in May 2016 both sides in the EU referendum campaign were accused of peddling 'misleading' figures and 'implausible assumptions' by the Treasury Select Committee), and the insistence by Conservative Prime Minister Theresa May – and then her successor Boris Johnson – that the result, despite the very slender margin, reflected 'the will of the people', so that there was no need to address the concerns of Remainers and no real attempt to build cross-party consensus. Under the circumstances, abiding by the result was regarded by Labour Remainers as a betrayal rather than a mere acceptance of the result of a democratic vote.

Overall therefore, the Brexit debate both exposed and deepened Labour's electoral weaknesses, such as the party's collapse in Scotland and the alienation of Leave voters, and organisational contradictions, reflected in the tensions between the parliamentary group, the leadership and the grassroots base.

2. The Ambiguities of the Labour Party: strategic fog?

Jeremy Corbyn was elected leader of the Labour Party in September 2015 with a mandate from a vastly expanded party grassroots to overhaul the terms of the UK's relationship with the EU and to place workers' rights front and centre, thus breaking away from the hitherto supposedly dominant business-oriented stance. The challenge for the Labour leadership was therefore to square the circle of voicing deep-seated popular resentment against the EU – relentlessly fanned by an overwhelmingly Eurosceptic conservative press (Daddow 2015) – while advocating continued membership.

The dilemmas resulting from the collision between the UK electoral arena and the EU arena were strikingly illustrated by the dual message displayed on the Party website's landing page during the Brexit campaign, asking supporters 'Can you help us fight back?' whilst declaring that 'Labour are in for Britain' (labour.org.uk, 22 May 2016): the Labour campaign consistently followed parallel tracks, simultaneously calling for a fightback against the Conservatives and advocating for a Remain vote. The two messages cohabited uneasily, especially as the precedent of the 2014 Scottish independence referendum, which 'saw Labour and Conservatives in an uncomfortable alliance under the umbrella of Better Together' (Mitchell 2015: 90), had worsened Labour's standing with Scottish voters and shown the potential electoral cost which might result from openly campaigning alongside the Conservative Prime Minister, David Cameron. It is revealing of the tension between the party political arena and the EU referendum arena that Corbyn's campaign speeches hammered the argument that the EU was not the real fight, and that the party needed to focus on attacking the Conservatives instead, a clear indication that his priority was to try and preserve the organisational unity of the Labour party, as opposed to maximise the pro-EU vote.

Turning to the substance of Labour's message, it is useful to take a closer look at Corbyn's three main campaign speeches. At the launch of the campaign, on 14 April 2016, Corbyn stated that 'It's perfectly possible to be critical and still be convinced we need to remain a member' and that 'It is not the EU that is the problem, but a Conservative government here in Britain' (Corbyn 2016a). At the relaunch, on 2nd June, after accusations that he had not been doing enough, he reiterated 'We, the Labour Party, are overwhelmingly for staying in' and 'The threat to the British people is not the European Union, it is a Conservative Government here in Britain' (Corbyn 2016b). The Conservatives and not the EU were the enemy (or the 'threat') and there should be no compromise on free movement. In his last speech on 22nd June, Corbyn, who until then had delegated the job of making the case for Remain to Alan Johnson, the former Labour Home Secretary and head of the *Labour In For Britain* campaign, realised that it was his own cue which really mattered. Although he continued to stick to his 'Remain and Reform' line and reasserted that there should be no limits to the number of EU workers who come to Britain, the message was more explicitly pro-EU, and this time he gave his personal endorsement, stating 'I want to stay in Europe' (Corbyn 2016c). So his eve of poll speech did show him stepping up, but came too late to make a difference.

Corbyn thus tried to straddle the two sides of the argument, by calling for a Remain vote while stressing the need to keep a critical distance. The ambivalence of the 'Remain and Reform' stance, with the EU defined as the best of two evils, was such that there was uncertainty among the public that Corbyn actually supported Remain at all. Indeed a leaked memo from the *Britain Stronger in Europe* campaign and based on data drawn from focus groups found that Labour supporters were 'uniformly uncertain' about the party's position on Europe (Ashmore 2016). Therefore throughout the campaign Corbyn tried to perform a balancing act, making enough pro-EU noise to reassure his pro-EU MPs, members and voters, but also dropping enough hints at anti-EU MPs and voters to indicate that he was on their side. In the context of the Brexit negotiations conducted by Prime Minister May, the overall ambiguity continued, so much so that Labour faced a barrage of criticism for its confused approach to Brexit, with a string of ex senior Labour figures – among whom ex Labour leaders Tony Blair and Neil Kinnock, as well as Blair's director of communications Alastair Campbell – urging Corbyn to take a clear stance (e.g. BBC News 2018b). The crisis culminated in February 2019 with the resignation of 8 Labour MPs (the rebels cited Brexit, the party's left turn as well as antisemitism as reasons for leaving the party) who joined forces with Conservative MPs to sit as The Independent Group, later officially established as a new centrist party named Change UK. This move prompted comparisons with the 'Gang of Four' who had left the Labour Party in 1981 to create the Social Democratic Party, in protest over Labour's policy over Europe. A YouGov poll conducted on 17–19 December 2017 suggested that even people who planned to vote Labour at the next election were unsure of the party's position, with nearly a quarter saying they thought Labour was completely against Brexit, while a third thought the party sat on the fence, and a tenth said they just had no idea (Lee 2018).

However, this continued confusion, with mixed messages being sent out (intentionally or not) by senior Labour figures, does not mean to say that the party remained static. Labour arguably travelled in fact a long way, albeit incrementally, in a succession of policy shifts, up to the point where the leadership had become, by the autumn of 2019, openly committed to the idea of a second vote on any Brexit deal. A close examination of Labour's stance on three of the main issues of Brexit, immigration, single market membership and a second referendum shows some marked evolution. On immigration, Labour remained fairly consistent, although the Shadow Cabinet was divided on the issue, with Emily Thornberry, the Shadow Foreign Secretary, advocating immigration controls, while Shadow Chancellor John McDonnell and Jeremy Corbyn were wary of full freedom of movement which they said negatively affects wages and conditions (Lee 2018). The challenge here was to find measures that could be introduced to curb EU immigration which would be compatible with EU freedom of movement rules, and idea encapsulated in the notion of 'managed migration' which seems to have become acceptable to all sides.

On single market membership, however, Labour struggled to keep a consistent line. Before and immediately after the June 2017 snap election, they were clear that the UK would have to leave the single market. But by the autumn of the same year, senior figures had begun to undermine that clarity by suggesting single market membership could continue indefinitely beyond the transition period. Indeed, John McDonnell – who had previously said that staying in the single market would be seen as 'not respecting' the referendum result – seemed to make a U-turn by suggesting that single market membership was not off the table (BBC News 2017). The next step, Shadow Secretary of State for Exiting the European Union Keir Starmer's 'internal market' proposal, which he put forward in

June 2018, was as close as the party could come to openly supporting single market membership, bearing in mind that full membership was seen as a problem because voters were demanding immigration control – a collection of essays published by left-wing think tank the Fabian Society stressed in 2016 that Labour 'must respect people's desire for control' (Fabian Society 2016) – and Corbyn wanted a free reign to intervene in the economy. The fact that Corbyn's most senior advisors, Seamus Milne and Karie Murphy, believed that 'EU membership will trammel a future government's capacity to pursue radical economic policies' accounts for their being relatively 'sanguine' about Brexit (Shaw 2019). The proposal was derided in a tweet by *Guardian* columnist Rafael Behr as 'a new tortured verbal convolution to avoid having a position' (6 June 2018), but was also clearly an attempt to nod at both sides of the debate. The position shifted markedly in early 2019 as Corbyn made staying in the customs union the first of the five conditions he presented to Theresa May in exchange for his support. This 'soft' Brexit position (which had caused angry clashes between supporters of the leadership's position and pro-EU campaigners during the party's annual conference in September) was confirmed when Labour's 2019 Election Manifesto stated that 'within three months of coming to power, a Labour government will secure a sensible deal', including a 'permanent and comprehensive UK-wide customs union', and maintaining 'close alignment with the Single Market', as well as 'dynamic alignment on workers' rights, consumer rights and environmental protections' (Labour Party 2019: 89–90).

Finally, on the matter of a second referendum, there were mixed messages from senior Labour frontbenchers for most of the period on whether a 'public vote' might be possible in the future. Tom Watson, the deputy leader, said in September 2017 that the party was 'not ruling it out' but that it was 'highly unlikely'. Two months later it emerged that Diane Abbott, the Shadow Home Secretary, had stated in letters to her constituents that she would 'argue for the right of the electorate to vote on any deal that is finally agreed.' (Lee 2018). While in December of the same year, Jeremy Corbyn said that 'We've not made any decision on a second referendum', on 14 January 2018, he seemed to have settled the issue, declaring on ITV's Peston on Sunday: 'We are not supporting or calling for a second referendum … what we've called for is a meaningful vote in Parliament.' Yet on the very same day Emily Thornberry – who would go on to become one of the most vocal proponents of this option – suggested on the BBC's Andrew Marr show that a second referendum wasn't completely ruled out (BBC News 2018a).

Crucially, the idea of a second referendum as an 'option' when all other routes have failed was endorsed at the annual conference in the autumn of 2018, the continued preferred option being to push for a general election: 'If we cannot get a general election Labour must support all options remaining on the table, including campaigning for a public vote.' (LabourList 2018), a line which was adhered to until very close to the December 2019 election. This was taken as a very encouraging sign by those supporting a second referendum, although the notion of 'public vote' was rather vague and the terms of a possible referendum, including what options would be included, were not yet specified. Further shifts in the first months of 2019, however, clarified that Labour was indeed moving more explicitly towards espousing a confirmatory public vote. Therefore even if a second referendum had not officially become party policy, since it had not been included in the 2017 manifesto and Corbyn had been very reluctant to take the step, many voices, including that of the Shadow Chancellor, were by then signalling that, failing a general election, this would become party policy. Thus on February 17, in an attempt to dissuade potential splitters from taking the plunge, John McDonnell said there was no need for a split over Brexit because the party may still back a people's vote: 'You'd only go back to the people in extremis, if you can't get a deal agreed through parliament or if a deal isn't going to protect jobs and the economy, you'd have to go back to the people' (McDonnell, 2019). Even if, by Spring 2019, the matter had yet to be settled, as attested by the internal wrangles over the content of Labour's 2019 European Election Manifesto (Stewart 2019a), the 2019 general election Manifesto took the plunge, committing Labour to giving the people 'the final say on Brexit' within six months of a Labour government being formed, with a deal being put to a public vote alongside, crucially, the option to remain.

Flexible ambiguity, in the shape of small incremental policy shifts while professing to respect the outcome of the Brexit vote, which had long precluded openly supporting a second referendum, had finally explicitly opened up the possibility of reversing the referendum vote, a move which, given the catastrophic results of the December elections for Labour, has proved highly controversial, with some critics considering that the prospect of a new Brexit deal and a public vote – alongside a marked lack of faith in Corbyn among these categories of voters – cost the Party its traditional working-class vote who just wanted 'Brexit done', and others holding the exact opposite view that Labour would have fared much better should it have stood more clearly on an anti-Brexit platform and maximised the pro-EU vote (on the two rival explanations see for example Quinn 2019).

While Corbyn's leadership on Europe was, from the referendum campaign, derided as simply non-existent, he himself claimed that his ambivalent stance resulted from a strategic choice to overcome the polarisation between Leavers and Remainers, as this was thought to be Labour's key asset to win in a general election. This idea was reiterated on the occasion of the launch of Labour's May 2019 Euro election campaign, when he declared: 'we insist the real divide in our country is not how people voted in the EU referendum. The real divide is between the many and the few' (Corbyn 2019), and throughout the December 2019 general election campaign he sought to portray Boris Johnson's government as divisive, presenting Labour as 'the only party that can heal the harmful divisions in our communities', and stating that 'while other parties have exacerbated polarisation, defining everyone by how they voted in the 2016 EU Referendum, Labour has consistently reached across this divide' (Labour Party 2019: 91). This was a means to put the Conservatives in a corner as the party of Brexit who would have to take the blame for any damaging consequence, but this also meant that while the Conservatives were set to become the dominant party of Leave voters, there was no one party consolidating the Remain vote (Mellon and Prosser 2017). The fact that the strategy failed spectacularly does not mean an absence of strategy, and the Conservative Party's impressive success in the 2019 election does not preclude a later downturn, since Brexit is in fact by no means 'done'. At the level of the intra-party game, although Corbyn's approach to Brexit has been consistently attacked by his internal opponents as a failure of leadership, his ambivalent stance can also be seen as a tool for managing dissent within his party and quelling rising discontent among his left-wing yet pro-European support base.

In this light, the seemingly over-careful use of language displayed by Corbyn over Brexit for most of the period between the referendum campaign and the December election can be taken to reflect his attempt at using negotiation tools rather than mere prevarication, allowing him to evade the more sensitive issue of Brexit, both externally and internally, while trying to make progress in other areas. Harold Wilson, who is said to have been fond of the aphorism that parliamentary politics is about being able to ride two horses at once, had successfully resorted to similar tactics when managing party splits over the same issue in the early 1970s, positioning himself as a broker between contending camps. 'Constructive ambiguity' is indeed one of the main weapons in the negotiating arsenal (see for example Mitchell 2009 on the effective use of this during the 1998 Belfast Agreement negotiations), as ambiguous language can be used 'to carve out spaces within which more than one interpretation is possible' (Usherwood 2017). In fact, such discursive strategy of deliberately crafting an ambiguous message to create more room for manoeuvre in highly constrained institutional environments, and to simultaneously advance other issues relatively unnoticed, is a discourse practice well-known to specialists of 'discursive institutionalism' (Bell 2011; Schmidt 2008). All these circumvolutions show that the game of Brexit cannot be seen in isolation from the games played in the other arenas and that these various dimensions are completely intertwined.

3. The Impact of the Brexit debate on the Labour Party

This section tracks the impact of the Brexit debate on the Labour Party's strategic position over the period so as to provide an organisational diagnosis based on the identification of the party's main strengths and weaknesses at the leadership, party, and societal levels, in the pursuit of a general election win. Holding power in the government is the official purpose of any majoritarian party, and even more so that of Her Majesty's Most Loyal Opposition, as well as being the stated purpose of Labour's leadership. Indeed achieving a general election was central to Labour's strategy throughout the debates over the UK's withdrawal from the EU, especially in the context of a Conservative party deeply divided on Brexit and emerging out of the June 2017 election with a minority in the House of Commons and thus dependent upon the unreliable support of the 10 Northern Ireland Democratic Unionist MPs.

The range of elements affecting a party's image and popularity with the voters is very wide, yet some elements may be seen as directly affecting voters' behaviour in a general election because of their prominence in the public debate at the time: the strengths and weaknesses of Corbyn as a leader, the changes in the party (the internal tensions within the parliamentary party which culminated in the summer 2016 leadership challenge, the vast expansion of the grassroots consolidated and exploited by Momentum) as well as in the party system as a whole (the rapid decline of UKIP following the vote, rising competition from other contenders such as the Scottish National Party, the Liberal Democrats and, in 2019, the newly created Brexit party), and the issues which had taken centre stage during and after the campaign (in particular immigration, the anti-establishment feeling, as well as some degree of backlash against austerity which Corbyn's rise seems to illustrate), including extensive negative media coverage of Jeremy Corbyn (see for example the audits of the 2017 and 2019 general election media coverage conducted by the Loughborough University's Centre for Research in Communication and Culture) and the impact of the antisemitism row (which saw the leadership accused of failing to efficiently deal with accusations of antisemitism in the party; on the list of antisemitism claims see BBC News 2019). The analysis of Labour's strengths and weaknesses at three different points from the 2016 referendum until the December 2019 thus helps account for the general trajectory of the Party, from a post-referendum troubled party, to a credible contender in 2017, to the collapse of 2019.

Starting with an evaluation of Labour's position at the beginning of 2017, seven months after the referendum, at a time when the party was struggling in the polls, still reeling from the 2015 general election defeat, the in-fighting which had followed the election of Corbyn as leader, and the shock of the Brexit vote, Labour's standing in the polls seemed to show how misguided the party's tactics had been since it now looked like the party would be almost certain to lose the next general election whenever it took place (YouGov's voting intention survey conducted on 9–10 January 2017 January saw the Conservatives on 39% and Labour 11 points behind on 28%).

The leadership level was the level at which the greatest imbalance between strengths and weaknesses was found, which obviously called for a change of leader. Corbyn's long-standing depiction of the UE as a capitalist club made him highly unsuited to the task of articulating pro-Remain sentiment in his party. But since the challenge against him in the summer of 2016 had in fact entrenched his position at the head of the party, the option of replacing him was not available in the short term. In the longer term, however, electoral disaster or a party split could lead to the emergence of a new, better suited leader, as later confirmed by the post-2019 general election leadership contest. But at this stage some of Corbyn's strengths did come through, particularly his perceived 'authenticity', his most significant leadership attribute but also a double-edged sword since 'ethical' leadership often correlates in media discourse with inefficient leadership (Bennister, Worthy, and Keith 2017; Iszatt-White et al. 2019).

At the organisational level (the party level), lack of cohesion and the ensuing cacophony were a major weakness, which called for an end to the ongoing war between the factions. Since there was no will to compromise on either side, this structural weakness was set to continue, hampering any attempt to put a coherent message across to the voters, at least until a new leader, able to straddle the factions and to unify the party, could emerge. As internal debates over Brexit developed, the two factions would turn out to be many. At this point, Labour's main competitor in the goal of recapturing the lost Labour voters was the Scottish National Party (SNP), but post-Scottish referendum and post-Brexit, it was too late to do much about this: while in the 2010 general election, Labour had won 41 out of Scotland's 59 Westminster seats, in 2017 it only managed to keep 7 seats, and 1 single seat in 2019. The danger from UKIP, on the other hand, seemed to have been over-estimated since the party's support slumped after the referendum vote now that the case for Brexit needed not be made any more (UKIP's vote share fell to about 2% in 2017, compared with 12.6% in 2015). There was also some competition from the Lib Dems but this was at this point too insignificant to be counted as a weakness. In this context, it may have been a good idea, as put forward in a Fabian Society analysis paper (Harrop 2017a), for Labour to abandon the idea that it could stand on its own and to forge an alliance with other parties.

The societal level was the one which presented the party with its greatest challenges, the main ones for Labour being negative media coverage of Corbyn (Cammaerts et al. 2016) and how to address anti-immigration sentiment. There has been a shift in public opinion which mainstream parties have been unable to contain or redirect and which insurgent populist parties – or populist factions within mainstream parties, such as the pro-Brexit conservative European Research Group – have been able to capitalise on. Anti-EU sentiment, combined with a rising distrust in the political elites (Jennings and Stoker 2016), has been stirred relentlessly for decades by the conservative press. The conundrum for Labour at this point was how to accept restrictions to free movement without pandering to racist discourse.

Overall, the post-Brexit referendum Labour Party was in very poor shape. Nevertheless, Corbyn's strong standing with the members and the rise in anti-establishment feelings in the public pointed to an obvious – but not necessarily wise – strategy. Labour released a document on 9 January stating that the Labour Party was going to put forward a 'populism of the left' in a bid to harness the anti-establishment and anti-elite wind (on Corbyn and populism see Martell 2018). A first example of this strategy was the announcement the following day of a proposed pay cap for the 'super-rich'. At the same time, there had also been a marked change from the posture of no compromise on free movement and from the idea that voters could be brought over to Corbyn's views which had been one of the pillars of Corbyn's EU referendum campaign (in his speech on 22nd June he stated 'if you have a rational discussion with people, as I try to do, and don't do it with rancour, you don't do with personal abuse, then you get a hearing'), to one where parties must follow the mood of the voters, as reflected in the idea of 'managed immigration'. This was a key shift from a position of trying to persuade the voters that the EU was the lesser of two evils, to talking to the concerns of Leave voters. There was the risk that the compromise position may blur the message even further, but clearly the party was trying to play on the few strengths that it had left.

Therefore at this point the paradox of the impact of Brexit on the party political arena was that the Conservatives, who were openly divided over the question, had come out of the campaign less damaged that Labour. This is because the referendum was a tool for Cameron to manage internal dissent and preserve party unity by shifting the question away from the party political arena. As a result, the conservative party was able to send out two messages at once so that there was a feeling among voters that Eurosceptics within the party would keep the government in check over the Brexit negotiations. Thus there is room for saying that Corbyn's ambivalent stance was as good as any to address that segment of the electorate which was not prepared to hear positive descriptions of the benefits of the EU. The problem for Labour was that ambivalence lay in Corbyn himself, casting doubt on his ability as a leader to set a direction to his party, whereas the organisation as a whole presented an unambiguously united pro-EU stance.

An analysis of Labour's standing 18 months later, in June 2018, shows that significant changes had taken place. By then Labour had managed to unexpectedly narrow the gap ahead of the June 2017 snap general election and then to win 34 extra seats, depriving Theresa May of a governing majority, a rare example of an election defeat being construed as a 'win' (e.g. Leftly 2017). This led many commentators within and without the party to revise their evaluation of Corbyn, until then almost universally derided as hopelessly unelectable, resulting in much more positive evaluations of his performance and handling of Brexit (a *Guardian* editorial stated on 2 June 2017 that 'Mr Corbyn is on to something resonant, something common, something good'). Indeed the ground had shifted significantly, Labour having 're-emerged as a viable contender for power in British politics' (Diamond and Cadywould 2017).

Overall, the number of weaknesses had declined at both the leadership and organisational levels, while at the societal level, anti-immigration sentiment was still a significant source of weakness but had receded and now looked as if it may eventually be counterbalanced by a stronger anti-austerity sentiment. Competition from UKIP had become too insignificant to even count as a weakness. On the other hand, the intensification of the antisemitism row was such that this now needed to be taken into account as a significant obstacle.

At the leadership level, whereas before the 2017 campaign had begun, voters rated Corbyn's likeability at 3.5 out of 10, by the end of the campaign, his rating had increased to 4.6 (Andersen 2019). Theresa May's lead over Corbyn, in terms of whom voters thought would make the best prime minister, had risen from 8 to 12 points in the previous month (she was now on 36% to Corbyn's 24%), but Corbyn had a significant 18-point lead when voters were asked which leader was 'in touch with ordinary people'. His perceived 'authenticity' and emotional empathy became a real asset during the campaign which pitched him against an opponent who came across as cold, remote and robotic (Wahl-Jorgensen 2018). Beyond the ups and downs, poll tracking by the Polling Report since the election showed Labour and the Conservatives to be neck and neck at around 40% each on average (http://ukpollingreport.co.uk/). Corbyn's lack of popularity as a potential Prime Minister was thus compensated by the party's good standing. Internal tensions continued to be a source of weakness, but it was then hard to gauge how influential internal critics (such as past party leaders) were on public perceptions. At the societal level, anti-immigration sentiment still posed a conundrum but the saliency of the issue had declined significantly, while the polarisation of public opinion between Leavers and Remainers seemed to have subsided.

Perhaps the most significant element in the context of this special issue, the 'blurred message' may no longer be seen as a source of weakness, and could even stand as a competitive advantage. In any case it seemed to be working in both directions. Indeed, by June 2018, the assessment of intentional and strategic fuzziness on the part of the Labour leadership seemed to have become widely shared. Observers who had previously been scathing of Corbyn's lack of clarity were now willing to grant him with some strategic acumen. Analysing the results in this new light, Menon (2018) even questioned whether Labour had anything to gain electorally by taking a clear stance against Brexit. Since changes are less noticeable when there is a perception that there is no position, this – often puzzling and frustrating – fuzziness could be seen as allowing Labour to gradually shift its stance without leaving itself open to accusations of having switched positions. Corbyn came across as being much more pragmatic than previously thought. He and his team were engaged in difficult and at times awkward electoral calculations, adopting the line that the result of the first referendum should be respected but trying to achieve the softest possible Brexit. The tactics consisted of engaging as little as possible with the issue of Brexit in the hope that Theresa May would sink herself, and her party.

As the original 29 March 2019 deadline came and went, and extension to 31 of October was granted (later to be pushed back again to the end of January 2020), and with Theresa May playing the clock in order to push her deal through the Commons, it looked increasingly as if Labour was not able to build on their 2017 relative success, as the very disappointing results in both the local and European elections of May 2019 attested (on 26 May, Labour came third behind the Brexit Party and the Lib Dems, with the Conservatives in 4th position behind the Greens). The failure to solve the Brexit issue had discredited the two main parties since both leaders stood accused of being mainly concerned with managing internal divisions within their parties and with shoring up their own positions rather than genuinely working at solving the nation's main problem. But Theresa May's resignation in June following her third defeat in the Commons over her Brexit deal, and her replacement by Boris Johnson in July, who stuck to the powerful line of getting 'Brexit done', allowed the conservative party to gain a clear advantage.

The prospect of a Labour victory had started receding when the route to a quick general election was cut off with the unsuccessful no-confidence vote of 29 January 2019 in which 26 Labour MPs supported the government and 14 abstained. At the time of the 2019 general election, the prospect of a Labour win now looked increasingly unrealistic. The overall picture was much more pessimistic for Labour than in earlier periods, since the balance between strengths and weaknesses had tilted strongly back toward the weaknesses.

At the leadership level, Corbyn found himself isolated both within the Parliamentary Labour Party, as he had been since his election as leader, and even within the Shadow Cabinet, and, this was a new development, in the wider party (Sleator 2019). He no longer benefited from facing a weak opponent, Boris Johnson having significantly changed the state of play with his unbending decisiveness over Brexit. The tensions over Corbyn's stance on Brexit had led to the creation of the new pro-EU centrist party Change UK.

At the organisational level, the main strengths were flagging whilst the main weakness, a fractured party, had gained much ground. The left was divided over Brexit between a traditional 'old' left, of which Corbyn and his highly influential aides were part, for whom Brexit was inescapable, acceptable or even desirable, and the anti-Brexit positions of some of his closest allies in the Shadow cabinet such as Diane Abbott, and, more significantly, the bulk of Momentum. Internal divisions also existed on the right, with some (among whom Stephen Kinnock) arguing that the referendum result must be abided so as not to alienate voters and most of the others who were determined to fight Brexit tooth and nail irrespective of the referendum result and of what the polls said regarding the intractable nature of pro-Brexit opinion. Brexit came to cut across the factions since the referendum presented an acute moral and strategic dilemma on whether to prioritise the process (the referendum) or the issue (Brexit). As a result there were people of both sides of the Brexit debate who argued that the referendum result must be respected. Thus, at party level, the main effect of the binary choice imposed by the referendum was to exacerbate intra-party strife, shattering the Corbyn coalition. But undoubtedly the most damaging aspect of these multiple layers of division over Brexit for Corbyn was that they generated a rift between the leadership and the grassroots base who were struggling to keep the faith, as illustrated through the slogan 'Love Corbyn. Hate Brexit'. A survey showed that 72% of Labour members wanted Corbyn to fully support a new referendum on Brexit (Bale, Webb, and Poletti 2019). Thus the benefits of a 'blurred message' for Labour were very much in question and, in light of Boris Johnson's clarity on the matter, now even looked like a suicidal stance.

The picture was getting increasingly confused as Labour's programme of reforms, once popular, at least among members and strong supporters, was completely drowned in the succession of Brexit manoeuvres on both sides. The game of party politics had been reduced to managing Brexit, which had now established itself as the single most first-order issue. At the societal level, public debate has shrunk to a bipolar tension between pro and anti-hard Brexit, while all other issues had been eclipsed or subsumed into the Brexit debate (Curtis 2017), a situation which worked against attempts to reconcile the two sides of the argument. In terms of party competition, while the SNP consolidated its grip on ex Labour voters in Scotland, Change UK failed to make any impact in the 2019 European elections (they only managed to get 3.3% of the vote and did not win a single seat) so that they disbanded following the December general election. As for the Liberal Democrat and Green surges at the May 2019 local and European elections, while they could not translate into similar hikes in a First-Past-The-Post general election, they again pointed to a possible change of strategy, as winning alone looked increasingly difficult for Labour. The remarkable success of the Brexit party, which gained 33% of the vote in the European election, and the collapse of the Conservatives, also showed that ambivalence was rejected at the polls and that recomposition on Brexit lines was taking root, at least until Brexit was resolved one way or the other. In the event, whereas a very efficient tactical alliance was forged between the Brexit

Party and the Conservative Party in the December general election, there was no such agreement among anti-Brexit parties, resulting in the fragmentation of the anti-Brexit vote among several parties.

Labour's strategic ambiguity over Brexit looked unlikely to succeed. In the 2017 election some voters, notably the young, had chosen Labour at the party 'not of Brexit', but Corbyn's stance – largely dictated by his closest aides – as seeming to favour a 'softer' Brexit left him open to accusations of not listening to his own party members and supporters and of acting in effect as a Brexit facilitator. As other tensions intensified, especially over the leadership's handling of anti-semitism, this strain was going to prove unbearable, and Corbyn, unable to navigate a chaotic intra-party environment, became insulated and failed to align himself on his party. With increasing suspicion that Corbyn's heart was not in the Remain cause, the rising levels of discontent which had spread to the pro-EU left and the activist base (which should have continued to be his strongest asset) were to prove deadly for the party.

The Labour leadership, by refusing to engage with the culture wars debate which posits that the emotion-based cultural divide between social liberals and authoritarians had supplanted the left/right divide (on the rise of identity politics see for example Goodhart 2017; Sobolewska and Ford 2020), and to accept the new polarisation of the electorate around Brexit, and trying instead to foster consensus around valence issues such as the defence of public services, navigated a middle ground between the two positions. But as the political ground kept shifting, 'constructive ambiguity' no longer seemed a credible strategy (Goes 2018; Starmer 2017). Corbyn thus ended up losing support on both sides of the argument, failed in his attempts to build a coalition (Menon and Wager 2019), and could no longer hold his acrobatic positioning.

Conclusion

What the nested games approach demonstrates is that analysis of Labour's handling of Brexit, rather than settling for a one-dimensional view of Jeremy Corbyn as solely responsible for Labour's Brexit prevarications and even for Brexit itself, must be based on a more nuanced and multidimensional approach, taking both structural and contingent factors into account. In this respect the analytical framework of nested games proves to be a very useful tool to conceptualise the way Labour navigated the contradictory forces at play. Even if, from an observer's viewpoint, Corbyn's approach seemed confused, it is unlikely that he himself felt his own actions to be irrational, as Brexit may only have been a 'subset' of his main goal: the economic and social transformation of Britain brought about by a general election win. Indeed, in trying to deal with the uncertain nature of the game and a constantly shifting environment, actors may devise 'mixed' strategies, privilege one level of the game over the other, or even attempt to innovate and change the rules of the game. Hence one of the main merits of this analytical framework is to take account of the fact that while the observer trying to make sense of events will tend to focus on one of the games, played in one specific arena considered to be the main arena, the player is in fact involved in a whole network of games playing out in various arenas (Tsebelis 1990 :7). As a result, focussing either on the Brexit arena, the electoral arena, or the arena of intra-party politics, each nesting its own sub-games, will only provide an incomplete picture of the complex multi-layered environment in which Corbyn was operating.

Disclosure statement

No potential conflict of interest was reported by the author.

ORCID

Emmanuelle Avril http://orcid.org/0000-0002-9084-2708

References

Ainsley, C. 2018. *The New Working Class: How to Win Hearts, Minds and Votes*. Policy Press.

Andersen, P. 2019. "Jeremy Corbyn: Election Study Data Suggests Labour Leader Faces a Tougher Struggle than in 2017", The Conversation. https://theconversation.com/jeremy-corbyn-election-study-data-suggests-labour-leader-faces-a-tougher-struggle-than-in-2017-120538

Ashmore, J. 2016. "Labour Voters Remain Unsure of Party's EU Referendum Position", PoliticsHome. https://www.politicshome.com/news/europe/eu-policy-agenda/brexit/news/75574/labour-voters-remain-unsure-partys-eu-referendum

Bale, T., P. Webb, and M. Poletti 2019. "Love Corbyn. HATE Brexit.", PSA Blog. https://www.psa.ac.uk/psa/news/love-corbyn-hate-brexit

BBC News. 2016a. "EU Vote: Where the Cabinet and Other MPs Stand". https://www.bbc.com/news/uk-politics-eu-referendum–35616946

BBC News. 2016b. "Corbyn Office 'Sabotaged' EU Remain Campaign - Sources". https://www.bbc.com/news/uk-politics–36633238

BBC News. 2017. "John McDonnell Not Ruling Out Single Market Membership". https://www.bbc.com/news/uk-politi cs–40726213

BBC News. 2018a. "Jeremy Corbyn: I'm Not Calling for Second EU Referendum". https://www.bbc.com/news/uk-politics–42681929

BBC News. 2018b. "Brexit: Jeremy Corbyn Must Change Stance, Says Lord Kinnock". https://www.bbc.com/news/uk-politics–44092538

BBC News. 2019. "A Guide to Labour Party anti-Semitism Claims". https://www.bbc.com/news/uk-politi cs–45030552

Bell, S. 2011. "Do We Really Need a New 'Constructivist Institutionalism' to Explain Institutional Change?" *British Journal of Political Science* 41 (4): 883–906. doi:10.1017/S0007123411000147.

Bennister, M., B. Worthy, and D. Keith. 2017. "Jeremy Corbyn and the Limits of Authentic Rhetoric." In *Voices of the UK Left. Rhetoric, Ideology and the Performance of Politics*, edited by J. Atkins and J. Gaffney, pp. 101–121, Palgrave Macmillan.

Berry, C. 2018. "Labour's Lost Tribe: Winning Back the Working Class." *Renewal* 26 (4): pp. 56–58.

Cammaerts, B., B. DeCillia, J. Magalhães, and C. Jimenez-Martínez. 2016. *Journalistic Representations of Jeremy Corbyn in the British Press: From Watchdog to Attackdog*. London School of Economics and Political Science.

Clarke, H. D., M. Goodwin, and P. Whiteley. 2017. *Brexit: Why Britain Voted to Leave the European Union*. Cambridge University Press.

Corbyn, J. 2016a. "Referendum Campaign Launch Speech". https://labourlist.org/2016/04/europe-needs-to-change-but-i-am-voting-to-stay-corbyns-full-speech-on-the-eu/

Corbyn, J. 2016b. "Referendum Campaign Relaunch Speech". http://www.ukpol.co.uk/jeremy-corbyn-2016-speech-on-the-eu–2/

Corbyn, J. 2016c. "Eve of Poll Speech". https://www.youtube.com/watch?v=DYeBVAbHRa0

Corbyn, J. 2019. Launch of Labour's campaign for the Euro elections.

Crerar, P. 2018. "Labour MPs' Fear of Brexit Voters Could Be Unfounded", Guardian. https://www.theguardian.com/politics/2018/may/29/labour-mps-fear-brexit-voters-unfounded-study

Curtice, J. 2017. "Is Labour's Brexit Dilemma Being Misunderstood?, What UK Thinks". https://whatukthinks.org/eu/is-labours-brexit-dilemma-being-misunderstood/

Curtis, C. 2017. "Has Labour Finally Found a Response to Its Brexit Dilemma?", YouGov. https://yougov.co.uk/topics/politics/articles-reports/2017/03/28/has-labour-finally-found-response-its-brexit-dilem

Daddow, C. 2015. "Performing Euroscepticism: The UK Press and Cameron's Bloomberg Speech." In *The UK Challenge to Europeanization. The Persistence of British Euroscepticism*, edited by C. Gifford and K. Tournier-Sol, pp 151–171, Palgrave Macmillan.

Datapraxis. 2019. "Tory Landslide, Progressives Split. A Datapraxis Analysis of the UK General Election". https://www.dataprax.is/tory-landslide-progressives-split

de Vreese, C. 2006. "Political Parties in Dire Straits? Consequences of National Referendums for Political Parties." *Party Politics* 12: pp. 581–98. doi:10.1177/1354068806066787.

Diamond, P., and C. Cadywould. 2017. "Don't Forget the Middle. How Labour Can Build a New Centre-Left Majority", Policy Network. https://policynetwork.org/wp-content/uploads/2017/07/Dont-Forget-The-Middle_FINAL.pdf

Electoral Commission. 2020. "Results and Turnout at the EU Referendum". https://www.electoralcommission.org.uk/who-we-are-and-what-we-do/elections-and-referendums/past-elections-and-referendums/eu-referendum/results-and-turnout-eu-referendum

Evans, G. 2000. "Europe: A New Electoral Cleavage?" In *Critical Elections: British Parties and Voters in Long-term Perspective*, edited by G. Evans and P. Norris, pp. 207–22, Sage.

Evans, G., and J. Tilley. 2017. *The New Politics of Class: The Political Exclusion of the British Working Class*. Oxford University Press.

Fabian Society (the). 2016. "Facing the Unknown: Building a progressive response to Brexit".

Fieldhouse, E. 2019. "Labour's Electoral Dilemma", British Election Study. https://www.britishelectionstudy.com/bes-findings/labours-electoral-dilemma/#.XkLYcCNCfb0

Goes, E. 2018. "Labour's 'Constructive Ambiguity' Is past Its Sell-by Date. It's Time to Come Clean about Brexit", The UK in a Changing Europe. https://ukandeu.ac.uk/labours-constructive-ambiguity-is-past-its-sell-by-date-its-time-to-come-clean-about-brexit/

Goodhart, D. 2017. *The Road to Somewhere*. New Tribes Shaping British Politics, Penguin Books.

Goodwin, M., and O. Heath. 2017. "UK 2017 General Election Vote Examined: Income, Poverty and Brexit", Joseph Rowntree Foundation. https://www.jrf.org.uk/report/uk-2017-general-election-vote-examined

Harrop, A. 2017a. *Stuck. How Labour Is Too Weak to Win, and Too Strong to Die*. Fabian Society.

Harrop, A. 2017b. *Labour's Brexit Dilemma*. Friedrich-Ebert-Stiftung London Office.

Heath, O., and M. Goodwin. 2017. "The 2017 General Election, Brexit and the Return to Two-Party Politics: An Aggregate Level Analysis of the Result." *Political Quarterly* 88 (3): pp. 345–358. doi:10.1111/1467-923X.12405.

Helm, T. 2018. "Corbyn Faces Clash with Labour Members over Second EU Referendum", Guardian. https://www.theguardian.com/politics/2018/sep/22/corbyn-under-pressure-from-labour-members-over-brexit

Hobolt, S. 2006. "Direct Democracy and European Integration." *Journal of European Public Policy* 13 (1): 153–166. doi:10.1080/13501760500380825.

Hobolt, S. 2009. *Europe in Question: Referendums on European Integration*. Oxford University Press.

Hobolt, S., T. Leeper, and J. Tilley. 2017. "Emerging Brexit Identities." In *The UK in a Changing Europe (2017). The UK in a Changing Europe (2017) Brexit and Public Opinion*, pp. 17–10. Economic and Social Research Council.

Hooghe, L., G. Marks, and C. Wilson. 2002. "Does Left/Right Structure Party Positions on European Integration?" *Comparative Political Studies* 35 (8): pp. 965–89. doi:10.1177/001041402236310.

Ipsos-MORI. 2016. "How Britain Voted in the 2016 EU Referendum". https://www.ipsos.com/ipsos-mori/en-uk/how-britain-voted-2016-eu-referendum

Iszatt-White, M., A. Whittle, G. Gadelshina, and F. Mueller. 2019. "The 'Corbyn Phenomenon': Media Representations of Authentic Leadership and the Discourse of Ethics versus Effectiveness." *Journal of Business Ethics* 159 (2): pp. 535–549. doi:10.1007/s10551-018-3838-x.

Jennings, W., and G. Stoker. 2016. *The Rise of Anti-politics in Britain*. Economic and Social Research Council.

Jennings, W., and G. Stoker. 2017. "Tilting Towards the Cosmopolitan Axis? Political Change in England and the 2017 General Election." *Political Quarterly* 88 (3): pp. 359–369. doi:10.1111/1467-923X.12403.

Labour Party (the). 2017. *Manifesto. For the Many, Not the Few*. Labour Party.

Labour Party (the). 2019. *Manifesto. It's Time for Real Change*. Labour Party.

LabourList. 2018. "Labour's Brexit Composite Motion in Full". https://labourlist.org/2018/09/labours-brexit-composite-motion-in-full/

Lee, G. 2018. "What Is Labour's Policy on Brexit?". Channel 4. https://www.channel4.com/news/factcheck/what-is-labour-policy-on-brexit

Leemann, L., and F. Wasserfallen. 2016. "The Democratic Effect of Direct Democracy." *American Political Science Review* 110 (4): 750–762. doi:10.1017/S0003055416000307.

Leftly, M. 2017 "How Labour's Jeremy Corbyn Can Win by Losing the U.K. Election", Time Magazine. https://time.com/4809394/british-election-2017-labour-party-jeremy-corbyn/

Martell, L. 2018. "Corbyn, Populism and Power." *Hard Times, N° 101*: pp. 1–11.

McCain, R. A. 2014. *Game Theory: A Nontechnical Introduction to the Analysis of Strategy*. World Scientific Publishing.

McDonnell, J. 2019. "Interview on the Andrew Marr Show, BBC One". https://www.youtube.com/watch?v=BOqQCuhdt9k

Mellon, J., and ProsserC. 2017. "Has Brexit Broken British Voting?", British Election Study. https://www.britishelectionstudy.com/bes-findings/has-brexit-broken-british-voting/#.XkL1iCNCfb0

Menon, A. 2018. "Why Would Labour Clarify Its Stance on Brexit? Ambiguity Is Working". Guardian. https://www.theguardian.com/commentisfree/2018/may/02/labour-clarify-position-brexit-vote-share-leave-remain

Menon, A., and A. Wager. 2019. "Corbyn's Brexit Ambiguity Is a Political Gamble", the UK in a Changing Europe". https://ukandeu.ac.uk/corbyns-brexit-ambiguity-is-a-political-gamble/

Mitchell, D. 2009. "Cooking the Fudge: Constructive Ambiguity and the Implementation of the Northern Ireland Agreement, 1998–2007." *Irish Political Studies* 24 (3): 321–336. doi:10.1080/07907180903075751.

Mitchell, J. 2015. "Sea Change in Scotland." *Parliamentary Affairs* 68 (1): pp. 88–100. doi:10.1093/pa/gsv029.

Quinn, T. 2019. "Two Tribes of Islington: The Real Challenge Ahead as Labour Seeks a New Leader", Conversation. https://theconversation.com/two-tribes-of-islington-the-real-challenge-ahead-as-labour-seeks-a-new-leader–129103

Schleiter, P., and V. Belu. 2016. "The Decline of Majoritarianism in the UK and the Fixed-term Parliaments Act." *Parliamentary Affairs* 69 (1): pp. 36–52. doi:10.1093/pa/gsv002.

Schmidt, V. 2008. "Discursive Institutionalism: The Explanatory Power of Ideas and Discourse." *Annual Review of Political Science* 11 (1): 303–326. doi:10.1146/annurev.polisci.11.060606.135342.

Shaw, E. 2019. "Labour's Political Calculations: Explaining the Party's Muddled Policy on Brexit", LSE blog. https://blogs.lse.ac.uk/politicsandpolicy/labours-muddled-policy-on-brexit/

Sleator, L. 2019. "Brexit: Where Labour's Factions Stand", BBC News. https://www.bbc.com/news/uk-politics–47062893
Sobolewska, M., and R. Ford. 2020. *Brexitland: Identity, Diversity and the Reshaping of British Politics*. Cambridge University Press.
Starmer, K. 2017. "No 'Constructive Ambiguity'. Labour Will Avoid Brexit Cliff Edge for UK Economy", Guardian. https://www.theguardian.com/commentisfree/2017/aug/26/keir-starmer-no-constructive-ambiguity-brexit-cliff-edge-labour-will-avoid-transitional-deal
Stewart, H. 2019a. "Watson Stages 'Polite' Walkout Over Labour's EU Election Manifesto". Guardian. https://www.theguardian.com/politics/2019/apr/30/watson-stages-polite-walkout-over-labour-eu-election-manifesto-brexit
Stewart, H. 2019b. "Corbyn Says Local Elections Show Voters Want Deal Done on Brexit". Guardian. https://www.theguardian.com/politics/2019/may/03/deliver-brexit-is-local-election-message-says-labour-mcdonnell
Tsebelis, G. 1990. *Nested Games: Rational Choice in Comparative Politics*. University of California Press.
Usherwood, S. 2017. "Regulatory Alignment, Constructive Ambiguity and Brexit", PSA Blog. https://www.psa.ac.uk/psa/news/regulatory-alignment-constructive-ambiguity-and-brexit
van der Eijk, C. 2017. "Is the Country Coming Together after the Brexit Referendum?", British Election Study. https://www.britishelectionstudy.com/bes-findings/is-the-country-coming-together-after-the-brexit-referendum/#.XNLF7vZuI2x
Wahl-Jorgensen, K. 2018. *Emotions, Media and Politics*. Polity Press.
YouGov. 2016a. "How Britain Voted at the EU Referendum". https://yougov.co.uk/topics/politics/articles-reports/2016/06/27/how-britain-voted
YouGov. 2016b. "Corbyn Loses Support among Labour Party Membership". https://yougov.co.uk/topics/politics/articles-reports/2016/06/30/labour-members-corbyn-post-brexit
YouGov. 2019 "YouGov Tracker. Voting Intention 2017 to Present". https://d25d2506sfb94s.cloudfront.net/cumulus_uploads/document/sviyn3n7wl/YG%20trackers%20-%20Voting%20Intention%20since%20GE%202017_W.pdf

Post-Brexit nationalism: challenging the British political tradition?

Emma Bell

ABSTRACT
In the UK, nationalism has been gaining ground for some time, yet Brexit appears to have exacerbated these trends and given legitimation to the nationalist cause. 'Taking back control' from the EU was widely regarded as a means of reinforcing parliamentary sovereignty, notably over national borders, but also, importantly, of legitimising popular sovereignty, of giving a voice to those who often feel unrepresented by their political leaders. The idea of popular sovereignty is closely linked to that of nationalism: the rise of national populism can partly be explained by the crisis of representativity in liberal democracies and the desire for more direct, participatory forms of democracy. This article seeks to analyse the British government's articulation of nationalism following the Brexit referendum in order to determine the impact that the rise of nationalism in this peculiar context might have on democracy in the UK. Will it be Westminster business as usual or may the unleashing of nationalist sentiment represent an opportunity to move beyond the current political model? The article also focuses on the Labour Party's approach to nationalism, analysing its capacity to mark a rupture from dominant forms of nationalism and thus challenge the British political tradition.

Introduction

Eric Hobsbawm, writing in 1992, declared, 'nationalism, however inescapable, is simply no longer the historical force it was in the era between the French Revolution and the end of imperialist colonialism after World War II' (1992, 169). He imagined that, with the rise of transnational and international political orders facilitating international collaboration, the nation state, along with nationalism, was on the wane. A quarter of a century later, it seems clear that these trends have actually had the opposite effect, unleashing new waves of nationalism, even among peoples such as the British who have often been thought of as 'reluctant nationalists' on account of their role as an imperial power, preoccupied with governing over foreign nations rather than with the need to assert a national identity under threat of foreign domination (Kumar 2003, 123). The referendum vote in favour of Brexit is widely thought to have been a victory for nationalism over internationalism, representing the collapse of the Anglo-British globalist worldview (Scotto, Sanders and Reifler 2018). Indeed, there is a close link between Euroscepticism and nationalism with the former helping to reinforce the latter (Gifford 2008; Wellings 2012). Reclaiming sovereignty from Europe has been presented by those in the 'Leave' camp as a nationalist cause. Such an idea is particularly resonant in Britain where parliamentary sovereignty, the founding idea of British democratic exceptionalism, is so intricately linked to national identity. The apparent superiority of this system over continental systems has long been a source of national pride.

Yet, it is doubtful whether British parliamentary sovereignty was really top of the agenda for nationalist 'Leave' voters. Indeed, it is more likely that the referendum result can be explained by the attraction of 'antimigrant cultural nationalism' (Evans 2017). Such nationalism may of course be in favour of the reassertion of parliamentary sovereignty in order to allow the British state to have greater control over its territorial borders by ending EU freedom of movement, yet it is above all characterised by a sense of alienation, a feeling of having been left behind by the political elites who have failed to address the economic dislocations of neoliberal globalisation (*ibid.*). Importantly, the referendum of 2016 allowed people who tend to experience a deep sense of powerlessness vis-à-vis the political establishment the chance to 'take back control', using their vote to profoundly upset the status quo. Brexit has arguably brought about a fundamental change in the way that British sovereignty is understood. There is now a popular expectation that the sovereignty of parliament is ceded to the 'sovereignty of the people' (Bogdanor 2016), or *peoples* in complex, multinational states such as the UK. The notion of popular sovereignty is hard to dissociate from nationalism. Indeed, the rise of national populism across Europe – defined as a promise to 'prioritize the culture and interests of the nation' and to 'give voice to a people who feel they have been neglected … by corrupt elites' – can partly be explained by a demand for more direct forms of democracy in the context of a crisis of representative democracy whereby people feel increasingly unrepresented by the political elites (Eatwell and Goodwin 2018, ix). In nations such as Scotland, nationalism cannot generally be associated with national populism – a very different form of civic nationalism has taken root there – but there is certainly a widespread demand for more direct, local democracy, particularly in the wake of the British government's decision to ignore the Scottish vote in the Brexit referendum. Different forms of nationalism are therefore challenging the British political tradition, associated with the practice of liberal democracy in the UK and defined as a solid belief in the superior capacity of elected representatives in Westminster to act in the national interest, and an aversion to extending popular participation in politics beyond periodic elections (Hall, Marsh, and Vines 2018). Ethnic and civic forms of nationalism therefore represent a significant challenge to the British political tradition.

This challenge has not emerged solely as a consequence of Brexit. Brexit is more a symptom than a cause of nationalism that has been rising over a longer period of time in a context of globalisation, multiculturalism, new forms of terrorism and rising migration. But Brexit does represent something of a watershed by giving vent and vindication to cultural and ethnic forms of nationalism, associated with increasingly disaffected segments of the population. Boris Johnson's conservative government may appear to be responding to this form of nationalism, notably by adopting strict controls on immigration, yet, in line with previous government policy, it is failing to respond to concurrent demands for popular sovereignty, instead shoring up parliamentary – or at least executive (Mabbett 2017) – sovereignty.

This article seeks to analyse in detail the British government's articulation of nationalism following the Brexit referendum in order to determine the impact that the rise of nationalism in this peculiar context might have on democracy in the UK. Will it be Westminster business as usual or may the unleashing of nationalist sentiment represent an opportunity to move beyond the current political model? The focus is on the Conservative Party as the party in power, but the influence of UKIP on this debate cannot be ignored. An analysis of the Labour Party is also relevant, especially as it enters a period of deep introspection following its catastrophic electoral defeat in December 2019. Nationalism is an issue that has – with some exceptions – been overlooked by the Party. The question is now whether it ought to start taking the issue more seriously as it seeks to carve out a new path to power. Drawing on policy discussion, speeches, manifestoes and intellectual debate, the focus is on the nationalism that is currently being articulated by the leadership of both parties, which is not to ignore the obvious tensions which exist within each party. It is hoped that this discussion will illuminate the interplay between the multiple levels on which the politics of nationalism are currently played out: the subnational, national, European and global arenas. Indeed, whilst the focus of the article is on the UK in the post-Brexit context, the conclusions will be of wider significance to parties throughout Europe and across the Atlantic who are dealing with the phenomenon of rising nationalism and numerous challenges to current models of liberal democracy.

Throughout the article, reference will be made to various forms of nationalism. Like democracy itself, it can be understood in many different ways. Here, we will deal primarily with economic, nativist, parliamentary and civic forms of nationalism. The precise meaning of these different forms of nationalism will emerge in the course of the following discussion. In practice, these different nationalisms constantly overlap and are by no means confined to one particular political party. A key distinction will be made between forms of nationalism that are 'descending', defined and promoted from above, rather than 'ascending', defined from below (Hall 1993). Obviously, the latter are more likely to foster participatory democratic politics and thus challenge the centrist, top-down British political tradition.

The article begins by examining the kind of nationalism that is currently being promoted by the British Conservative Party post-Brexit, analysing whether its attempts to reconcile nationalist sentiment with its project for a 'Global Britain' can widen democracy in any meaningful sense. It then looks at the Labour Party's approach to nationalism, discussing its failure to address this issue in an original way until fairly recently, and the possible alternative nationalisms that it might promote that could present a challenge to the British political tradition.

The Conservative Party: nationalism in the service of neoliberalism

The Conservative Party is currently divided between hyperliberal 'hard Brexiteers', who place a premium on the liberation of the market from all possible constraints, and those who are willing to accept a 'softer' form of Brexit that would see the UK continuing to accept some EU market regulation. With the victory of Boris Johnson at the 2019 general election, it is this former wing that is now governing the country. Yet, Johnson, perhaps in a cynical attempt to secure the political support of the economically marginalised, is prepared to accept a degree of state intervention in the market by providing government aid to deprived areas and to companies to offset the negative economic consequences of Brexit. This is coherent with his promises, following his predecessor Theresa May, to tackle the problems of the 'left behind', even if this means increased state interventionism. Colin Crouch thus sees the party as splitting into nationalist and neoliberal wings, as economic protectionism gains ground (Crouch 2017). This is to assume that neoliberalism is incompatible with both state protectionism and nationalism.

Yet, in practice, neoliberalism has always entailed a significant degree of interventionism in order to guide markets and make them behave in a certain way (Dardot and Laval 2009; Peck, Theodore, and Brenner 2010; Harcourt 2012). It has also worked to ensure that private enterprise is supported through various forms of corporate welfare (Farnsworth 2013). Crouch cites the example of the government reassurances made to the Nissan motor company in 2016 that it would not be adversely affected by Brexit as evidence that the government is moving 'in protectionist directions' (Crouch 2017, 227). Yet, this is nothing new: government assistance to the company began under the Thatcher governments in 1984, allowing it to benefit from £797 million in various forms of corporate welfare such as loans, research and development grants and tax relief between 1984 and 2017 (Farnsworth, Cola and Conn 2017). Economic protectionism has always sat alongside neoliberalism – it would thus be a mistake to regard such measures as threatening the neoliberal project (Bell and Christoph 2019).

Similarly, economic protectionism, often associated with nationalism, should not necessarily be assumed to run contrary to neoliberalism. To the extent that economic nationalism can be defined as a desire to reinforce national identity and the prosperity and power of the nation state, it has always been compatible with liberalism (Helleiner 2002). In the nineteenth century, liberal economic nationalism emerged as a means of maintaining Britain's economic superiority – this was the main justification provided by Robert Peel for the repeal of the Corn Laws in 1846 (320). The gold standard, often considered as an emblematic policy of economic liberalism, was actually a nationalist policy, primarily aimed at restoring national prestige (321). Today, the neoliberals continue to promote liberal economic policies on the grounds that they are most beneficial for the nation state in terms of promoting prosperity at home and allowing the UK to punch above her weight abroad (323). Margaret Thatcher pursued a form of 'nationalist neoliberalism' whereby economic liberalism was presented as being deeply rooted in the traditions and character of the British nation, associated with individualism and Britain's pride in her historic role in developing the global economy (Gifford 2008, 68). Neoliberals in general tend to simultaneously adopt internationalist discourse to promote economic globalisation and nationalist discourse to resist political globalisation, considered as a barrier to the free market and the sovereign power of the nation state (Harmes 2012). The Conservative Party's discourse is indeed simultaneously nationalist and internationalist. Whilst recognising that the vote in favour of Brexit can partly be interpreted as a vote against globalisation and its elites, former leader Theresa May insisted that free trade and open markets are in the best interests of the nation state and its citizens, especially the worst off (May 2016). Presenting economic liberalism in nationalist terms is a very effective way of presenting it as a force for progress (Fekete 2016). As highlighted above, nationalism is essential in ensuring popular support for free market policies (Rosamond 2018). There is significant irony in this, given that the economic dislocations caused by neoliberalism are widely considered as having been a major driver behind the rise of right-wing ethnic nationalism (Evans 2012).

Regardless of their differences over the form that Brexit should take or the degree of state interventionism in the market that is considered permissible, the Conservative Party Brexiteers appear to be united in regarding Britain's departure from the EU as an opportunity to reassert neoliberalism. They are also united in using nationalism to advance this cause. Two key interlinked forms of nationalism are invoked here: parliamentary nationalism and ethnic nationalism. Contrary to claims that Brexit is primarily about promoting democracy, these forms of nationalism actually represent a threat to the enhancement of popular participation in politics and are instead likely to simply bolster the highly centralised British political tradition. They are defined from above and eschew participatory politics. Let us examine each in turn:

Asserting parliamentary nationalism

Arguments in favour of the repatriation of sovereignty from European institutions to the Westminster parliament are nationalist in two senses: firstly, they aim to 'give back control' to 'the people'; secondly, they appeal to national chauvinism, presenting British institutions as being inherently superior to those in continental Europe. In her first speech on the government's negotiating objectives for leaving the EU, Theresa May noted the differences in political traditions between the UK and the rest of Europe, highlighting the importance of parliamentary sovereignty for the British, implying that this is a principle that continental Europeans have difficulty understanding (May 2017). This is a view shared by current Prime Minister Boris Johnson and other conservative supporters of the so-called Anglosphere who favour a closer relationship between Britain and countries such as the United States, Great Britain, Canada, Australia and New Zealand than with continental Europe, on account of the common values that bind them together (Gardiner 2010, 3). The profoundly eurosceptic European Research Group within the Conservative Party goes further, suggesting that the traditions of the Westminster parliament are superior to the political traditions that can be found on continental Europe, considering that forming a close union with states that are considered as inherently inferior somehow devalues Britain's status (McKay 2019). Parliamentary nationalism is therefore a means of legitimising the British political tradition.

The use of the referendum to instigate the UK's departure from the EU suggested a challenge to this tradition and a promise of more popular participation in politics. Yet, the close association of nationalism with Parliament means that it is Parliament itself that is ultimately strengthened (Vines

2015). Indeed, although 'the people' are regularly invoked to justify going through with Brexit, 'the people' were largely excluded from decision-making processes beyond the referendum. One way put forward to encourage more democratic participation in the process was the establishment of numerous 'citizens' assemblies' which would bring together randomly selected representative groups of citizens to discuss the possible options following the Brexit referendum. The idea was modelled on the Irish Citizen's Assembly set up in 2016 to discuss contentious issues such as the legalisation of abortion. Yet, an amendment (put forward by Labour MPs Stella Creasy and Lisa Nandy) to the legislation intended to enact the Withdrawal Deal negotiated between the British government and the EU which would have created such assemblies on a widespread basis in the UK was not even selected for debate in January 2019. Similarly, the conservative government rejected any attempt to involve the electorate in discussions over the form that Brexit might take via a second referendum.

Parliament as a whole has been strengthened to a certain extent in the post-referendum debates over Brexit, inflicting many defeats on the government, most notably with the successive defeat of the former Prime Minister's Brexit deal. Yet, more than anything, it appears to have been executive power that has been strengthened by post-Brexit appeals to parliamentary nationalism, thus helping to ensure the survival of a British political tradition characterised by strong executive power (Hall, Marsh, and Vines 2018). In rejecting any jurisdiction of the European Court of Justice post-Brexit, the government alone will have the power to decide on economic relationships with its EU partners, international diplomacy being a prerogative power reserved to the executive (Mabbett 2017, 169). Furthermore, it is the executive that claims to be the sole legitimate interpreter of the will of 'the people' (169). Despite the Miller case whereby the Supreme Court reasserted parliamentary authority regarding the UK's triggering of article 50 of the Lisbon Treaty on the basis that a referendum is merely advisory unless explicitly stated otherwise (R. [Miller] v. Secretary of State for Exiting the European Union [2016] EWHC 2768 [Admin]), the executive has constantly reaffirmed that it must respect the will of 'the people' in ensuring that Brexit goes ahead, regardless of the democratic will of those people who voted to remain in the European Union.

'The people' is a useful, malleable term which is generally used by conservative MPs to refer to 'the British people'. Indeed, the conservative appeal to nationalism is dressed in the language of unionism, with Theresa May constantly referring to the need to protect 'the precious union' (for example, May 2018). Yet, this is a nationalism that conflates English and British interests. It is in reality Anglo-British nationalism which can trace its roots back to the eurosceptic debates of the 1970s, notably those put forward by Enoch Powell (Vines 2015). Powell's nationalism was 'a consistent English nationalist position' (Gamble 2003, 28). His reverence for the Westminster model of government stemmed from the fact that he situated the tradition of parliamentary democracy firmly in the English inheritance (Kenny and Pearce 2018, 89). Consequently, his staunch defence of the British union had to be on English terms (Gamble 2003, 28). This is also true of Theresa May and Boris Johnson who have talked up the importance of the union whilst simultaneously excluding political leaders from Scotland from the Brexit negotiations and refusing to grant any special concessions that may placate the majority of Scottish people who voted to remain in the EU (whilst political leaders from Northern Ireland were initially given somewhat more attention, largely due to May's dependence on 10 DUP MPs to support her minority government and on account of the threat that Brexit poses to the Northern Irish peace process, Boris Johnson's majority government has largely ignored their concerns). This reflects a long-held conservative (and, indeed Labour) belief in the primacy of the unitary state. Such nationalism appeals more to the English majority that supported a referendum on EU membership in the first place and subsequently voted 'Leave'. English conservative Brexit-supporting voters, it seems, are prepared to sacrifice the 'precious union' in favour of a clean break with the EU that would satisfy their nationalist demands to see sovereignty returned to the UK Parliament: 79% of English conservatives would support Scottish independence as the price of Brexit, whilst 75% would accept the collapse of the peace process in Northern Ireland as a price worth paying (Henderson and Jones 2018). These voters also show a clear dissatisfaction with the

Westminster model as it currently stands, with almost half of English conservative voters believing that Scottish MPs should not sit in the UK Parliament (*ibidem.*). It is perhaps unsurprising that the notion of 'taking back control' has more resonance amongst an English population that, lacking local democratic structures of governance akin to those of other nations in the UK, feels a particularly acute need to address this democratic deficit (Barnett 2016). Indeed, 79% of those who voted 'Leave' in the 2016 referendum identified themselves as 'English, not British' (Ashcroft 2019). Furthermore, 42% of those who identify as English rather than British believe that an English Parliament should have more influence than either the UK government (25%) or local councils (15%) over how England is run (Jeffrey et al. 2014, 18). Yet, the Anglo-British nationalism promoted by the Conservative Party is currently doing little in practice to address the democratic deficit in England, largely ignoring English nationalist demands (O'Toole, 2018). Deprived of these democratic structures, 'normal' democratic nationalism (Nairn 2003) could easily give way to ethnic nationalism. Indeed, in the absence of political and institutional conduits for national pride, people may be more prone to seek exclusive, ethnic forms of national expression (Nodia 1992). The Conservative Party's failure to take English political nationalism seriously and to rethink the democratic process and the executive sovereignty of the UK parliament, so closely linked with the British political tradition, may unleash 'uglier' forms of nationalism. Yet, rather than resisting such forms of nationalism, it seems the Conservative Party has been actively promoting them.

Appealing to nativism

The Conservative Party deliberately eschews the ethnic nationalism often associated with Enoch Powell and his infamous 'Rivers of Blood' speech (Powell, 1968). In recent years, it has sought openly to defend and promote racial equality. As Home Secretary, Theresa May expressed concern about police stop and search powers which disproportionately target ethnic minorities (May 2013) and introduced a revised code of police practice aimed at curbing their use. The appointment of Asian Sajid Javid to the post of Home Secretary in 2018 helped to project an image of a modern Conservative Party at ease with multiculturalism. In Boris Johnson's new Cabinet, Priti Patel of Indian origin was given the job of Home Secretary whilst Javid was given the post of Chancellor before resigning and being replaced by Rishi Sunak, also of Indian origin.

Yet, conservative immigration policy appeals to nativist sentiment in promoting the rights of British citizens over those of citizens of other nations. Nativism may be understood as distinct from ethnic nationalism: while the latter seeks to establish a homogeneous ethno-nation, the former focuses on preserving a particular ethnic configuration from change (Kaufman 2018). The British Conservative Party tones down the ethnic aspect of its discourse but nonetheless seeks to protect those who have attained British citizenship – the natives – from citizens of other countries. Amber Rudd, former Home Secretary under the May government, considered that native British people should have priority access to the labour market, stating that when companies recruit from abroad, they 'should ensure people coming here are filling gaps in the labour market, not taking jobs British people could do' (Rudd 2016). Native British people are also given priority over access to welfare services. From 2014, under the Conservative–Liberal Democrat coalition government, the criteria for determining whether EEA citizens are 'habitually resident' in the UK in order to have access to means-tested benefits were made more stringent, notably limiting the rights of jobseekers without 'a genuine prospect of finding work'. In 2015, in response to concerns about 'health tourism' whereby people come to the UK specifically to benefit from NHS treatment (although it is estimated that spending on non-UK citizens is negligible, representing 0.3% of total annual health spending in the UK – Factcheck 2016), since October 2017 providers of NHS treatment have been required to ensure that patients are eligible for free healthcare and to apply charges if they are not. Such measures contribute to creating a 'hostile environment' for migrants, building on Theresa May's policies as Home Secretary to extend identity controls from physical borders to the domestic arena, forcing employers, landlords, doctors and teachers to check the immigration status of people they provide services to. It was this policy which led directly to the Windrush scandal in Spring 2018 following revelations by *The Guardian* that immigrants who arrived in Britain between 1948 and 1973 and who, as Commonwealth citizens, had an automatic right to settle in the UK, found themselves deprived of medical treatment and employment and, in some case, threatened with deportation, should they fail to be able to prove their status as British citizens. These measures were accompanied by the immigration acts of 2014 and 2016 intended to make entry into the country more difficult, notably introducing an income threshold of £18 600 for non-EEA citizens wishing to bring their spouses to Britain.

Post-Brexit, immigration controls will become stricter. In 2019, Parliament voted the Immigration and Social Security Co-ordination (EU Withdrawal) Act to end the free movement of EU citizens to the UK (with the exception of Irish citizens), rendering them subject to UK immigration law. The changes are dressed in the language of equality. The former Prime Minister, in her foreword to the White Paper preceding the Bill highlighted 'the huge contribution' migrants have made to the UK and promised that the system would be based on skills alone, not the country that migrants come from (HM Government 2018a, 3). In an earlier speech outlining the core elements of the Withdrawal Deal between the UK and the EU, May stated that EU nationals would no longer be able to 'jump the queue ahead of engineers from Sydney or software developers from Delhi' (BBC 2018). Whilst this latter statement sparked controversy for suggesting that EU nationals were failing to respect existing rules, such language did imply that future immigration controls would be colour and race-blind. Similarly, the current Conservative government's new points-based immigration system is to accept applications for residency on criteria that are based on skills and earnings rather than on country of origin These policies are far-removed from Powell's ethnic nationalism which specifically sought to limit immigration 'of colour'. Yet, racism is today simply articulated in more subtle ways. Measures to restrict access to public services and benefits reinforce the idea articulated so successfully by Powell that migrants avail of Britain's public services to the detriment of native British citizens. Powell would also surely have approved of May's and Johnson's constant reassertion of the need for the UK 'to take back control of its borders' (HM Government 2018a, 3) and thus reassert the sovereignty of the Westminster Parliament over the issue.

Furthermore, despite the language of equality, it is unlikely that the conservative immigration policy will be colour-blind in practice. The 'hostile environment' policy is set to continue: despite the Conservatives' preference for the term 'compliant environment' over 'hostile environment', and government plans to give the Home Office 'a more human face' and to fully compensate those affected by the scandal (HM Government 2018b; Conservative Party 2019, 21), no substantial policy change has so far been implemented at the time of writing (March 2020). Given the lack of commitment on the part of the Johnson government to roll back the immigration legislation that led to the 'hostile environment' policy, it seems will continue in all but name. The risk is that racial discrimination will be encouraged. According to the UN Special Rapporteur on Contemporary Forms of Racism, Racial Discrimination, Xenophobia and Related Intolerance:

> a hostile environment ostensibly created for and formally restricted to irregular immigrants, is in effect, a hostile environment for all racial and ethnic communities and individuals in the UK. This is because ethnicity continues to be deployed in the public and private sector as a proxy for legal immigration status. Even where private individuals and civil servants may wish to distinguish among different immigration statuses many likely are confused among the various categories and thus err on the side of excluding all but those who can easily and immediately prove their Britishness, or whose white ethnicity confer[s] upon them presumed Britishness (Achiume 2018, para. 38).

Beyond mere suspicion on grounds of race, racial hatred may even be fuelled by the government's tendency to play to public fears regarding immigration, as exemplified by the former Home Secretary's reaction to 40 refugees crossing the English Channel in small boats during the Christmas period in 2018. Questioning the legitimacy of their claims to asylum before their demands had been properly processed, he asserted that Britain should do all that it could to ensure such claims generally do not succeed (Dearden 2019).

Despite attempts to reject ethnic nationalism, the Conservative Government's determination to reinforce Britain's borders and repatriate immigration control to Westminster, whilst ensuring that British citizens are given priority access to jobs and services in the UK in an environment that is increasingly suspicious towards migrants, appeals to nativist nationalist sentiment. Appeals to nativism and ethnic nationalism are often regarded as a threat to liberal democracy. For European Commission President, Jean-Claude Juncker, 'exaggerated nationalism' that 'projects hate' is a 'poison' that 'destroys all in its path', including presumably liberal democracy (2018). Yet, such nationalism can be regarded as forming part of the liberal political tradition. Alongside the tradition of liberal internationalism which sees all nations as being capable of embracing liberal politics, there is a nationalist liberal tradition that regards only specific nations as culturally predisposed to develop and nurture liberal democracy (Kosc 2017). For the latter tradition, which can be traced back to the American Founding Fathers, political liberalism 'was a uniquely British inheritance that could be undermined by French, German, and Irish migrants with radical political views or foreign loyalties' (Kosc 2017). In contemporary Britain, the threat to liberal values is seen as coming from migrants with different cultural values, from those who live 'in segregated communities', leading 'separate lives, apart from each other and apart from the mainstream', often 'behaving in ways that run completely counter to our values' (Cameron 2011). Migrants are presented as lacking the liberal values of self-help and responsibility, drawn to Britain by 'our generosity' and 'the attractiveness of our benefits system' (Cameron 2013). Due to their different values, they make it 'impossible to build a cohesive society' (May 2015). Furthermore, some of them are thought to harbour 'real hostility towards Western democracy and liberal values', such as respect for gender equality (Cameron 2011). The focus on culture rather than race enables the Conservative Party to differentiate its nationalism from that of the extreme right and, significantly, to present it as being compatible with liberal democracy.

The Conservative Party approach to promoting a national identity based on liberal values fails to enhance democracy. It seeks to apply 'muscular liberalism', as opposed to 'passive tolerance' in order to 'actively promote' liberal values (Cameron 2011) and a certain kind of national identity. This has entailed stricter controls on immigration, together with the increased surveillance of Muslim communities in particular though the anti-terrorism strategy, *Prevent* (Kundnani 2009), aimed at tackling extremism. Such measures may be experienced as authoritarian rather than liberal governance by the communities concerned, even if authoritarianism is not overt (Bell 2015). Furthermore, nationalism may help to generalise authoritarian governance throughout the broader populace as neoliberal governments use it to police inequality to ensure that social disorder does not create unstable political conditions threatening to global capital (Fekete 2016). Increased surveillance measures may be accepted by nationalists lured by the promise of national security faced with the threat of the immigrant other. Consequently, 'nationalism could well provide the route into the "strong state"', providing 'the climate that allows for its break from democracy' (Fekete 2016, 18). A hard or 'no deal' Brexit paving the way for a deregulated, hypercompetitive Britain, as desired by the Brexit neoliberal utopians (Bell, 2019), will surely generate exacerbated social insecurity, strengthening the appeal to nativist nationalism and the need for politicians to invoke it to garner electoral support and justify the implementation of more authoritarian policies. Liberal nativist nationalism thus risks tipping over into authoritarian nativist nationalism, shoring up the power of the central state. The promotion of nativist nationalism may appear to be a challenge to the British political tradition to the extent that it responds to genuine fears about immigration. Indeed, 'strong public concerns over immigration, and its perceived effects on the country and on communities, were central to explaining the 2016 vote for Brexit' (Goodwin and Milazzo 2017, 13). 'Leave' voters tended to see the EU as the best way to allow Britain to reclaim control over its borders and reduce immigration that they believe has negative effects on the welfare state, the economy and cultural life of the nation (10). According to Evans, these sentiments cannot be dissociated from economic deprivation linked to the post-industrial service economy which has helped to fuel a sense of xenophobia or 'placeism', defined as 'a fierce sense of territoriality and a social preoccupation with a hierarchy of born-and bred belonging [which] implie[s] a generalized suspicion of outsiders of all kinds' (2017, 217). It is a sentiment which was effectively exploited by the British National Party and repackaged by UKIP which managed to sanitise the immigration debate and shift the political centre to the right (*ibid.*). This in turn allowed the Conservative Party to pick up the debate, to present itself as being more 'in tune' with popular concerns and simultaneously to stave off the electoral threat from UKIP and then the Brexit Party (which risked dividing the conservative vote).

Yet, it doing so, the Conservative Party has adopted national populism, leading the debate from above, whilst presenting its policy as one that is informed only from below. It is a policy that 'give[s] voice to a people who feel they have been neglected ... by corrupt elites' (Eatwell and Goodwin 2018, ix). Yet, the Party has failed to address the underlying question of deprivation or, more importantly for this debate, to inform the public about the facts of immigration, propagating rather than challenging myths. The first myth is the notion that post-Brexit Britain will be able to gain full control of immigration policy. Given the Conservatives' commitment to pursuing the ideal of a 'Global Britain' via trade deals with the rest of the world, it is likely that it will have to grant some concessions on immigration restrictions to countries, such as India, that it hopes to trade with. Furthermore, whilst neoliberalism can sit comfortably alongside nativism, the free movement of people tends to underpin the free movement of capital. Secondly, the government has tended to exaggerate the extent of immigration to Britain. Politicians often refer to a 'migrant crisis', despite the relatively low numbers of migrants living in the UK compared to other countries: in 2016, there were nine non-national citizens per 100 000 inhabitants living in the UK, compared to 38 in Malta or 18 in Ireland (Eurostat 2018). The government also fails to inform the public of important facts about immigration which tend to run counter to people's concerns about its negative impact, such as: the positive impact migration has on stimulating demand in the economy; large increases in EU immigration did not cause falls in wages; EU migrants can help to reduce the budget deficit and fund public services by paying more in taxes than they take out in benefits (Wadsworth et al. 2017). The government has also played down the potential negative impact of post-Brexit immigration restrictions. Whilst it is difficult to establish post-Brexit immigration growth models, Portes and Forte (2017) suggest that the impact on GDP per capita will be 'almost certainly negative' whilst any possible increase in low-skilled wages will be 'relatively modest' (2017, S40).

Rather than engaging in genuine democratic dialogue, capable of promoting deliberative participatory democracy, the Conservative Party has been happy to tap into public fears about migration for political gain. The Conservative Party thus promotes a 'descending' nationalism (Hall 1993, 355) that is defined from above and excludes ordinary people from the democratic process of defining the contours of national identity, despite appearing to be responding directly to their concerns. Nativist nationalism therefore becomes yet another way of shoring up executive sovereignty, albeit in the guise of responding to popular fears. Such a strategy is likely to exacerbate sentiments that liberal democracy is not working in the popular interest if the public see no long-term positive impacts following Brexit. We will now move on to a discussion of the Labour Party's articulation of nationalism in order to determine if it may be capable of articulating a more democratic version of post-Brexit nationalism that goes beyond the British political tradition and allows alternative democratic models to develop.

The Labour Party: building nationalism from the bottom up?

Although nationalism is often associated with right-wing governments, particularly at the present time, it is not a naturally conservative ideology. Historically, it has often been associated with radicalism and popular movements seeking to overturn the status quo (Miller 2003, 309), even if Conservative Prime Ministers such as Benjamin Disraeli and Winston Churchill drew upon nationalism. Disraeli appealed to nationalist sentiment to advance the spread of democracy and unite people under one nation, whilst Churchill sought to unite the nation in the face of a common enemy. Margaret Thatcher also drew on nationalism to bring people together against a common enemy 'without' in the Falklands War and the trade unionists and left-wing activists she described as 'the enemy within'.

Nationalism has been treated with some suspicion by the Left, particularly by international socialists such as G.D.H. Cole and Harold Laski who regarded the nation state and the nationalism associated with it as an obstacle to international peace, with Laski even going so far as to propose the creation of a 'world community' in which nations would give up ideas of national sovereignty (Matthews 2013, 33–35). New Labour followed a very different political trajectory, but it also advocated going beyond nationalism, embracing post-nationalism in an attempt to deepen globalisation and Europeanisation (Kenny 2014, 33). Yet, paradoxically, its refusal to appeal to nationalist sentiment only helped to fuel it. In the wake of the London terrorist attacks of 2005, perpetrated by British-born citizens, Gordon Brown did address the question of patriotism, launching a national debate on the meaning of Britishness. For him, it entailed celebrating national symbols such as the Union Jack and associating being British very clearly with values, notably those of 'responsibility, liberty and fairness' (Brown 2006). He was essentially promoting a civic form of nationalism and focussing on what could bring multicultural Britain together as a nation. But white British people who rejected this multicultural model were largely ignored in this discussion, as was the rise of nationalism, in England or elsewhere. Whilst Brown recognised Britain as 'a country of different nations and thus of plural identities', he argued that a British identity should be celebrated 'which is bigger than the sum of its parts'. This was to ignore the rise of political nationalism in Scotland and in England, and, perhaps more seriously, the rise of 'antimigrant cultural nationalism' (Evans 2017). This form of nationalism became increasingly prevalent in the context of the post-class politics pursued by New Labour whereby Tony Blair sought to follow a new politics which would go beyond class binaries and 'liberate Britain from the old class divisions' (Blair 1999). Failing to address the specific problems of those who were being left behind by the new neoliberal post-industrial economy, New Labour thus paved the way for people to self-identify in terms of place and local identity rather than class (Evans 2012). The rejection of internationalism and multiculturalism that ensued was easily exploited by racist parties such as the BNP and later by the forces of Euroscepticism, first the UKIP and then the Conservatives, who helped to stoke fear about migration, particularly from the EU. Despite adopting populist tropes about 'bogus asylum seekers' and the need to prevent migrants from becoming a 'burden' for the welfare state (Mulvey 2010), New Labour was perceived as being 'soft on immigration' (Evans and Chzhen 2013, 142), to such an extent that the party adopted 'controls on immigration' as a key slogan in the 2015 general election. This perception was far from justified: although in 2004 the Blair government decided to join just two other EU countries (Sweden and Ireland) in placing no immediate restrictions on migrants from the ten new EU member states, his government also introduced legislation to significantly limit the rights of asylum seekers and to deter them from seeking asylum in the UK, and led an escalation in detention and deportation (Gibney 2008). Nevertheless, the party was perceived as ignoring the interests of its key working-class electorate by both failing to address economic hardship and rising concerns about immigration. In seeking to combine Thatcherite neoliberal economics with an internationalist, multicultural outlook, it failed to address nationalistic sentiment in a way that Thatcher herself had done, providing the 'glue' that allowed people to coalesce around her project.

Yet, the Labour Party has not always ignored the question of nationalism Clement Attlee invoked civic nationalism to rally popular support around a universal welfare state. Tony Benn, despite his international socialism, grounded his opposition to Britain's membership of the European Union in a defence of the sovereignty of the Westminster parliament (Vines 2015; Gifford 2008, 63). This was in many ways a natural position to hold given the Party's long-term commitment to parliamentary sovereignty and the British state (Jones and Keating 1985). The Labour leadership under Michael Foot also demonstrated a preference for such nationalism in its support of British intervention in the South Atlantic during the Falklands War (Williams 1984, 371). In its historical defence of parliamentary nationalism, Labour differs little from the Conservative Party. This attitude perhaps results from the confusion it makes between parliamentary and popular sovereignty, assuming that the former is the embodiment of the latter (*ibid.*, 187–8). This would suggest that the Party is ill-equipped to respond to popular challenges to the British political tradition that are being fuelled by new forms of national populism. As with the Conservatives, it has largely adopted a descending form of nationalism, defined from above and closely associated with the institutions of the British state.

However, in response to the revival of nationalism on the right of the political spectrum, some voices on the Left have highlighted the urgency of challenging the Right on its own terms. Through his exploration of the dissonance between politics and identity, Stuart Hall explained how Thatcher successfully managed to link the two together by appropriating national identity to create 'an active popular consent' for her policies (cited in Matthews 2013, 180). These policies became part of identity itself: it became British to be in favour of the free market and against socialist policies. To challenge the hegemony of neoliberalism, Hall believed the Left would have to create a new version of the national popular by taking identity seriously. This call has been taken up more recently by Anthony Barnett who explains, 'A class-based anger expressed in patriotic themes cannot just be answered by economic policies', suggesting that Labour will have to go beyond policies of redistribution and the reduction of inequalities of wealth if it is to be successful (Barnett 2016, 242). Similarly, John Denham, Labour MP and founding member of the English Labour Network, a group launched in 2017 to further discussion on the political identity of England, has underlined the need for the Labour Party to embrace 'a new progressive patriotism' grounded in 'nation, people and place' if it hopes to secure popular support for its policies (2016). Although it is questionable that such a form of nationalism can be furthered if the focus is on addressing concerns about immigration (as Denham suggests) – there is a risk of mimicking the nativist nationalism of the Conservative Party – Denham's focus on the importance of place may pave the way for a progressive nationalism that would no longer be 'banal', limited to the symbolic 'flagging' of symbols of national identity in our daily lives (Billing 2002). It could become a positive force, underpinning a new democratic politics. How might Labour go about doing this?

From parliamentary sovereignty to popular sovereignty: fostering civic nationalism?

Contrary to the Conservative Party, Labour could promote 'ascending' nationalism (Hall 1993), defined from below and associated with the everyday practices of ordinary people rather than with the institutions of the State. Indeed, 'democracy is not just a set of institutional arrangements but a culture and a spirit, a way of doing politics' (Wright 2017, 195). Democratic involvement can itself become a way of expressing one's identity and pride in the nation. Yet, such involvement is meaningless if confined to voting every few years in elections or in a referendum. It must be something that is integrated into people's daily lives, that starts at the level of community and works upwards to the level of national institutions. Indeed, feelings of identity and belonging have always been rooted in the community first and in the nation second. This is not about rejecting existing institutions – that is the stuff of anti-establishment populism – but rather about transforming them from below so that they can work better in the national interest.

For Raymond Williams, nationalism did not have to be about the nation state – indeed, such nationalism is essentially regressive. A positive nationalism is linked not to the unitary state but rather grounded in the 'politics of place' (1984). The sentiment of 'placeism' identified by Evans (2017) does not therefore have to lead to negative, nativist nationalism. Evans would undoubtedly agree with Williams when he suggested that place becomes particularly important as a site for social bonding when other means of bonding through class or institutions such as trade unions has broken down in the wake of deindustrialisation and globalisation (373–4). Attachment to place can encourage new forms of democratic participation aimed at tackling issues which affect the locality, whilst participation in local politics can help to reinforce attachment to place. Thus, there exists a positive symbiotic relationship between a locally based nationalism and democracy. Given that localities – cities and regions – are 'natural units of government' (Williams 1984, 372), what happens there necessarily relates to wider issues that affect the nation as a whole. In this way, local politics necessarily impact upon the national.

The Labour Party is currently proposing policies which seek to empower local communities, allowing them to take decisions about issues that affect them directly, such as housing and urban planning. Reviving the old tradition of 'municipal socialism', it has promised to devolve power from the centre to local councils but, importantly, also to give more direct control to local communities over the actions of those councils (Corbyn 2017). Labour has also proposed cooperative ownership of newly-nationalised services such as railways and energy companies, combining state ownership with local, regional and community ownership and ensuring that consumers and employee representatives sit together on boards with representatives of state, regional and local government (Labour Party 2017, 31, 2019).

Local control of the economy and public services is potentially a very effective way of tackling the feelings of disempowerment engendered by conditions of post-democracy whereby power has been increasingly displaced from national representatives to multinational corporations (Crouch 2012 (2004)). In taking power away from international capital, it might be considered as a form of economic nationalism. It entails turning the policy of holding capital to account into a 'progressive national cause' by placing national interest first (Denham 2017, 102). The popularity of such a cause may be grounded in place, through local participation in economic decision-making, fostering the development of civic nationalism that links identity to popular democracy and cooperativism. This may be a good way of tapping into feelings of political disempowerment that may have helped inform the decision to vote in favour of leaving the European Union.[1]

Yet, just as for the Conservative Party, there are risks that, rather than promoting popular democratic participation, nationalism could undermine democracy. Labour is not immune from the ethnic nationalism that taints the Conservatives. There is always a danger that suspicion towards foreign capital may tip over into hostility for foreign workers, especially if Labour fails to make the case for immigration. Despite the generally positive views of immigration on the part of Corbyn, including his calls to avoid scapegoating immigrants for the problems encountered by public services (Corbyn 2018), the party leadership has largely accepted the need for stricter immigration controls post-Brexit. The Opposition failed to mount an effective opposition to the Conservatives' Immigration and Social Security Co-ordination (EU Withdrawal) Bill 2019, discussed above, allowing the Bill to pass with 76 Labour MPs absent (after changing its position from abstention to imposing a mere one-line whip). In doing so, it responds to Denham's call for Labour to make the case for an end to freedom of movement in its current form in order to dissociate the Party from 'massive and rapid immigration' (Denham 2017: 100, 105). Blindly responding to popular sentiment about immigration without engaging in meaningful debate about the issue risks creating exclusive communities that would undermine attempts to increase popular, inclusive participation in local decision-making processes. Such an approach also ignores the fact that nationalist sentiment is not driven solely by an anti-immigration stance. Whilst regaining control over immigration was cited as the second main reason for voting 'Leave' by Leave voters (Ashcroft 2019) in the general population, anti-immigrant sentiment amongst the white working class tends to be regarded as a legitimate way of expressing what is essentially anti-establishment sentiment (Flemmen and Savage 2017). Labour's focus on the local has real potential to take nationalism beyond its association with the institutions of Parliament by addressing that anti-establishment feeling, creating 'multiple sites of sovereign' (Keating 2001) in localities across this country. Importantly, this would allow it to accommodate multiple identities in the way that the Good Friday Agreement allows the people of Northern Ireland to be British or Irish or both. It could accommodate nationalist sentiment in Scotland, Wales or England whilst bringing people together to fight for the common national cause of genuinely taking back control from both transnational capital and central government. A truly democratic culture fostered by a 'new politics' which rejects both neoliberalism and socialist statism could be what unites the country behind a new progressive nationalism.

For such a project to be successful, Labour's focus on the local should not ignore the national: micro-level politics can only be facilitated by ambitious reform of macro-level politics, starting with the Westminster Parliament. The Labour Party promised in its last general election manifesto to establish a Constitutional Convention, led by a citizens' assembly to 'answer crucial questions on how power is distributed in the UK today, how nations and regions can best relate to each other and how a Labour government can best put power in the hands of the people' (Labour Party 2019, 81). This follows the model of the Scottish Constitutional Convention established following the failure of the Scottish referendum on devolution in 1979. It brought together the Labour, Liberal Democrat, Green and Communist parties, the Scottish Trades Union Congress, local government, churches and other representatives of civil society to put forward proposals for constitutional reform regarding Scotland. Its ideas were eventually taken up by Labour when it came to power in 1997, paving the way for the creation of the Scottish Parliament. A new Constitutional Convention could go some way towards addressing the democratic deficit that is currently being reinforced by the Conservative Party's promotion of parliamentary nationalism post-Brexit. Furthermore, the Labour Party is committed to abolishing the House of Lords and replacing it with a second elected chamber.

Yet it remains to be seen exactly how the Party would ensure that such a reform does not end up reinforcing the strength of Parliament to the detriment of ordinary citizens, ensuring that it is accompanied by electoral reform to ensure a more proportional representation of the nation's political preferences. A truly representative parliament should be capable of representing multiple identities and multiple sites of sovereignty in order to promote a truly progressive 'ascending' nationalism that can accommodate democratic expression from below. Whilst Brexit may have opened up opportunities in this regard by encouraging popular expectations of more participatory politics, the Labour Party seems to have considerable difficulties breaking from the constraints of the centralised Westminster political tradition. Similarly, to the Conservatives, it has eschewed continuing involvement of the wider public in the debate over Brexit, slow to embrace unconditionally a second referendum or to address the denial of the democratic will of the majority of the Scots and Northern Irish who voted to remain in the European Union. In doing so, it also risks advancing descending nationalism and ultimately failing to treat the current ills of British democracy.

Conclusion

The Conservative government under Boris Johnson certainly appeals to nationalism, yet it does so primarily to build popular support for a hyperliberal project that aims to reinforce the power of global capital, failing to empower ordinary people. It is a good example of descending nationalism, firmly entrenched in the centralised British political tradition. In the context of Brexit, 'taking back control' has translated as the reinforcement of executive power as government appeals to parliamentary nationalism to protect the institutions of the British State, failing to recognise multiple identities and to address the democratic deficit that exists within the UK. It also fuels exclusionary populism through its appeal to nativism, instrumentalising fears from below in order to secure support for its own political project. It has let the nationalist genie out of the box and will find it very hard to control, especially if it fails to address popular demands for greater representativity and participation.

The Labour Party should ignore nationalism at its peril – ignoring English nationalism was considered to be one of the main reasons for its electoral defeat in December 2019 (English Labour Network 2020). But this does not mean mimicking the Conservative Party: Labour does show some potential to promote a radically different form of nationalism, defined from below and articulated through popular democratic participation in local government. Following Williams, it could reappropriate the politics of 'placeism' (Evans 2017) to develop a genuine ascending form of nationalism, built from the bottom-up. Yet, in supporting post-Brexit immigration controls, there is a danger that it may also appeal to an exclusionary form of nationalism that excludes certain citizens from the democratic polity. It has also ultimately failed to challenge the British political tradition in excluding the wider public – and even political representatives of the three devolved nations – from the Brexit process. A truly progressive nationalism should be 'ascending', capable of recognising multiple sites of identity and encouraging genuine dialogue about the contours of nationhood. Identification with the national begins with the local.

A progressive nationalism does not represent a retreat from the international arena. On the contrary, it might be regarded as a means of making people comfortable with multi-level governance that can sit more easily alongside cosmopolitanism. Indeed, if people feel properly anchored in place and believe that they have real control, they may be more willing to adopt a global perspective. At a time when post-Brexit nationalism appears to herald the end of cosmopolitanism, there is a strong imperative to promote an alternative nationalism capable of promoting international cooperation to find solutions to global problems.

Whilst Brexit may represent an obstacle to the development of a more open form of nationalism that does not preclude internationalism, it may also be regarded as an opportunity for politicians seeking to promote a genuine ascending nationalism as a means of empowering local communities and sating their demands to seize control of the political process. In order to avail of such contingent factors, it will first be necessary to address the structural deformities of the British state and its dominant centralised political tradition which currently frustrate the exercise of multi-level democracy. Similarly, in Europe, the rise of exclusionary nativist nationalism might be countered by reforming national and European structures in such a way that they enable citizens to participate more actively in the shaping of the contours of their national and European identities.

Note

1. It is obviously rather difficult to measure such feelings, but it might be assumed that the popularity of the slogan 'take back control' appealed to many who felt marginalised by the current political system. Through qualitative research methods, Flemmen and Savage have identified a distinct anti-establishment feeling amongst those who are often considered as the 'left behind' in the UK (2017).

Disclosure statement

No potential conflict of interest was reported by the author.

References

Achiume, T. 2018. "End of Mission Statement of the Special Rapporteur on Contemporary Forms of Racism, Racial Discrimination, Xenophobia and Related Intolerance at the Conclusion of Her Mission to the United Kingdom of Great Britain and Northern Ireland". *United Nations Human Rights Office of the High Commissioner*. Accessed February 2019. https://ohchr.org/EN/NewsEvents/Pages/DisplayNews.aspx?NewsID=23073&LangID=E

Ashcroft, L. 2019. "How the UK Voted on Brexit and Why: A Refresher." 4 February. Accessed March 2020. https://lordashcroftpolls.com/2019/02/how-the-uk-voted-on-brexit-and-why-a-refresher/

Barnett, A. 2016. "Blimey, It Could Be Brexit." Accessed February 2019. https://drive.google.com/file/d/0B6iE9UndVXNKSlVfMkZ0RGNuN1k/view

BBC. 2018. "Brexit Plan Will Stop EU Migrants 'Jumping the Queue' – May". 19 November. Accessed February 2019. https://www.bbc.com/news/uk-politics-46257168

Bell, E. 2015. *Soft Power and Freedom under the Coalition*. Basingstoke: Palgrave.

Bell, E., and G. Christoph. 2019. "The Slow Retreat of Neoliberalism in Contemporary Britain?" In *Neoliberalism in Context*, edited by S. Dawes and M. Lenormand, 19–38. Basingstoke: Palgrave.

Billing, M. 2002(1995). *Banal Nationalism*. London: Sage.

Blair, T. 1999. "Speech to the Labour Party Conference." Accessed March 2020. https://www.theguardian.com/politics/1999/sep/28/labourconference.labour14

Bogdanor, V. 2016. "Europe and the Sovereignty of the People." *The Political Quarterly* 87 (3): 348–351. doi:10.1111/1467-923X.12297.

Brown, G. 2006. "Speech to the Fabian Society." 14 January. Accessed March 2020. https://www.sneps.net/t/images/Articles/06brown%20-%20fabian%2006%20-%20The%20future%20of%20Britishness.pdf

Cameron, D. 2011. "Speech on Multiculturalism." Munich, 5 February. Accessed February 2019. https://www.gov.uk/government/speeches/pms-speech-at-munich-security-conference

Cameron, D. 2013. "Speech on Immigration." University Campus Suffolk, Ipswich. 25 March. Accessed February 2019. https://www.gov.uk/government/speeches/david-camerons-immigration-speech

Conservative Party. 2019. *Let's Get Brexit Done: Unleashing Britain's potential*. Accessed March 2020. https://vote.conservatives.com/our-plan

Corbyn, J. 2017. Speech to the Labour Party Conference, Brighton, 27 September. Accessed February 2019.

Corbyn, J. 2018. "Speech to the Labour Party Conference." 26 September. Accessed February 2019. https://www.mirror.co.uk/news/politics/read-jeremy-corbyn-speech-full-13311639

Crouch, C. 2012 (2004). *Post-Democracy*. Cambridge: Policy Press.

Crouch, C. 2017. "Neoliberalism, Nationalism and the Decline of Political Tradition." *The Political Quarterly* 88 (2): 221–229. doi:10.1111/1467-923X.12321.

Dardot, P., and C. Laval. 2009. *La nouvelle raison du monde: Essai sur la société néolibérale*. Paris: La Découverte/Poche.

Dearden, L. "Sajid Javid Says UK Will Do 'Everything We Can' to Thwart Asylum Claims from People Crossing Channel." The Independent. 2 January. 2019. Accessed February 2019. https://www.independent.co.uk/news/uk/home-news/migrant-crossings-sajid-javid-english-channel-asylum-seekers-refugees-home-secretary-a8707646.html

Denham, J. 2017. "A New Progressive Patriotism." *The Political Quarterly* 88 (1): 97–105. doi:10.1111/1467-923X.12326.

Eatwell, R., and R. Goodwin. 2018. *National Populism: The Revolt against Liberal Democracy*. Milton Keynes: Penguin Random House.

English Labour Network. 2020. *Labour Election 2019: How Labour Lost England*. Accessed March 2020. https://englishlabournetwork.files.wordpress.com/2020/02/ge2019-how-labour-lost-england-pdf.pdf

Eurostat. 2018. "Migration and Migrant Population Statistics." Accessed February 2019. https://ec.europa.eu/eurostat/statistics-explained/index.php/Migration_and_migrant_population_statistics

Evans, G. 2012. "'The Aboriginal People of England': The Culture of Class Politics in Contemporary Britain." *Journal of Global and Historical Anthropology* 62: 17–29.

Evans, G. 2017. "Brexit Britain: Why We are All Postindustrial Now." *American Ethnologist* 44 (2): 215–219. doi:10.1111/amet.12470.

Evans, G., and K. Chzhen. 2013. "Explaining Voters' Defection from Labour over the 2005–10 Electoral Cycle: Leadership, Economics and the Rising Importance of Immigration." *Political Studies* 61 (S1): 138–157. doi:10.1111/1467-9248.12009.

Factcheck. 2016. "Health Tourism: What's the Cost?". Accessed February 2019. https://fullfact.org/health/health-tourism-whats-cost/

Farnsworth, K. 2013. "Public Policies for Private Corporations: The British Corporate Welfare State." *Renewal* 24 (4): 51–65.

Farnsworth, K., L. Cole, and M. Conn 2017. "Oiling the Wheels: Nissan, Private Investment and British Corporate Welfare." *Corporate Welfare Watch*. Accessed January 2019. http://www.corporate-welfare-watch.org.uk/wp/wp-content/uploads/2017/10/170927-nissan-report-final.pdf

Fekete, L. 2016. "Flying the Flag for Neoliberalism.." *Race & Class* 58 (3): 3–22. doi:10.1177/0306396816670088.

Flemmen, M., and M. Savage. 2017. "The Politics of Nationalism and White Racism in the UK." *British Journal of Sociology* 68 (1): 234–264. doi:10.1111/1468-4446.12257.

Gamble, A. 2003. *Between Europe and America: The Future of British Politics*. Basingstoke: Palgrave.

Gardiner, N. 2010. "The Anglosphere and the Defence of Freedom." *Heritage Lectures N°1176. The Heritage Foundation*. Accessed February 2019. https://www.heritage.org/report/the-anglosphere-and-the-advance-freedom

Gibney, M. 2008. "Asylum and the Expansion of Deportation in the United Kingdom." *Government and Opposition* 43 (2): 146–167. doi:10.1111/j.1477-7053.2007.00249.x.

Gifford, C. 2008. *The Making of Eurosceptic Britain: Identity and Economy in a Post-Imperial State*. Farnham: Ashgate.

Goodwin, M., and C. Milazzo. 2017. "Taking Back Control? Investigating the Role of Immigration in the 2016 Vote for Brexit." *British Journal of Politics and International Relations* 1–15. doi:10.1177/1369148117710799.

Hall, M., D. Marsh, and E. Vines. 2018. "A Changing Democracy: Contemporary Challenges to the British Political Tradition." *Policy Studies* 39 (4): 365–382. doi: 10.1080/01442872.2018.1451504.

Hall, S. 1993. "Culture, Community, Nation." *Cultural Studies* 7 (3): 349–363. doi:10.1080/09502389300490251.

Harcourt, B. 2012. *The Illusion of Free Markets: Punishment and the Myth of Natural Order*. Cambridge MA: Harvard University Press.

Harmes, A. 2012. "The Rise of Neoliberal Nationalism." *Review of International Political Economy* 19 (1): 59–86. doi:10.1080/09692290.2010.507132.

Helleiner, E. 2002. "Economic Nationalism as a Challenge to Economic Liberalism? Lessons from the 19th Century." *International Studies Quarterly* 46 (3): 307–329. *JSTOR* 10.1111/1468-2478.00235.

Henderson, A., and R. Wyn Jones. 2018. "May's 'Precious Union' Has Little Support in Brexit Britain." 8 October. Accessed February 2019. https://www.centreonconstitutionalchange.ac.uk/news/press-release-may's-'precious-union'-has-little-support-brexit-britain

HM Government. 2018a. "The UK's Future Skills-Based Immigration System." December. Accessed February 2019. https://assets.publishing.service.gov.uk/government/uploads/system/uploads/attachment_data/file/766465/The-UKs-future-skills-based-immigration-system-print-ready.pdf

HM Government 2018b. "The Windrush Generation: Government Response to the Committee's Sixth Report of Session 2017–19." Accessed February 2019. https://publications.parliament.uk/pa/cm201719/cmselect/cmhaff/1545/154502.htm

Hobsbawm, E. 1992. *Nationals and Nationalism since 1780*. Cambridge: Cambridge University Press.

Jeffrey, C., R. Wyn Jones, A. Henderson, R. Scully, and G. Lodge. 2014. "Taking England Seriously: The New English Politics." *The Future of England Survey 2014*. Accessed February 2019. https://www.centreonconstitutionalchange.ac.uk/sites/default/files/news/Taking%20England%20Seriously_The%20New%20English%20Politics.pdf

Jones, B., and M. Keating. 1985. *Labour and the British State*. Oxford: Clarendon Press.

Juncker, J.-C. 2018. "State of the Union Address: The Hour of European Sovereignty." Accessed February 2019. https://ec.europa.eu/commission/sites/beta-political/files/soteu2018-speech_en_0.pdf

Kaufmann, E. 2018. "Interview. E-International Relations." 25 October. Accessed 27 May 2019. https://www.e-ir.info/2018/10/25/interview-eric-kaufmann/

Keating, M. 2001. *Plurinational Democracy: Stateless Nations in a Post-Sovereignty Era*. Oxford: Oxford University Press.

Kenny, M. 2014. *The Politics of English Nationhood*. Oxford: OUP.

Kenny, M., and N. Pearce. 2018. *Shadows of Empire: The Anglosphere in British Politics*. Cambridge: Polity Press.

Kosc, J. A. 2017. "The Liberal Roots of Nativism." Foreign Affairs. 29 September. Accessed February 2019. https://www.foreignaffairs.com/articles/united-states/2017-09-29/liberal-roots-nativism

Kumar, K. 2003. *The Making of English National Identity*. Cambridge: Cambridge University Press.

Kundnani, A. 2009. *Spooked: How Not to Prevent Violent Extremism*. London: Institute of Race Relations.

Labour Party. 2017. *Alternative Models of Ownership*. Accessed February 2019. http://labour.org.uk/wp-content/uploads/2017/10/Alternative-Models-of-Ownership.pdf

Labour Party. 2019. "It's Time for Real Change." Accessed March 2020. https://labour.org.uk/wp-content/uploads/2019/11/Real-Change-Labour-Manifesto-2019.pdf

Mabbett, D. 2017. "Parliamentary Sovereignty and Brexit." *The Political Quarterly* 88 (2): 167–169. doi:10.1111/1467-923X.12364.

Matthews, W. 2013. *The New Left, National Identity, and the Break-up of Britain*. Leiden: Brill. doi:10.1163/9789004253070.

May, T. 2013. "Stop and Search: Time to Get It Right, Says Theresa May". *Cited by the BBC*. 2 July. Accessed February 2019. https://www.bbc.com/news/uk-23140505

May, T. 2015. "Speech to the Conservative Party Conference." 6 October. Accessed February 2019. https://www.independent.co.uk/news/uk/politics/theresa-may-s-speech-to-the-conservative-party-conference-in-full-a6681901.html

May, T. 2016. "Speech to the Lord Mayor's Banquet." 14 November. Accessed February 2019. https://www.gov.uk/government/speeches/pm-speech-to-the-lord-mayors-banquet-14-november-2016

May, T. 2017. "Speech Setting Out the Government's Negotiating Objectives for Exiting the EU." 17 January. Accessed February 2019. https://www.gov.uk/government/speeches/the-governments-negotiating-objectives-for-exiting-the-eu-pm-speech

May, T. 2018. "Speech on Our Future Economic Partnership with the EU." 2 March. Accessed February 2019. https://www.gov.uk/government/speeches/pm-speech-on-our-future-economic-partnership-with-the-european-union

McKay, D. 2019. "What Really Motivates the European Research Group?". *Prospect*. 11 January. Accessed January 2019. https://www.prospectmagazine.co.uk/politics/motivates-tories-erg-jacob-rees-mogg-european-research-group-brexit

Miller, D. 2003. "In Defence of Nationality." In *Debates in Contemporary Political Philosophy: An Anthology*, edited by D. Matravers and J. Pike, 301–317. London: Routledge.

Mulvey, G. 2010. "When Policy Creates Politics: The Problematizing of Immigration and the Consequences for Refugee Integration in the UK." *Journal of Refugee Studies* 23 (4): 437–462. doi:10.1093/jrs/feq045.

Nairn, T. 2003. *The Break-Up of Britain: Crisis and Neo-Nationalism*. Champaign: Common Ground.

Nodia, G. O. 1992. "Nationalism and Democracy." *Journal of Democracy* 3 (4): 3–22. doi:10.1353/jod.1992.0053.

O'Toole, F. 2018. *Heroic Failure: Brexit and the Politics of Pain*. London: Head of Zeus.

Peck, J., N. Theodore, and N. Brenner. 2010. "Postneoliberalism and Its Malcontents." *Antipode* 41 (1): 94–116. doi:10.1111/j.1467-8330.2009.00718.x.

Portes, J., and G. Forte. 2017. "The Economic Impact of Brexit-Induced Reductions in Migration." *Oxford Review of Economic Policy* 33 (1): S31–S44. doi:10.1093/oxrep/grx008.

Powell, E. 1968. "Rivers of Blood Speech." Accessed February 2019. https://www.telegraph.co.uk/comment/3643823/Enoch-Powells-Rivers-of-Blood-speech.html

Rosamond, B. 2018. "Brexit and the Politics of UK Growth Models." *New Political Economy*. doi:10.1080/13563467.2018.1484721.

Rudd, A. 2016. "Speech to the Conservative Party Conference." Accessed February 2019. http://press.conservatives.com/post/151334637685/rudd-speech-to-conservative-party-conference-2016

Scotto, T. J., D. Sanders, Reifler, and J. Reifler. 2018. "The Consequential Nationalist-Globalist Policy Divide in Contemporary Britain: Some Initial Analyses." *Journal of Elections, Public Opinion and Parties* 28 (1): 38–58. doi:10.1080/17457289.2017.1360308.

Vines, E. 2015. "A Common Appeal: Anglo-British Nationalism and Opposition to Europe, 1970–1975." *Australian Journal of Politics and History* 61 (4): 530–545. doi:10.1111/ajph.12117.

Wadsworth, J., S. Dhingra, G. Ottaviano, and J. Van Reenen 2017. "Brexit and the Impact of Immigration on the UK." *LSE Brexit Paper 5*. Accessed February 2019. http://cep.lse.ac.uk/pubs/download/brexit05.pdf

Wellings, B. 2012. *English Nationalism and Euroscepticism: Losing the Peace: British Identities since 1707*. Oxford: Peter Lang.

Williams, R. 1984. "Decentralism and the Politics of Place: An Interview with Raymond Williams." *Interviewer: P. Cooke. Environment and Planning, Society and Space* 2: 369–374.

Wright, T. 2017. "Democracy in Britain." *Retrospect and Prospect". The Political Quarterly* 88: 189–197. doi:10.1111/1467-923X.12342.

Theresa May, the Brexit negotiations and the two-level game, 2017–2019

Pauline Schnapper

ABSTRACT
For the two years between the activation of article 50 of the Lisbon treaty and the expected withdrawal on 29 March 2019, Theresa May was confronted with an apparently classical two-level game, where she needed to find a compromise between what Brussels could find acceptable, especially as far as trade relations were concerned, and what her domestic constituency demanded. This was made more complex by the fact that the latter was itself divided between Remainers, Soft and Hard Brexiters and multiple other sub-groups. Based on a discursive institutionalist approach, this article suggests that the Prime Minister was caught in a contradiction between her 'hard' rhetoric at home and the reality of her bargaining position in Brussels. Tsebelis' nested games theory explains why her communicative discourse was politically rational but ultimately incompatible with the reality of the European power game.

1. Introduction

Theresa May's government embarked on a two-year negotiation with the European Union (EU) when it activated article 50 of the Lisbon Treaty on 29 March 2017, with the view to both find an agreement on the British exit from the EU and on their future relations.[1] The negotiation was mainly conducted, on the British side, by the newly-formed Department for Exiting the EU (DexEU). Its first Permanent Secretary, Oliver Robbins, joined 10 Downing Street as the Prime Minister's Europe adviser in September 2017 and played a pivotal role in the whole process, arguably more important than the Brexit Secretaries – first David Davis, then Dominic Raab and finally Stephen Barclay – according to some commentators. On the EU side, Commissioner Michel Barnier and his team negotiated on behalf of the 27 member states following guidelines agreed at the April 2017 European Council (European Council 2017).

The negotiation proceeded in two phases. The first one ended in December 2017 with a putative deal on the divorce bill, the EU citizens' rights and a statement on the Irish border. The second one covered 2018 and ended in 22 November 2018 when the May government signed a legally-binding 585-page withdrawal document with the EU, which covered the transition period until December 2020, and a 25-page political declaration on the future relation between the UK and the EU. The core point of the agreement was that the UK as a whole would stay in the EU customs union during the transition period and possibly beyond in order to prevent a hard border between Northern Ireland and the Republic in the south – the so-called backstop. This was well short of the 'red lines' that Theresa May had been defending at home since 2016, and did not satisfy supporters of staying in the single market (soft Brexiters) or remainers either. With a hung Parliament and the government relying on the ten votes of the Democratic Unionist Party of Northern Ireland to remain in power, the ratification of this agreement in Parliament proved impossible, with different factions from different parties coalescing into opposition to the government.

This seems the perfect illustration of Robert Putnam's classical 'two-level game' theory of international negotiations, which sees them as taking place simultaneously at the domestic (level II) and the international (level I) levels, each one impacting the other (Putnam 1988). Negotiations can only succeed if a 'win-set' exists which can satisfy both levels. In this case, a multiplicity of domestic constraints proved overwhelming: the Conservative party was divided, the views of the public were unclear and there had been different votes in the 2016 referendum in Scotland and Northern Ireland. Theresa May was therefore confronted with different domestic expectations.

Yet we will see that the two-level game theory does not fully account for the Brexit negotiation as it assumes that the two partners are equal and that there are relatively coherent and consensual preferences put forward at level I, conditions which were not met in this case. This paper will therefore make three different arguments. One is a theoretical one, emphasizing both the usefulness but also the limits of Putnam's theory when analysing the Brexit negotiations. The second, methodological, one makes the case for a constructivist approach based on the discrepancies between rhetoric and reality, in this case the contradictions between Theresa May's discourse aimed at her domestic audience and the constraints imposed by her European partners. It will be based on an analysis of her speeches about the negotiations at home (2016 Conservative party conference, Lord Mayor's Speech, Mansion House, Lancaster House and Belfast) and on the continent (in Florence and Brussels) between 2016 and 2018. The third, empirical argument looks at how the negotiations progressed in Brussels while at the same time domestic support for the government inevitably unravelled as a result of the fragmentation of the domestic constituency at level II. This can be to a large extent explained by the discrepancy between the political rhetoric necessary at home and the reality of the balance of power in Brussels. What was rational at the domestic level was doomed at level I and the other way round.

So the first section of this article will discuss the theoretical framework which I use to analyse the UK/EU bargaining. The following sections will then look at the two different stages in the negotiation – broadly speaking 2017 and 2018, focusing on the way May dealt with the different actors at the different levels and the evolution – or rather lack of – of her discourse.

2. Theoretical framework

Our theoretical starting point is the two-level game theory, which as Hooghe and Marks have shown is particularly suited in a domestic environment marked by a high-level politicisation of European issues and a strong sense of national identity (Liesbet and Marks 2005). Putnam (1988) shows that in international negotiations representatives from national governments are constrained by domestic actors and need to achieve two goals simultaneously: 'At the international level, national governments seek to maximize their own ability to satisfy domestic pressures, while minimizing the adverse consequences of foreign developments'. Leaders need therefore to find compromises around the negotiating table that will be acceptable both to their foreign counterparts (Level I) and their constituency at home (Level II). In order to achieve this, 'there are likely to be prior consultations and bargaining at Level II to hammer out an initial position for the Level I negotiations. Conversely, the need for Level II ratification is certain to affect the Level I bargaining.'

Putnam also tells us that the key to reaching an agreement is the size of the win-set, which is 'the set of all possible Level I agreements that would "win" – that is, gain the necessary majority among the constituents – when simply voted up or down'. This is the deal that can be acceptable to both the international partners and the domestic constituency and prevents 'involuntary defection' where the leader can't achieve ratification. The more contested the issues are at either or both levels, the smaller the win-set is. So normally, the bigger the win-set, the more likely ratification will be possible, although there can be some benefits in having a small win-set while bargaining, since it enables the negotiator to argue: 'I'd like to accept your proposal, but I could never get it accepted at home' (p. 440). But this implies that there is a clearly defined and more or less consensual position at home that can be defended at level I.

In the case of Theresa May's negotiation with the EU-27, it was difficult to define the win-set, even to assess whether there was one. According to the Prime Minister's own early speeches, the government's aim was to leave the single market and customs union, withdraw from the jurisdiction of the European Court of Justice (ECJ), put an end to the free circulation of people, achieve a 'bespoke' agreement that would enable 'frictionless trade' and sign cooperation agreements with the EU on security issues (May 2017). On the EU side instead, it was to keep the integrity of the single market, keep the unity of the EU, prevent a hard border in Ireland, prevent 'cherry-picking' (allowing the UK to choose among the four freedoms of circulation which ones it would accept and which ones it would not apply) and the undermining of the regulatory regime (European Union Council 2017). At the start of the negotiation at least, there was very little if any overlap between the two, meaning that one would have to give in or there would be no agreement.

Although a small win-set can be a bargaining advantage according to Putnam, it is doubtful whether this could apply in this case because of the divisions within the domestic constituency. The two main political parties were split, with a very large spectrum of opinions ranging from advocating a second referendum with the hope of remaining in the EU to leaving in March 2019 without a deal and resorting to WTO rules, the so-called Canada and Norway options being somewhere in the middle. Theresa May was actually quite isolated in this varied landscape.

The Prime Minister's position was also undermined by the fact that, following the botched 2017 general election in which she lost her majority and had to rely on the DUP votes, she was a weak leader at home with no majority in Parliament and a divided party. She was faced with both the Foreign and Brexit Secretaries resigning in July 2018 and although she survived as Prime Minister, she had a low level of credibility in Brussels because, as Putnam put it, she could not guarantee the ratification of a future deal (p. 439). Another difficulty came from the fact that the cost of no agreement was higher for the UK than for the EU-27. If no agreement was reached by the end of March 2019 the UK would face the so-called 'cliff-edge', where it returned to basic WTO trade rules, with tariffs and border controls in place. Instead, this would have much less dramatic consequences for the rest of the EU, which are less dependent on trans-Channel links, even though it would disrupt supply chains for them too. Negotiators in Brussels were fully aware of this imbalance and were in a stronger position to impose their views.

These specific circumstances mean that Putnam's traditional model cannot fully apply here. On the one hand, there was no 'objective' set of national preferences articulated by the Prime Minister nor a widespread consensus. Her constituents at the different domestic levels were divided and she lacked the kind of leverage described by Putnam. On the other hand, the asymmetry in the bargaining power of the two sets of negotiators in Brussels, never acknowledged by the British government, meant that the UK's 'red lines' would not be accepted. As Schimmelfennig (2018) showed, the government failed to realise that once no longer a status-quo actor in the EU (as it had been in the past, which enabled it to obtain opt-outs from a number of policies) its bargaining power would be radically reduced. Finally, Putnam's model implies a type of rationality and fixed interests among negotiating partners which was lacking in the British government. Indeed, if the Prime Minister's position was rational in domestic *political* terms, since she needed parliamentary ratification, in many ways her 'red lines' were less *economically* rational for the long-term future of her country and traditional economic and business voices were not listened to (Dunlop, James and Radaelli 2019). Yet she felt compelled to stick to them and refused to contemplate forms of a softer Brexit which would have been more in tune with the reality of interconnected economies in Europe, but unacceptable to parts of her domestic constituency.

This is why the two-level game needs to be supplemented with two additional considerations. The first one is Tsebelis's idea of the 'nested games' referred to in the introduction to this special issue, i.e the idea that an apparently sub-optimal approach (to negotiations in this case) can only be explained if a broader political context is taken into account. Here Theresa May's red lines were consistent with the expectations if not of a majority of British voters, at least with a majority of her own party, even if they were not fully rational in terms of the long-term economic and political interests of her country.

The second one is the need to adopt a constructivist framework, based on the premise that it is necessary to analyse the role of ideas and discourse to understand the unfolding of events which may appear as sub-rational at first sight. Vivien Schmidt's discursive institutionalism is particularly helpful here. She defines discourse 'not just as the representation of ideas but also as the interactive process of exchanging ideas which appears in two basic forms: the "coordinative" discourse among policy actors and the "communicative" discourse between political actors and the public' (2008, 2). This can be applied to the two-level model of the UK/EU negotiations, where the coordinative discourse took place in Brussels with the other member-states and the European Commission and the communicative discourse with a multi-faceted domestic audience in the UK. Actors in Brussels proved more united and aligned with each other than May's audience in her communicative discourse and the imbalance between the two levels added to her difficulties. Schmidt also shows that there are different levels of ideas and discourse that come into play, from the philosophical (in this case parliamentary sovereignty or the collective memory of the second world war) to the programmatic (here May's commitment to implement Brexit even though she was originally a remainer) and the immediate policy ideas (here expressed in her different speeches and statements) (Schmidt 2013, 7).

The crucial point here is that discourse, in this case the Prime Minister's, was also constructed, rather than simply emanating from 'objective' material interest. Policy choices were elaborated and explained as a result of a specific interpretation of the context in which these decisions were taken, in this case the 2016 EU referendum. May thought she would draw her legitimacy from an understanding of the popular vote as a rejection of immigration and a yearning for sovereignty, also assuming that Leave voters had shared the same intentions when casting their votes and a univocal vision of the future relation between their country and the EU. This chimed with and was made easier by long-held ideas, in the sense used by Schmidt of frames of references, about British exceptionalism and scepticism towards the European project (George 1998). Similarly, Martill and Staiger (2018) suggest that the apparently uncompromising strategy pursued by the government was a direct consequence of 'underlying cultural and ideational factors', especially the Conservative type of statecraft and more generally the Westminster model which favours confrontational politics. Dunlop, James and Radaelli (2019) add an important policy-making, as opposed to political, dimension to our understanding of what they call the 'Brexit fiasco', stressing the lack of reflexive learning within government and antipathy towards outside expertise.

Schmidt and Crespy also assert that discourse influences negotiations both at the European and domestic levels. In particular, they stress the fact that preferences may change over the course of the negotiations and are 'constructed, reconfigured and communicated simultaneously to national constituencies and other European decision makers' (2014, 3). This applies to the May government which started from a very 'hard' stance and gradually moved, in practice but not in rhetoric, to making major concessions to Brussels. The Prime Minister trapped herself in communicative discourse for her domestic audience which made a coordinative discourse and therefore successful negotiations impossible. The next section will analyse how this played out in the first phase of the negotiations.

3. The first phase, 29 March–December 2017

May's legitimacy, as a former Remainer, was first discursively established by the repeated tautology that 'Brexit means Brexit', first expressed when she ran for the leadership of the Conservative party on 11 July 2016. It was meant to underline the fact that Brexit would be delivered, that there would be no turning back and no second referendum. But the phrase said nothing about how the UK would leave the EU or what their future relationship would be like.

Her policy ideas for the negotiation, as expressed later in her speeches and statements, were broad but clear. She developed a narrative around the 2016 referendum which interpreted the voters' choice in normative terms, as the (legitimate) aims of stopping EU immigration and retrieving lost sovereignty:

> Our laws made not in Brussels but in Westminster. Our judges sitting not in Luxembourg but in courts across the land. The authority of EU law in this country ended forever ... But let me be clear about the agreement we seek ... I want it to involve free trade, in goods and services. I want it to give British companies the maximum freedom to trade with and operate within the Single Market – and let European businesses do the same here. But let's state one thing loud and clear: we are not leaving the European Union only to give up control of immigration all over again (May 2016a).

> So we will take back control of our laws and bring an end to the jurisdiction of the European Court of Justice in Britain. Leaving the European Union will mean that our laws will be made in Westminster, Edinburgh, Cardiff and Belfast. And those laws will be interpreted by judges not in Luxembourg but in courts across this country (May 2017a).

> Yes, the United Kingdom will be a fully independent, sovereign country, free to make our own decisions on a whole host of different issues such as how we choose to control immigration. But we still want to trade freely – in goods and services – with Europe (May 2016b).

This interpretation could have been different, it was neither 'natural' nor 'objective', but constructed as a response to the successful referendum Leave campaign which had articulated this vision. The 'Take Back Control' theme, directly inherited from it, was present in these early speeches and remained constant throughout the negotiation. As early as October 2016, the central contradiction between wanting to abandon EU laws, to control immigration on the one hand and to trade freely with the EU (which implied accepting the four freedoms of circulation) on the other was apparent but never acknowledged. There were only very short and vague references to possible difficulties in the future: seven words after the October 2016 EU Council and in her speech to the Conservative Party conference ('It will require some give and take') and a few lines in the Florence speech (2017): 'Of course, we recognise that we can't leave the EU and have everything stay the same. Life for us will be different.' But on the whole, in her communicative discourse May described the process as relatively straightforward, due to the UK's unique status as a previous member. The aim of the negotiation was to find a 'bespoke' agreement on 'frictionless trade' which would be neither simply a free trade deal (the so-called Canada option) nor remaining in the European Economic Space like Norway, as it required accepting the free circulation of people:

> That is also why, in our negotiations on leaving the European Union, we are not trying to replicate the deal that any other country has with the EU. And we are not going for an off-the-shelf solution (2016c).

> We do not start with a blank sheet of paper, like other external partners negotiating a free trade deal from scratch have done ... As for a Canadian style free trade agreement, we should recognise that this is the most advanced free trade agreement the EU has yet concluded and a breakthrough in trade between Canada and the EU. But compared with what exists between Britain and the EU today, it would nevertheless represent such a restriction on our mutual market access that it would benefit neither of our economies. Not only that, it would start from the false premise that there is no pre-existing regulatory relationship between us (2017b).

Finally, this is also when the 'No deal for Britain is better than a bad deal' phrase first appeared in May's speeches (May 2017a). It found its way in the Conservative manifesto in June 2017 and she repeated it many times, e.g in September 2018, without ever expanding on what she meant by a 'bad' deal. The repeated mantra also ignored the fact that 'no deal' did not mean the status quo but the imposition of checks at the UK borders, including in Ireland, on 29 March 2019.

Theresa May therefore expressed early on a number of principles or 'red lines', not as preliminary statements which would then evolve in the course of the negotiations in order to reach a realistic compromise, but as non-negotiable items. It was a hard-bargaining tactic which later clashed with the reality of the balance of power in Brussels. It entailed that either the EU would make all the effort to reach an agreement or that she would have to make concessions in the negotiation without acknowledging it, a contradiction which eventually blew up in her face. At the same time, she had not agreed on her strategy with the different groups and sub-groups within her party and Parliament in general (level II), therefore had no consensual policy to defend in Brussels (level I). This was risky especially as she faced a united European Union speaking with a single voice and never managed to divide her partners in the negotiation in Brussels.

This hard rhetoric was meant to satisfy the Leavers in her own party, who were keen to embark on trade deals with third countries and would not accept remaining under the jurisdiction of the European Court of Justice. It succeeded in appeasing them at first (Glynn and Menon 2018, 34). In the two-level game, they were her main constituency because she depended on their ratification. Neither the interests of the 48% of Remainers in the electorate nor, for example, of the business community, which traditionally were close to the Conservative party, were taken into account in her negotiating strategy. She did not attempt to reach out to opposition parties either, although there might have been a cross-party majority in favour of a soft Brexit in the House of Commons (with Labour, Liberal Democrats, Greens, SNP and about two dozen Conservative MPs). Her domestic strategy was a classical one in a two-party system of maximising support within her own party, which was a rational one as long as her party had a majority in Parliament. But even within her own party, she ignored the supporters of a soft Brexit, for whom the priority was to mitigate the economic harm caused by leaving the EU and stay as close as possible to the single market. After May lost her majority in the House of Commons in the snap general election in June 2017, the parliamentary arithmetic became even more complex and the need to maintain unity behind her strategy more pressing. On the Conservative Leave side, Jacob Rees-Mogg led the European Research Group of about 60 Conservative MPs who supported a hard Brexit and opposed any concessions to Brussels. They supported the hard Brexiters in the Cabinet, who pledged not to give in to what Liam Fox called 'blackmail' from Brussels. As for Boris Johnson, he said Brussels could 'go whistle' as far as exit payments were concerned.[2] Their views on Brexit could accommodate no compromise, it was an absolute version of sovereignty which was not compatible with any remaining ties with the EU, seen as bureaucratic, undemocratic and in terminal economic decline anyway.

Because Theresa May felt compelled to appease the hard Brexiters, she met with some difficulties on the other side of the debate. An All-party parliamentary group on EU relations was created by Chuka Umunna for Labour and Anna Soubry for the Conservatives, who then launched the Independent Group/Change UK with a few other MPs, to argue for a 'close relationship with the European Union'. The pro-Remain Conservatives were only a handful as a whole but could have a disproportionate impact in the absence of a government majority, provided they chose to use their power. On the Labour benches, MPs were divided on the merits of staying in the single market. The leadership opposed staying in the single market because they wished to stop the free movement of people, but 30 MPs signed an open letter in September 2017 in favour of staying in the single market and the customs union.[3] In December 2017 the House of Commons voted the amendment to the EU Withdrawal Bill sponsored by Dominic Grieve which gave Parliament a 'meaningful vote' on the future deal negotiated by the government in Brussels. This proved a major hurdle a year later when it came to ratifying the Brussels deal.

The fragmentation of parliamentary opinion and the lack of consensus at level II were compounded by the devolved regions. In Scotland, the pressure expected from the Scottish nationalist government following the different referendum result (Scotland voted to remain by 62%) failed to materialise. The government published its proposals in a document, *Scotland's Place in Europe*, in late 2016 where Nicola Sturgeon insisted on her 'determination to ensure Scotland's voice is heard and acted upon'. She wished the UK, or at least, Scotland to stay in the single market and customs union and more powers to be devolved to the Scottish Parliament (Scottish Government 2016). In March 2017, she formally asked the government to grant the Scottish Parliament the power to organise a second referendum on independence, to which Theresa May replied that 'now is not the time' (quoted in Hassan 2018, 134). But in the general election that followed, the SNP lost 21 seats (from an unprecedented high of 54) and the Conservative party won 12 in Scotland (from a very low base of one). This subdued the SNP's ambition to have a second referendum on independence before March 2019, the official line being that the plan would be on hold until the terms of Brexit were clear. In the meantime, the Scottish government's successive demands to be associated to the negotiations and to stay in the single market were ignored in London, raising tensions in Scotland. So Theresa May was able to take advantage of Nicola Sturgeon's new relative weakness to limit the need to take Scottish views into account.

But things turned out differently in Northern Ireland, thanks to the leverage the 10 DUP MPs suddenly gained over the May government following the 2017 general election. The paradox here is that the DUP hardline stance over Brexit did not correspond to the wishes of a majority of the Northern Irish population, which had voted to remain in the 2016 referendum by 55%. Indeed, it was the only party in Northern Ireland which advocated leaving the EU. But the collapse of the assembly and power-sharing government in Belfast in January 2017 and Sinn Fein's policy of not taking up their seats in Westminster gave the DUP the opportunity to be the only voice for Northern Ireland in London and therefore disproportionate power (Murphy 2018). This was also helped by the fact that the Irish border soon became the most difficult issue in the Brussels negotiation. In early December 2017, Arlene Foster torpedoed an agreement on the Irish border which would have aligned Northern Ireland with EU laws in a telephone conversation with Theresa May.[4] It forced Theresa May to accept that there would be no border on the Irish sea.

In contrast to the government's intransigent communicative discourse in London, the picture in Brussels was one of the successive concessions by the government or what the journalist Paul Taylor called 'managed surrender' (2018). May gradually yielded to a number of EU demands. First, the Commission imposed a separation between the negotiation on the transition period and the negotiation on the final deal, which the government first resisted and finally agreed to in December. This reduced May's leverage in the negotiation on the transition period as she was not able to use the trump card of a future security cooperation. The government had no say either on the three issues to be discussed first, namely the Brexit bill, the rights of UK citizens in the EU and European citizens in the UK and the Irish border. Then, Theresa May accepted the principle of a transition (or implementation) period including the free movement of people which was accepted by the Cabinet in July.[5] She also had to agree that the jurisdiction of the ECJ would apply during the transition.[6] Finally, she accepted that the UK could not sign a trade deal during that period.[7] All of this was different from what she had first claimed and was confirmed in her Florence speech (May 2017b).

In the end, the December 2017 deal on the transition period guaranteed the same rights for the 'Brexit citizens', including EU citizens who would be coming to the UK during the transition period. The UK government also accepted to pay about £50 billion to settle the different bills.[8] The Irish border issue was not solved except for a statement of principle that there would be no hard border between the north and south of Ireland and that there would be full alignment with the rules of the single market and customs union as a last resort. In spite of the strength of the hard Brexit group within the Conservative party, May managed to get eurosceptic support for the agreement with the EU because it was only for the duration of the transition period. Eurosceptics chose to focus on the future instead, with Rees-Mogg saying the deal 'is tolerable if the end state is a clean Brexit'.[9] The second phase proved much more difficult and the gap between May's communicative rhetoric and the coordinative needs of negotiations in Brussels widened.

4. The second phase: January–November 2018

The second phase was about what the transition phase would look like in concrete terms since Brussels had refused to start talks on the future relation between the EU and UK until this issue was settled. In theory, it was supposed to be completed by the October 2018 EU Council, in time for ratification before the Brexit date in March 2019. Instead, it ended with the November 2018 585-page deal on the transition phase and the political declaration on the future of UK–EU relations. During that period, May continued to defend the same principles in the negotiation – frictionless trade, neither Canada nor Norway-type relations with the EU in the future, an end to free movement, no hard border in Ireland, freedom to sign trade deals with third countries – continuing to brush aside the fact that some of these demands were incompatible. The only qualification she added to her previous stance, in an effort to reassure both her European partners and working-class voters at home, was there would be no social dumping post-Brexit:

> As I said in Florence, we share the same set of fundamental beliefs; a belief in free trade, rigorous and fair competition, strong consumer rights, and that trying to beat other countries' industries by unfairly subsidising one's own is a serious mistake. And in other areas like workers' rights or the environment, the EU should be confident that we will not engage in a race to the bottom in the standards and protections we set. There is no serious political constituency in the UK which would support this – quite the opposite (May 2018a).

As a result of this continuity in public statements, a similar pattern of parallel and incompatible negotiations continued. The outcome of domestic negotiations was a proposal (the so-called Chequers plan) which was unacceptable to the Level I negotiators. In the end, the government backed down in the face of Brussels pressure and agreed to stay in the customs union during the transition period and possibly beyond if no deal was reached at the end of 2020, in order to prevent a hard border in Ireland. But this time the contradiction between the two types of discourse came to a head when the House of Commons refused to ratify the agreement.

By March 2018 the EU Council had agreed that negotiations on the future UK–EU relations could start. But they immediately stalled as the government made no specific proposals to the Commission for fear of inflaming tempers in London. A sort of phoney war ensued, where Michel Barnier repeated the EU red lines and waited for British proposals:

> After Brexit, we want an EU-UK ambitious partnership on trade as well as security. But we have to base this partnership on our values and principles, respecting also the UK red lines. That means for us integrity of the single market, indivisibility of the four freedoms, autonomy and the decision-making of the EU, and the protection and respect of the fundamental rights of EU citizens.[10]

This meant in practice that every time the government aired a proposal it was slapped down by Brussels because it did not comply with these principles. It was the case with the 'Norway minus' proposal, May's 'customs partnership' proposal or the backstop for the whole UK, whereas the Commission's preferred option was that Northern Ireland alone stayed in the customs union.[11] The EU's hard stance was confirmed when it expelled the UK from the Galileo satellite project and stated that post-Brexit Britain would not be able to use the European Arrest Warrant and access to security data.

The government continued to insist that it would protect the open border in Ireland and Theresa May visited Belfast in July, shortly after the Chequers plan was published and again in February 2019. The DUP position remained intransigent and out of step with what an increasing part of the Northern Irish population wished, including businesses and farmers in Northern Ireland who traditionally provide their electoral basis (McHugh 2018). It supported the hardest of hard Brexits, i.e the possibility of no deal, even though it would entail the introduction of a hard border which they also claimed to reject. As a result, they remained aligned with Jacob Rees-Mogg's ERG group, for example, voting in favour of their amendment on the customs bill which called for a single UK customs territory, therefore ruling out a border in the Irish sea. Arlene Foster, the DUP leader, met with Michel Barnier in Brussels in October 2018 and complained about his supposed 'hostility' to her concerns.

Scotland continued to be totally marginalised in this second phase, for lack of leverage over the government. Nicola Sturgeon tried to take advantage of the dispute over the Irish border in order to extract a special status for Scotland post-Brexit. She tweeted in February 2018: 'If NI stays in single market, the case for Scotland also doing so is not just an academic "us too" argument – it becomes a practical necessity. Otherwise, we will be at a massive relative disadvantage when it comes to attracting jobs and investment.'[12] This was immediately ruled out by the London government. She could not achieve anything either on what became the main issue between Edinburgh and London, i.e the contentious clause 11 of the Withdrawal bill, which returned powers exercised by the EU to the central government in London and not the devolved governments.[13] Instead, the Scottish government quoted the Scotland Act 1998 which states that all non-reserved powers are devolved and demanded that Edinburgh obtain full powers over, for example, agriculture. The dispute grew in February 2018 when the Welsh and Scottish governments decided to pass legislation to transfer EU powers to Edinburgh and Cardiff.[14] Confronted with London's refusal to change article 11, the Scottish Parliament rejected the EU withdrawal bill in May.[15] Although the British Prime Minister had repeatedly insisted that she was working for the whole of the UK in her Brexit negotiations, for instance in her Belfast speech (2018b), the bill was actually a breach of the Sewel convention by which Westminster does not legislate on devolved powers without the consent of the Scottish Parliament. In the short term, the SNP government failed again to have an impact on the UK government's Brexit policy but in the longer term causing a constitutional crisis between London and Edinburgh was a risky strategy for the central government. The danger, from a British unionist point of view, was that it might lead to more support for independence in Scotland in the future.

Meanwhile, because divisions remained in Cabinet over the future trade relations and the related issue of the Irish border, proposals were only put on the table at a Cabinet meeting at Chequers on 6 July and then in a white paper. May's plan suggested that the UK could stay in the free trade area for goods only in order to maintain the cross-border supply chains running and limit border controls on goods, with a 'facilitated customs arrangement' by which the UK would collect customs duties at its borders on behalf of the EU and therefore avoid a border in Ireland (HM Government 2018). This meant that the insurance policy known as the backstop, where Northern Ireland would stay in the customs union until a free trade agreement was signed with the EU, would not need to be used. Yet even this was a concession to a softer Brexit that was anathema to the radical Brexiters in the Cabinet and after a few days David Davies, the Brexit Secretary, and Boris Johnson, the Foreign Secretary, both resigned in the first major political crisis for Theresa May, protesting that following the EU rulebook was in contradiction with the referendum result. There were neither mass resignations nor a leadership contest against Theresa May, which required a letter from 15% of the Conservative MPs, in the immediate aftermath of the Chequers meeting. This allowed her to stay in power and present the plan to the EU-27 but the crisis contributed to undermining the authority of the Prime Minister.

The Chequers plan was May's relatively successful attempt to reconcile the different factions of her party behind a strategy for the transition period. But it was soon clear that May would not be able to sell it to Brussels, even on the basis that it was the only option acceptable to her domestic constituency. When the government published its white paper in July, reactions from Brussels were at first muted as the taskforce did not want to weaken Theresa May's position any further. So the Commission welcomed the principle of a UK plan but made it clear it did not find its content satisfactory since staying in the single market only for goods would undermine the indivisibility of the four freedoms (Grant 2018). The 'facilitated customs arrangement' was not really considered as feasible either. On the Irish border, Barnier continued to suggest that Northern Ireland could stay in the customs union, therefore removing the need for customs checks at the border.

The showdown came at the informal Salzburg EU summit on 20 September 2018, when the EU-27 publicly rejected Theresa May's proposals, which to them would undermine the single market and give British companies unfair advantage. They also issued her with an ultimatum, giving her until October to provide a solution to avoid a hard border in Ireland. The clash of 'red lines' had occurred and the EU gave no sign of being ready to compromise on theirs. This was interpreted as a 'humiliation' in the British press.[16] The Salsburg episode illustrated the extent to which the two or three levels of negotiation had been taking place in parallel universes, rather than impacting on each other. Theresa May seemed surprised that the red lines she had constantly repeated in London were not accepted in Brussels and that the Commission was not making any concessions on them, sharing a widely held illusion in London that the UK and the EU-27 were equally powerful in the negotiations. Her threat to walk out without a deal, issued at that point, was part of the same idea that a no deal would be at least as dangerous for the EU as for the UK and therefore lead to concessions on the EU side.[17]

In the last round of negotiations in Brussels which ended with the November agreement, May made two further concessions to the EU. She stated that she would be ready to extend the two-year transition if a trade deal had not been achieved and she accepted that the backstop, because it was an insurance policy, could not be time-limited. This time, the Brexiters and the DUP reacted angrily, claiming that it was unacceptable to be tied to the EU without a clear end limit.[18] May postponed the vote on the deal, originally planned on 11 December, to 15 January 2019 but could not prevent the biggest defeat for a government in modern times, with the deal rejected by 432 votes against 202, including 118 Conservative MPs and the 10 DUP MPs.

Two weeks later, the House of Commons voted the so-called Malthouse compromise, supported by both the ERG and some Remainers, which asked the government to renegotiate the backstop and was agreed by Theresa May, although the EU had made clear it would not reopen negotiations on the agreement. May attempted to go back to Brussels on the back of this vote in a typical move in terms of this two-level game. She presented the deal again to Parliament on 12 March where it was again rejected, albeit by a smaller majority, by a combination of hard Brexiters, Remainers and opposition Labour MPs. At this point, and faced with the possibility of a no-deal Brexit on 29 March, the European Council granted a six-month delay to the British government, in the hope that it would either pass the withdrawal deal or suggest another solution, including a second referendum.

Theresa May's domestic troubles did not end though. She attempted, for the first time since the referendum, to widen her negotiation to the Labour Party, which was invited to take part in talks at 10 Downing Street. Labour's line in the six-week discussions that followed was that the UK should remain in the customs union, which was obviously unacceptable for the Conservative Brexiters. The negotiation impasse therefore remained while Conservative discontent with the Prime Minister grew when the local elections in May yielded disastrous results for the party. The emergence of the new Brexit Party led by Nigel Farage and its success in the European election later that month, where it got over 30% of the votes, sealed May's fate. She announced her resignation as leader of the party and therefore as Prime Minister for 7 June 2019. The two-level game had proved too difficult for her.

5. Conclusion

The two-level model of negotiations provided a useful starting point to analyse the EU/UK negotiations between 2017 and 2019 but their dynamics did not follow the traditional pattern by which bargaining at each level is played out against one another with a convergence taking place between the different positions. Instead in this case, the two negotiations ran on parallel and antagonistic lines with May torn between different discourses in Brussels and in London. The analysis of her rhetoric, in a constructivist perspective, proved useful in understanding her failure to reach a deal in Brussels which would be acceptable in London. Vivien Schmidt's distinction between coordinative and communicative discourses on the one hand and the Tsebelis' nested games on the other helped us analyse the gap between what the Prime Minister was presenting at home and what she could achieve with the EU-27. Theresa May successfully muddled through in the first phase of the negotiations but the gap between what she said in London and ultimately did in Brussels could not be sustained.

Other factors also contributed to making the traditional framework of the two-level negotiation unworkable. First, the domestic constituency was much more fragmented and divided than in the Putnam model, making it impossible for the government to defend a clear line in Brussels or to use it as a springboard in the discussion. As a result, the win-set, in other words the areas of compromise between the two starting positions, was impossibly small. May's red lines, based on a specific interpretation of the referendum result and the reliance on hard Brexiters, made it impossible to find an accommodation with the principles defended by the EU-27. Second, the bargaining power of the British government was much smaller than anticipated. This in turn was due to its future position outside the EU, which reduced its leverage, especially in comparison with countries like Ireland, which could rely on the EU to support it precisely because it was a member-state. The 'red line' attitude which had worked well under previous governments to extract opt-outs on the single currency or the Schengen agreement, when it was a recalcitrant member of the EU, were no longer tenable once the UK had become a prospective third country.

More generally, the government's attitude showed a fundamental misunderstanding of the functioning of the EU and illustrated its weak socialisation into European institutions in spite of over forty years of membership. This is hardly surprising in the context of embedded euroscepticism in the UK historically, and the strength of British – or rather English – nationalism, particularly conspicuous in the Leave campaign in 2016 and which May used again in her different speeches. The constant use of the rhetoric of 'take back control' and 'Global Britain' led the government to downplay the political and economic importance of its relations with the continent when addressing its domestic audience and ultimately overstate its bargaining power in Brussels.

Notes

1. For their comments on earlier drafts, I would like to thank Filipa Figueira, Emmanuelle Avril, Vivien A. Schmidt, Nicholas Startin and the other authors of this special issue.
2. "European leaders can 'go whistle' over EU divorce bill, says Boris Johnson." *The Guardian*, 11 July 2017.
3. "Labour should commit to staying in the single market and customs union", *The Observer*, 23 September 2017.
4. "May's weakness exposed as DUP derails Brexit process", *The Guardian*, 4 December 2017.
5. "Free movement could go on during post-Brexit transition, says May", *The Guardian*, 4 April 2017; "Cabinet accepts Brexit transition will mean years of free movement", *The Guardian*, 20 July 2017.
6. "UK government concedes transitional role for ECJ after Brexit", *Financial Times*, 11 July 2017.
7. "'A fantasy': EU leaders dismiss UK's post-Brexit customs plan", *The Guardian*, 15 August 2017.
8. "Brexit divorce bill: UK could pay £50bn after bowing to EU pressure", *The Guardian*, 29 November 2017; "May forges surprise consensus as Eurosceptics fall into line", *Financial Times*, 30 November 2017.
9. "Theresa May under fire over Brexit transition deal", *The Guardian*, 19 March 2018.
10. Quoted in "EU-UK divide poses serious threat to Brexit talks, says Barnier", *The Guardian*, 29 June 2018.
11. "Barnier criticises May's UK-wide Brexit backstop plan", *The Guardian*, 8 June 2018.
12. Quoted in "Brexit plan to keep Northern Ireland in customs union triggers row", *The Guardian*, 9 February 2018.
13. John Swinney and Michael Russell, 'Westminster is using Brexit to put devolution at risk. Scotland will not stand for it', *The Guardian*, 21 February 2018; 'Sturgeon accuses UK ministers of threat to veto Scottish powers', *The Guardian*, 22 February 2018.
14. 'Scots and Welsh set up Brexit legislative stand-off with Westminster', *Financial Times*, 28 February 2018.
15. 'Constitutional Crisis looms as MSPs prepare to reject UK's Brexit Bill', *The Scotsman*, 15 May 2018. 'Scotland withholds consent for Brexit bill', *Financial Times*, 16 May 2018.
16. "'Humiliation' and 'disaster': how the UK press covered May's Salzburg ordeal", *The Guardian*, 21 September 2018.
17. "EU's brexit hard line angers Theresa May", *Politico*, 20 September 2018, https://www.politico.eu/article/theresa-may-reacts-angrily-to-uk-brexit-plan-rejection-eu-summit-salzburg/.
18. "DUP accuses May of breaking Brexit pledge over 'Irish Sea border'", *The Guardian*, 9 November 2018.

Disclosure statement

No potential conflict of interest was reported by the author.

References

Crespy, A., and V. Schmidt. 2014. "The Clash of Titans: France, Germany and the Discursive Double Game of EMU Reform." *Journal of European Public Policy* 21 (8): 1–17.

Dunlop, C. A., S. James, and C. M. Radaelli. 2019. "Can't Get No Learning: The Brexit Fiasco through the Lens of Policy Learning." *Journal of European Public Policy*. doi:10.1080/13501763.2019.1667415.

European Council. 2017. "European Council (Art. 50) Guidelines for Brexit Negotiations." April 29 https://www.consilium.europa.eu/en/press/press-releases/2017/04/29/euco-brexit-guidelines/

George, S. 1998. *An Awkward Partner: Britain in the European Community*. Oxford: Oxford University Press.

Glynn, J., and A. Menon. 2018. "Brexit." In *The British General Election of 2017*, edited by P. Cowley and D. Kavanagh, 21–40. Basingstoke: Palgrave Macmillan.

Grant, C. 2018. "Europe's Response to May's Plan Could Cost Her More Ministers." *The Guardian*, July 10.

Hassan, G. 2018. "Still Different, Only Slightly Less So: Scotland." In *The British General Election of 2017*, edited by P. Cowley and D. Kavanagh, 125–148. Basingstoke: Palgrave Macmillan.

HM Government. 2018. "The Future Relationship between the United Kingdom and the European Union." Cm 9593, July. https://www.gov.uk/government/publications/the-future-relationship-between-the-united-kingdom-and-the-european-union

Liesbet, H., and G. Marks. 2005. "Calculation, Community and Cues: Public Opinion on European Integration." *European Union Politics* 6 (4): 419–443. doi:10.1177/1465116505057816.

Martill, B., and U. Staiger. 2018. "Cultures of Negotiation: Explaining Britain's Hard Bargaining in the Brexit Negotiations." Dahrendorf Forum Working Paper No. 4, September 14.

May, T. 2016a. "Speech to the Conservative Party Conference." October 5. https://www.independent.co.uk/news/uk/politics/theresa-may-speech-tory-conference-2016-in-full-transcript-a7346171.html

May, T. 2016b. "Press Statement after the European Union Council." October 21. https://www.gov.uk/government/speeches/european-council-october-2016-prime-ministers-press-statement

May, T. 2016c. "Speech to the Lord Mayor's Banquet." November 14. https://www.gov.uk/government/speeches/pm-speech-to-the-lord-mayors-banquet-14-november-2016

May, T. 2017a. "The Government's Negotiating Objectives for Exiting the EU." Speech at Lancaster House, January 17. https://www.gov.uk/government/speeches/the-governments-negotiating-objectives-for-exiting-the-eu-pm-speech

May, T. 2017b. "A New Era of Cooperation and Partnership between the UK and the EU." Speech in Florence, September 22. https://www.gov.uk/government/speeches/pms-florence-speech-a-new-era-of-cooperation-and-partnership-between-the-uk-and-the-eu

May, T. 2018a. "Mansion House Speech on Our Future Economic Partnership with the EU." March 2. https://www.gov.uk/government/speeches/pm-speech-on-our-future-economic-partnership-with-the-european-union

May, T. 2018b. "Speech in Belfast." July 20. https://www.gov.uk/government/speeches/pm-belfast-speech-20-july-2018

McHugh, M. 2018. "Brexit: Northern Ireland Support to 'Remain' in EU Soars to 69%." *The Belfast Telegraph*, May 21.

Putnam, R. D. 1988. "Diplomacy and Domestic Politics: The Logic of Two-Level Game." *International Organization* 42 (3): 427–460. doi:10.1017/S0020818300027697.

Schimmelfennig, F. 2018. "Brexit: Differentiated Disintegration in the European Union." *Journal of European Public Policy* 25 (8): 1154–1173. doi:10.1080/13501763.2018.1467954.

Schmidt, V. A. 2008. "Discursive Institutionalism: The Explanatory Power of Ideas and Discourse." *Annual Review of Political Science* 11 (1): 303–326. doi:10.1146/annurev.polisci.11.060606.135342.

Schmidt, V. A. 2013. "Speaking to the Markets or to the People? A Discursive Institutionalist Analysis of the EU's Sovereign Debt Crisis." *British Journal of Politics and International Relations* 16 (1): 188–209. doi:10.1111/1467-856X.12023.

Scottish Government. 2016. "Scotland's Place in Europe." December 20. https://www.gov.scot/publications/scotlands-place-europe/

Taylor, P. 2018. "Brexit: A Managed Surrender." *Politico*, March 23.

From UKIP to the Brexit party: the politicization of European integration and disruptive impact on national and European arenas

Karine Tournier-Sol

ABSTRACT
The British referendum on EU membership was both the result and the cause of major ruptures and reconfigurations of the British political order. It also marked the climax of the politicization of European integration, as highlighted by the post-functionalist theory. The UK Independence party (UKIP) is pivotal in this process: it is both a product of this politicization and one of its major agents. As such, from a European viewpoint, UKIP stands as a case in point, an illustration of the potentially disruptive impact of such parties on national and European arenas. Building on Putnam's two level-game, on Tsebelis' nested games and on Reif and Schmitt's first and second order, this article aims to show that UKIP stands as the very embodiment of the interaction between these two arenas – between first- and second-order games. It perfectly illustrates the fact that the referendum reconfigured the national game that created it. This paper will therefore explore those two aspects: how UKIP impacted the first-order game, and conversely how the referendum impacted UKIP. Finally, the paper will analyze the disruptive impact of UKIP's successor, the Brexit party, on the British and European arenas.

Introduction

The referendum on the UK's membership of the European Union (EU) which took place on 23 June 2016 was a landmark political event. At the core of this special issue is the idea that, with hindsight, it proved to be a critical juncture – both the result *and* the cause of major ruptures and reconfigurations of the British political order (see Alexandre-Collier, Schnapper and Usherwood in this issue).

The referendum also marked the climax of the politicization of European integration, as highlighted by the post-functionalist theory according to which 'permissive consensus' has been replaced by 'constraining dissensus' (Hooghe and Marks 2009; Schimmelfennig 2014), with the Maastricht treaty as a major turning point in this process (Usherwood and Startin 2013; Vasilopoulou 2013). Since 1991, the European issue has entered the public sphere, beyond the political and economic elites, and public opinion has proved willing and sometimes able to restrain European integration, which has become politicized in national arenas: 'Engaging mass publics and extending into the domain of domestic politics, European integration has become salient and contested in public opinion and party competition' (Schimmelfennig 2014, 321).

The UK Independence party (UKIP) is particularly pivotal in this respect: it is both a product of this politicization – out of which it was born when it was set up in opposition to the Maastricht treaty in 1991 as the Anti-Federalist League, and then as a fully fledged political party in 1993 – and one of its major agents, as epitomized by the party's success, leading up to the Brexit vote.

As such, from a European viewpoint, there are certainly lessons to draw for Europe as UKIP stands as a case in point, an illustration of the potential impact of such parties on domestic and European arenas through the politicization of European integration. These two political arenas have become increasingly interwoven in recent years. This article builds on Reif and Schmitt's work on first and second order – which describes European affairs as typically second-order, with political actors making decisions on the basis of domestic considerations (Reif and Schmitt 1980) – combined with Putnam's two-level game theory and Tsebelis' 'nested games' (Putnam 1988; Tsebelis 1990), in order to underline and explore the overlapping and interconnections between the national game and the European game. The aim is to show that UKIP stands as the very embodiment of the interaction between the domestic political arena and the European one – between first- and second-order games – resulting from the politicization of European integration. It perfectly illustrates the two-way process addressed by this special issue, the fact that 'the referendum in effect reconfigures the national game that created it' (see Alexandre-Collier, Schnapper and Usherwood in this issue).

This paper will therefore explore those two aspects: how UKIP impacted the first-order game, and conversely how the referendum impacted UKIP. The first section will study how UKIP, by moving from the margins to the mainstream, acted as a game changer and disrupted the national game. It will demonstrate that the party was a major agent of the rupture provoked by the referendum it contributed to bringing about. The second section will analyze how, conversely, the party was also a major casualty of this disruption: UKIP came out as the main victim of the reconfiguration of the national game it helped to trigger, being sent back to the margins of British politics, and undergoing an internal split – another rupture. Finally, the third section will focus on UKIP's successor, the Brexit party, and on its impact on the British and European arenas: Nigel Farage's new party played an instrumental role in shaping British politics, with an influence on the Conservative party, proving another agent of the politicization of European integration and of the interconnection between the two arenas.

How UKIP disrupted the first-order game

This first section will therefore show how UKIP moved from the margins to the mainstream, from second-order to first-order, which allowed the party to have an impact on the national game of British politics.

UKIP was born out of Euroscepticism when it was founded back in 1993. It was created as a single-issue party (Usherwood 2008) advocating the withdrawal of the UK from the EU. It therefore stands in the Eurosceptic tradition as a 'hard Eurosceptic' party according to the typology of Taggart and Szczerbiak, *ie* opposed to the very principle of European integration (Taggart and Szczerbiak 2004, 3). UKIP's discourse is articulated around the defence of British national sovereignty which has been 'destroyed' by the Maastricht treaty (Farage 2011, 70). While this limited positioning quickly allowed it to gain representation in the European Parliament following the introduction of proportional representation in 1999, it also restricted the impact of the party on the national game, as Europe is typically a second-order issue (Reif and Schmitt 1980). For a long time, UKIP was therefore limited to playing a role only in the European elections once every five years.

Yet, several factors combined to push the party to the first-order game of national politics. First, UKIP undertook a strategic populist shift under the leadership of Nigel Farage: it rebranded its original Euroscepticism by incorporating it into a wider populist narrative, an anti-establishment discourse, while at the same time making immigration the party's number one priority (Tournier-Sol 2015a). UKIP successfully connected its core policy on Europe, which was a low salience issue for voters, to immigration, which on the contrary was a high salience issue. This decisive strategic shift was made possible following the expansion of the EU's free movement zone to Eastern European countries (the A8 countries[1]) in 2004 in the UK.

This opportunity for UKIP was created by the interplay between the European level and the domestic level (Putnam 1988). As argued by Hooghe and Marks, mainstream parties were reluctant to politicize European integration, as the issue cut across traditional left-right cleavages and was therefore potentially divisive, both internally (as for the Conservative party in the 1990s) and electorally (Hooghe and Marks 2009). This strategic dilemma was compounded by the fact that mainstream parties had been at the very origin of the project and process of European integration. On the contrary, UKIP seized the opportunity and skillfully capitalized on this politicization, building upon it to devise its own 'winning formula' (Kitschelt 1995). UKIP was therefore a major agent of the politicization of European integration in the UK, as other comparable *tan* (traditionalism/authority/nationalism) parties elsewhere in Europe (Hooghe and Marks 2009).

Second, the party also benefited from the reconfiguration of the British political order. In terms of political environment, of opportunity structure, the party enjoyed a uniquely favourable political context, resulting from the shifting nature of British politics, of the national game (Evans and Menon 2017), with an ideological convergence of both major parties towards a centrist, socially liberal consensus – first with Tony Blair and New Labour, and then with David Cameron and the Conservative party. Both leaders took their parties to the centre of British politics. This process was reinforced by the coalition government between the Conservatives and the Liberal Democrats, and resulted in a reconfiguration of the national game. Indeed, this ideological convergence alienated part of the electorate and fueled the revolt of what UKIP would call 'the people's army' (Farage 2015, 14), while giving the party political space. This led to UKIP's unprecedented surge after 2010, starting in the opinion polls and then translating in the ballot box from 2012 to 2013 to reach its climax with the party's historic victory in the 2014 European elections. This course of events in turn allowed the party to have an actual effect on the national game.

UKIP therefore gradually moved from second-order to a position where it was able to have an impact on the first order, and to act as a game-changer, contributing to shaping events. The party's growing electoral success indeed partly accounts for David Cameron's referendum pledge in his 2013 Bloomberg speech, as UKIP was increasingly seen as a threat to the Conservative party's electoral prospects. The referendum was therefore a tactical move to 'shoot the UKIP fox' – making it obsolete by depriving it of its very rationale – though this commitment was also called for by an increasing part of the Conservative parliamentary party, whose Euroscepticism had hardened, with 26.5% identifying as hard Eurosceptics, i.e. advocating withdrawal or referendum (Heppell 2013, 347).

Moreover, as a major agent of the politicization of European integration in the UK, the party also had an impact on the terms of the political debate on Europe and immigration. As other opponents of European integration elsewhere in the EU, UKIP actually framed the debate on Europe. In response to the UKIP challenge, mainstream parties reacted by radicalizing their own discourse on immigration and Europe: there was a spill-over effect. UKIP therefore contributed to framing politics on these subjects. The party had a disruptive effect on the national game, and contributed to making the referendum on EU membership possible.

This contagion effect was mostly visible during the referendum campaign, which was marked by a form of mainstream populism. Indeed, UKIP had undoubtedly an impact on the referendum campaign, and not only via its organization, *Leave.EU*. The official pro-Leave group, *Vote Leave*, with Boris Johnson as a key figure, adopted part of the party's rhetoric and arguments in its own campaign, while claiming to be different from UKIP. *Vote Leave* ran a mainstream populist campaign, combining a strategy of inclusion and exclusion (Mudde 2004, 563): inclusion of UKIP's rhetoric and ideas, and exclusion of UKIP as a political actor, by constantly and deliberately distancing itself from the toxicity associated with Nigel Farage's party. This toxic dimension was demonstrated in a study carried out by Robert Ford prior to the referendum campaign (*The Guardian*, 4 October 2015), pointing to a repelling effect. It showed that voters tended to reject a policy if it was overtly associated with UKIP and its leader, even in policy areas such as immigration, where UKIP's stance was popular and which was the main driver of UKIP's success. This was of course highly problematic in the context of a referendum in which moderate and undecided voters had to be reached out to in order to get more than 50% of the vote. Well aware of this, the more mainstream Conservative Eurosceptics of *Vote Leave* kept dissociating themselves publicly from *Leave.EU*, UKIP and Nigel Farage, with the aim of decontaminating the pro-Leave debate and arguments.

In terms of impact on the referendum result itself, UKIP's role is less obvious, yet no less interesting. Arithmetically, the party probably accounts for a quarter of the Brexit vote, although the extreme volatility of the UKIP vote makes it difficult to get a precise idea (Mellon and Evans 2016). The party was therefore not the main provider of Brexit votes – which actually mostly came from the Conservative party. But it can be argued that the party's influence went beyond mere arithmetics by indirectly infusing the political debate through its politicization of European integration and by successfully fueling the disaffection of part of the electorate towards the traditional parties – 'the elite' in its populist discourse.

Looking into the nature of the vote, there are clear correlations between the Brexit vote and the UKIP vote: the electoral profile of the Brexit supporter shares striking similarities with that of the average UKIP voter – described as a white male, over the age of 55, with no educational qualification and with a working-class background (Ford and Goodwin 2014; Goodwin and Heath 2016). But over and above this, in-depth studies of the Brexit vote demonstrate that beyond demographics, identity and values played a major part in the result (Swales 2016). The vote was in fact more split along values lines than along party lines, or by age, class or sex. Those questions of values and identity are precisely those on which UKIP had been building its success in previous years – they formed the basis of its unprecedented rise, the very territory on which the party had been thriving following its populist shift. There was a powerful link between social values and votes in the referendum: 80% of the most socially conservative voters voted to leave, compared to fewer than 10% of the most socially liberal (Evans and Menon 2017). Similarly, the Libertarian-Authoritarian scale proved to be a strong indicator of the vote according to the Natcen report: people who identified as authoritarian were more likely to vote Leave (66%) than those who identified as libertarian (18%) (Swales 2016). This is congruent with previous studies on UKIP voters which show that most of them are socially conservative and authoritarian (Curtice 2015; Jeffery et al. 2014).

Identity was therefore a major factor in the Brexit vote. This corroborates the post-functionalist stress on identity/nationalist politics and cleavages in contemporary European debates: 'identity is critical in shaping contestation on Europe' (Hooghe and Marks 2009). Identity was also a decisive factor in the UKIP revolt which preceded the Brexit vote. Even though the Brexit vote is not reducible to UKIP, there are clear echoes between the two which seem to stem from similar values and concerns, and testify to a comparable kind of revolt against the political establishment – be it British or European.

UKIP was thus instrumental in securing the referendum, and also to a certain extent in winning it, albeit more indirectly: its impact went beyond its mere electoral weight; it had a disproportionate and indirect influence on its outcome, resulting from its ability to frame the political debate on Europe and to politicize the issue in the years preceding the referendum. UKIP both benefited from and actively fueled a political climate amenable to the Brexit vote. It acted as a major agent of politicization, a major agent of the rupture provoked by the referendum. Yet the disruptive effect of UKIP also affected the party itself, as the result of the referendum had a decisive impact on its own fate.

How the referendum impacted UKIP: back to the margins of British politics

When the official results confirming the victory of the Leave vote came in the early morning hours of 24 June 2016, the only clear winner was UKIP – although its members were as confounded as anyone else, with Nigel Farage himself conceding defeat after the closing of the polling stations the night before, before triumphantly proclaiming June 23 the UK's 'Independence Day' six hours later. Not only did the referendum result come to vindicate UKIP's very existence and purpose, its original fight, which had been long derided by the traditional political class, but UKIP was actually the only party with a clear, unambiguous pro-Brexit stance in this campaign, fighting unanimously to leave the EU. The party therefore emerged as the main winner of the rupture it had been calling and working for.

Yet, UKIP also soon turned out to be the major victim of the disruptions and reconfigurations which followed the referendum and which it had contributed to provoking. Paradoxically then, the party was therefore the agent of its own demise, although it will be argued that this was not completely inevitable. The referendum had multiple repercussions on UKIP – direct and indirect, immediate and delayed.

First, to some extent, the adverse effect of the Brexit vote on UKIP was predictable, as the party lost its very purpose and *raison d'être* with the Leave victory – 'shooting the fox' had been one of David Cameron's aims with his referendum pledge back in 2013. Yet the party's situation was made even more difficult by the resignation of Nigel Farage only ten days after the referendum, declaring 'mission accomplished'. Though this departure was also foreseeable, it came very early, thereby depriving UKIP of its charismatic and emblematic leader. Additionally, Farage's swift resignation seemed to substantiate the idea that UKIP was over, that it had no purpose and no future after the result, and that it was now an empty shell. Though this may not have been intentional from Nigel Farage, it certainly added to the impression that it signaled the end of UKIP.

The Brexit victory therefore had a major immediate and direct impact on UKIP, raising the question of the very relevance of the party post-referendum. Unfortunately, as UKIP went through an existential crisis, it reverted to its old habits of internal factions, leadership quarrels and endless scandals, further hampering its necessary mutation and undermining its very survival. Actually, this was not new for UKIP, as this self-destructive tendency had been part and parcel of the party's history since its foundation in 1993, pointing to its major weakness, namely its lack of professionalism and its amateur nature which had already been a limit to its evolution before (Tournier-Sol 2015b). Although UKIP had already evolved from its status as a single-issue party to a more conventional form of populist party in the years preceding the referendum, its difficulty to find a new purpose and identity was exacerbated by its inherent lack of ideological coherence (Usherwood 2019). While this feature had previously allowed the party to adapt to its environment thanks to its chameleonic nature (Taggart 2000) and to broaden its electoral appeal, it turned out to be a major hindrance on its way towards self-redefinition. The departure of Nigel Farage was another compounding factor in this process, as he had been the binding agent, the 'glue' holding the different factions together and giving the party cohesion in the eyes of the public and the media, though this did not go without some internal disagreements, for example, in the aftermath of the 2015 general election (Goodwin and Milazzo 2015). Yet, despite these inherent difficulties, it is important to underline that UKIP bears some responsibility for its own failure, which was not unavoidable, as the potential for a populist force does exist in the UK – as demonstrated by UKIP's unprecedented success in the years prior to the referendum.

Second, the seismic effect of the referendum results reconfigured the British political order and the national game, with UKIP a major casualty in the process. The Brexit vote opened a new cycle in British politics: the political environment which had been so beneficial for the insurgent party after 2010 was radically reordered, leaving no political space to UKIP. There was a repolarization of British politics after Brexit and along Brexit lines. In a clear attempt to woo UKIP voters, the Conservative party of Theresa May repositioned itself as a less socially liberal party, and, crucially, as the party of Brexit, with May's new mantra 'Brexit means Brexit'. In the new emerging political order, the Conservative party was then seen as the best placed to deliver Brexit, so that a large number of UKIP supporters started to defect to the Tories, which was made easier by their adoption of flagship UKIP policies (among which immigration control and support for grammar schools). Ironically, in a reverse process that mirrored UKIP's previous ability to attract voters from other parties (and particularly from the Conservative party), there was a haemorrhage of UKIP voters, which was not restricted to the Conservative party though it represented the largest part (47% by the start of the 2017 general election campaign, Mellon et al. 2018). The party also lost voters to non-voting (Tilley and Evans 2017).

This process of realignment was illustrated by the 2017 general election, which was marked by the reassertion of the two-party system and the collapse of UKIP, gathering only 1.8% of the vote cast – 10.8 down from its historic 12.6% score in the 2015 general election. It was also reflected by the sharp drop in UKIP membership figures: by December 2017 UKIP had lost half of its members down from its peak of 46,000 in May 2015 (House of Commons Library 2018).

One year after the Brexit vote, the disruptive effect of the referendum on UKIP was clear. The party lost its position in the first-order arena and was sent back to the margins of British politics where it came from. Once more, even though this was part of a larger reconfiguration of the national game going beyond UKIP itself, the party bears part of the responsibility: embroiled in its own internal crisis, it failed to capitalize on the difficulties of the Brexit negotiations and was hardly audible on the political stage. The fact that voting intentions for UKIP rose after the Chequers plan in July 2018 shows that the party was still seen by some voters as the recipient of their dissatisfaction with Brexit, and could have taken full advantage of that had it not been caught up in endless political drama (the Henry Bolton episode is particularly instructive in this respect) and had it been represented by a credible leadership figure.

Third, the party itself underwent a radical transformation, with decisive consequences on its electoral fate. After two and a half years of disarray, Gerard Batten took over as leader in 2018 and initiated a significant shift of the party to the far-right, choosing to focus on anti-Islam policies. Batten sparked controversy by hiring Tommy Robinson, aka Stephen Yaxley-Lennon, as a political advisor. Robinson is a former member of the British National Party (BNP) who in 2009 founded and led the English Defence League before resigning in 2013 to set up Pegida in 2015. This move testifies to a radicalization of UKIP, a major change in the nature of the party, both ideologically and strategically. It breaks with Nigel Farage's earlier attempt to detoxify the UKIP brand and present the party as a 'non-sectarian, non-racist party'. It de facto reduces the electoral appeal of such a political force, with an apparent strategic shift towards a form of street protest group and away from a regular political party aiming at winning elections and getting representation.

It therefore marks a profound change in the evolution of UKIP, with a high risk of marginalization in the British political system, the potential of such parties being very limited as exemplified by the BNP (Eatwell and Goodwin 2010). So far, UKIP had succeeded in absorbing the electorate of the far-right while maintaining a 'reputational shield' (Ivarsflaten 2006) due to its origin in the Eurosceptic tradition, which had allowed it to transcend traditional political cleavages and broaden its appeal. The new face of UKIP clearly jeopardizes this ability and the party's future.

Eventually, this radical redefinition of the party post-referendum brought about another rupture for UKIP: the party suffered an internal split, with Nigel Farage and several other UKIP senior figures and MEPs leaving in disagreement over its new direction in December 2018. Farage declared that he did not recognize the party which he had joined 25 years before anymore (*Telegraph*, 4 December 2018).

UKIP therefore failed to adapt and fill the political space available for a more conventional populist force on the British political stage. Though the reordering of the national game following the referendum undeniably made it difficult for the party to continue to exist, UKIP also bears part of the responsibility for its own failure. However, as the probability of the UK taking part in the 2019 European elections increased, the heart and soul of UKIP was (unsurprisingly) taken up by Nigel Farage with his new 'Brexit party', leading to yet more ruptures and reconfigurations of the British political order.

The Brexit party's impact on the political game

This third and final section will focus on UKIP's successor, the Brexit party, and its disruptive impact on the national and European arenas, from the 2019 European elections to the general election six months later.

Shortly after leaving UKIP, Nigel Farage created a new political force to achieve what his former party had proved unable to do: capitalize on Theresa May's failure to deliver Brexit. He skillfully took advantage of the British conundrum and of the Prime Minister's incapacity to gather support for her EU withdrawal agreement, which came under fire from her own hard-Brexiteers and was denounced by Nigel Farage as 'the great Brexit betrayal'. As the UK prepared for a European election which should never have taken place three years after the Brexit vote, Nigel Farage seized the opportunity to reframe the political debate on Brexit and occupy the political space with his new Brexit party – a kind of UKIP 2.0, with a clear continuity in terms of policy but a very different structure and party machine (*Guardian*, 12 April 2019). One of the advantages of starting afresh for Farage was to be free from the historical baggage and the toxicity associated with the UKIP brand – the limitation though being his own toxicity and divisive image in the public opinion. The recruitment of European parliamentary candidates from very diverse political, social and ethnic backgrounds and of well-known figures such as the former Conservative MP Ann Widdecombe, or Annunziata Rees-Mogg, came to offset Farage's own shortcomings, helping him decontaminate his own brand. It also substantiated his claim to transcend the traditional left and right cleavages, thereby widening his potential electoral appeal beyond former UKIP supporters. The Brexit party was meant to be an alliance ranging across the political spectrum, as shown for instance by the recruitment of Claire Fox, a former member of the Revolutionary Communist party, as MEP candidate for the North West. The idea was to go beyond party politics.

Farage thereby displayed an undeniable political instinct, tapping into the frustration of Brexit voters and their feeling of 'betrayal', and understanding the need for a clear stance, in contrast with that of the two major parties and their inner divisions on the subject. Nigel Farage took ownership of the issue (Budge and Farlie 1983; Petrocik 1996). Yet, the Brexit party is not just about Brexit: it is a populist movement, claiming to uphold democracy and aiming at challenging the establishment, with its slogan 'change politics for good'. Its overt purpose is to 'launch a revolution in British politics', to send a shockwave through the political system. Farage resorted to the same populist rhetoric as when he was UKIP leader, castigating 'career politicians' and 'Westminster traitors'.

The Brexit party was officially launched on 12 April 2019, only six weeks before the European elections. It led an extensive campaign, on social media and on the ground, with Nigel Farage relentlessly touring the Leave-voting constituencies to rally support. The party did not present a manifesto or any kind of precise policies. The message was supposed to be loud and clear, and conveyed by the very name of the party: countering the 'betrayal' of the establishment and delivering a 'clean break' Brexit – the phrase was preferred to a 'no deal' Brexit during the campaign, probably because it sounded more appealing and less alarming (Barnard and Menon 2019).

The new party quickly surged ahead in the opinion polls, showing that it had struck a chord with the pro-Brexit electorate. As anticipated, it stormed to victory on election day, securing 31.6% of the vote and returning 29 MEPs to the European parliament. The Brexit party thereby caused a further shock to the political order, with UKIP and the Conservative party as its main victims. It absorbed the UKIP vote, which was reduced to 3.3%, down from 27.5% in the 2014 European elections. The party was wiped out of the European parliament, returning no MEP. The Conservative party suffered a crushing defeat, coming fifth with only 8.8% of the vote and four MEPs, its worst result since 1832. Labour also performed badly, coming third after the Liberal Democrats which got 20.3% of the vote share. The election was marked by an increased polarization of public attitudes towards Brexit (Curtice 2019a). The pro-remain vote was also strong, albeit more fragmented between the Liberal Democrats, the Greens and Change UK (which were competing nationally), and the Scottish and Welsh nationalists, with a total of 40%.

The Brexit party therefore acted as a disruptive force in this election. Though European elections are second-order, the party's historical score sent a shock wave through the first-order and the national game of British politics, especially affecting the Conservative party's position. Indeed, the Brexit party mainly took votes from disaffected Conservative voters. According to a survey conducted by Paul Whiteley just before election day, 64% of the Brexit party vote came from Conservatives, that is three times as much of the vote as it took from Labour (22%) and six times as much as it took from the Liberal Democrats (11%) (Whiteley 2019). This explains why the Conservative party's score was reduced to simple digits. The Brexit party's win in the European election therefore gave it a disproportionate role (considering that it was a newcomer with no representation at the national or local level) and allowed Nigel Farage to shape politics once again, as he had done with UKIP in the years prior to the referendum. In the context of the election of Theresa May's successor at the head of the Conservative party, it clearly put pressure on the leadership contenders, with the future leader and Prime Minister tempted to push for a no deal Brexit to be able to meet the 31 October deadline and therefore defuse the Brexit party's threat.

And this is exactly what the new Conservative Prime Minister Boris Johnson did: in order to fight off the Brexit party's challenge and recapture its electorate, Johnson co-opted the party's ideas (Schain 2006), promising to deliver Brexit on 31 October 2019 'do or die' and pitching Parliament against the people, in a populist narrative framing the Conservative government as the voice of the people who had been betrayed by the political class, those "forces in this country that simply don't want Brexit delivered at all" (Johnson 2019). Boris Johnson did not refrain from the confrontation which ensued with Parliament and the Supreme Court and which actually strengthened his positioning against the Westminster and judicial elite. The purge of 21 Tory moderates who had supported a bill to prevent a no-deal Brexit marked a further step towards the radicalization of the Conservative party, its final transformation into a homogeneous hard-Brexit party, which de facto made the Brexit party redundant, obsolete, by taking up its very clothes.

Nigel Farage tried to resist, fighting for relevance in the new political order resulting from the realignment of the Conservative party he had contributed to accelerating. First by offering an electoral pact to Johnson, which the latter flatly rejected, and then by denouncing the new deal secured by the Prime Minister with the EU as 'Brino' (Brexit in name only). As the general election drew nearer, the Brexit party leader finally yielded to the pressure from the Conservative party and from within his own ranks, withdrawing his candidates in the 317 constituencies won by the Conservatives in the 2017 general election, so as to avoid splitting the Leave vote and risking a Labour victory – thereby threatening the very idea of Brexit. However, Boris Johnson's ruling out of any extension of the transition period beyond 31 December 2020 and his commitment that the future trade deal with the EU would not entail any political alignment may be seen as a final concession to reach out to Farage and his supporters in the run up to the election.

It testifies to the Brexit party's impact on the national and European arenas, as it actually brings back the possibility of a no-deal Brexit on 31 December 2020 at the end of the transition period, given the short time it leaves for negotiating a new trade deal with the EU. The resounding victory won by the Conservative party vindicated Boris Johnson's strategy and spelt the end of the Brexit party which only gathered 2% of the vote, while UKIP got 0.1% with its far-right shift. Yet, the very small vote share of the Brexit party in the 2019 general election is not representative of its actual impact on the political game. In the continuity of its predecessor, the Brexit party has been a major agent of the reordering of the British political order, sending a shock to the political system in the 2019 European election which reverberated through the political landscape in general and the Conservative party in particular, with consequences on the European game as well in the context of Brexit. Like UKIP, the party therefore illustrates the interaction between the domestic and European arenas resulting from the increasing politicization of European integration.

Conclusion

The British referendum on EU membership caused a seismic shock to the British political order, which was followed by several aftershocks, as demonstrated by the 2017 general election, the 2019 European elections and the 2019 general election. UKIP, and subsequently the Brexit party, proved instrumental in this process, demonstrating the ability of populist Eurosceptic parties to impact the national game through the politicization of European integration, even from an outsider position.

At the domestic level, Nigel Farage's successive parties acted as some sort of pressure groups on the British political system and on the Conservatives in particular. They contributed to the progressive radicalization of the Conservative party from the outside, with a direct effect on Britain's relationship with the EU. Although this redefinition of the party is also the result of an endogenous process, as it corresponds to one of the ideological tendencies within the Tory party's broad church

(Seyd and Whiteley 1996, 85), it was reinforced by UKIP and the Brexit party. This is not surprising though, as it corroborates the fact that there has always been some degree of porosity between the Conservative party and UKIP (before its far-right turn), which ideologically borrows from the Conservative political tradition (Tournier-Sol 2015a). UKIP's platform has been close to that of the right-wing of the Conservative party, leading UKIP to be seen as a mere Tory splinter group for a long time. The idea of a pact between the two parties had already been mooted under David Cameron's leadership (Fabricant 2012). Despite the apparent failure of his successive parties to gain substantial representation in Westminster, Nigel Farage has actually demonstrated the significant influence that outsider populist Eurosceptic parties can have on shaping politics. The Brexit party's crushing victory in the 2019 European elections accelerated the process of radicalization initiated by the Conservative party after the referendum and amplified by the election of Boris Johnson as party leader – a change of leadership which marked a change of dominant faction within the party (Lynch and Whitaker 2018), in line with Nigel Farage's positioning.

At the European level, UKIP and the Brexit party perfectly illustrate the growing interaction between the domestic and European arenas taking place across the EU. They therefore stand as examples of the potential disruptive effect of such parties on the increasingly interwoven national and European games – examples from which there are certainly lessons to draw for Europe.

Such parties represent a challenge to the established political parties which have been steering European integration since its origin, and which are losing ground across the EU, as demonstrated by the 2019 European elections. The two major party groups (the centre-right European People's Party and the centre-left Socialists and Democrats) suffered a major blow, losing their majority for the first time since the first direct elections to the European parliament in 1979. They are proving unable to address the new identity cleavages which cut across the traditional left and right lines and on which Eurosceptic populist parties have been thriving. Yet, the populist surge which had been anticipated in the run-up to the European elections did not materialize, although populist parties from left and right made substantive gains in the European Parliament, securing 29% of the seats (up from 24% in 2014), as pro-European Liberal and green parties also made significant gains, providing a different alternative to major parties. The result is a more fragmented and polarized European parliament (Hobolt 2019), echoing the British case. Though populist parties may try to act as a disruptive force in the European parliament, they will remain divided between different groups, which means that their influence will be limited. The good news for the EU is that the increased politicization of European integration has produced the highest turnout in the history of direct elections to the European parliament, with an average of 50.6% in the 28 member-states. It means that EU voters are increasingly aware of the interlocking between the domestic and European arenas, and are showing a willingness to take ownership of the European issue and of their elected representation in Strasbourg. This European election therefore opens a new cycle in European politics, with potential new challenges to the political order.

Brexit itself has had an unexpected and positive effect on the EU, which seems to have been consolidated by the negotiations with the UK, as the 27 member-states stood together, united through the whole process (see Chopin and Lequesne in this issue). The spill-over effect of the Brexit vote which had been feared has not materialized either, the complicated and disruptive dimension of Brexit probably acting as a deterrent. Significantly, neither Matteo Salvini in Italy nor Marine Le Pen in France advocates their country's exit from the EU, which they plan to reform from within through their Identity and Democracy group in the European parliament.

Britain eventually left the EU on 31 January 2020, more than two and a half years after the referendum. Yet, the country's new relationship with the EU is still left to define, and the consequences of Brexit are yet to come. As for the Brexit party, it has lost its representation in the European Parliament, as well as its very *raison d'être*. Nigel Farage has already announced the creation of a new political force, the Reform party, with a platform focused on constitutional issues such as the electoral system, the House of Lords or direct democracy. Brexit has not put an end to the disaffection of part of the British electorate towards its political class. Nigel Farage might succeed in mobilizing support for his new party as Brexit unfolds and (inevitable) disappointments kick in. But that's another story.

Note

1. The Czech Republic, Estonia, Hungary, Latvia, Lithuania, Poland, Slovakia and Slovenia.

Disclosure statement

No potential conflict of interest was reported by the author.

References

Barnard, C., and A. Menon. 2019. "Clean Brexit' Sounds so Simple, Doesn't It? Trouble Is, It Doesn't Exist." *The Guardian*, May 21. https://www.theguardian.com/commentisfree/2019/may/21/clean-brexit-party-no-deal

Brexit party. 2019. "Brexit Party's Constitution." *Electoral Commission*, March 12. https://www.electoralcommission.org.uk/__data/assets/pdf_file/0010/254791/FOI-030-19-Response.pdf

Budge, I., and D. Farlie. 1983. "Party Competition - Selective Emphasis or Direct Confrontation? An Alternative View with Data." In *Western European Party Systems. Continuity & Change*, edited by H. Daalder and P. Mair, 267–305. Beverly Hills: Sage.

Curtice, J. 2015. "A Revolt on the Right? The Social and Political Attitudes of UKIP Supporters." *British Social Attitudes*, 32, Natcen Social Research.

Curtice, J. 2019. "Fracture and Polarisation? Lessons from the Euro-election." *The UK in a Changing Europe*, June 3. https://ukandeu.ac.uk/fracture-and-polarisation-lessons-from-the-euro-election/

Eatwell, R., and M. Goodwin, eds. 2010. *The New Extremism in 21st Century Britain*. Oxon: Routledge.

Evans, G., and A. Menon. 2017. *Brexit and British Politics*. Cambridge: Polity Press.

Fabricant, M. 2012. "The Pact? The Conservative Party, UKIP and the EU." *A Discussion Paper*, November. http://thepactreport.wordpress.com/

Farage, N. 2011. *Flying Free*. London: Biteback Publishing.

Farage, N. 2015. *The Purple Revolution: The Year that Changed Everything*. London: Biteback Publishing.

Ford, R. 2015. "David Cameron's Third Act: The EU Referendum." *The Guardian*, October 4.

Ford, R., and M. Goodwin. 2014. *Revolt on the Right: Explaining Support for the Radical Right in Britain*. Abingdon: Routledge.

Goodwin, M., and C. Milazzo. 2015. *UKIP: Inside the Campaign to Redraw the Map of British Politics*. Oxford: Oxford University Press.

Goodwin, M., and O. Heath. 2016. "The 2016 Referendum, Brexit and the Left Behind: An Aggregate-level Analysis of the Result." *The Political Quarterly* 87 (3): 323–332. doi:10.1111/1467-923X.12285.

Heppell, T. 2013. "Cameron and Liberal Conservatism: Attitudes within the Parliamentary Conservative Party and Conservative Ministers." *The British Journal of Politics and International Relations* 15 (3): 340–361. doi:10.1111/j.1467-856X.2012.00546.x.

Hobolt, S. B. 2019. "EU Elections Analysis: Centrists in Retreat but No Far-right Populist Surge." *Sky News*, May 27.

Hooghe, L., and G. Marks. 2009. "A Postfunctionalist Theory of European Integration: From Permissive Consensus to Constraining Dissensus." *British Journal of Political Science* 39 (1): 1–23. doi:10.1017/S0007123408000409.

House of Commons Library. 2018. "Membership of UK Political Parties." *N° SN05125*, September 3. https://researchbriefings.parliament.uk/ResearchBriefing/Summary/SN05125#fullreport

Ivarsflaten, E. 2006. "Reputational Shields: Why Most Anti-Immigrant Parties Failed in Western Europe, 1980–2005." *Annual Meeting of the American Political Science Association, Philadelphia*, August 31. http://www.nuffield.ox.ac.uk/politics/papers/2006/ivarsflatenapsa2006.pdf

Jeffery, C., R. W. Jones, A. Henderson, R. Scully, and G. Lodge. 2014. "Taking England Seriously: The New English Politics". *The Future of England Survey*, Centre on Constitutional Change. http://www.centreonconstitutionalchange.ac.uk/sites/default/files/news/Taking EnglandSeriously_The New English Politics.pdf

Johnson, B. 2019. "Speech at the Conservative Party Conference." October 2 https://vote.conservatives.com/news/prime-minister-party-conference

Kitschelt, H. 1995. *The Radical Right in Western Europe: A Comparative Analysis*. Ann Arbor: University of Michigan Press.

Lynch, P., and R. Whitaker. 2018. "All Brexiteers Now? Brexit, the Conservatives and Party Change." *British Politics* 13: 31–47. doi:10.1057/s41293-017-0064-6.

Mellon, J., and G. Evans. 2016. "Are Leave Voters Mainly UKIP?" *British Election Study*, July 8.

Mellon, J., G. Evans, E. Fieldhouse, J. Green, and C. Prosser. 2018. "Brexit or Corbyn? Campaign and Inter-Election Vote Switching in the 2017 UK General Election." *Parliamentary Affairs* 71 (4): 719–737. doi:10.1093/pa/gsy001.
Mudde, C. 2004. "The Populist Zeitgeist." *Government and Opposition* 39 (4): 541–563. doi:10.1111/j.1477-7053.2004.00135.x.
Petrocik, J. R. 1996. "Issue Ownership in Presidential Elections, with a 1980 Case Study." *American Journal of Political Science* 40 (3): 825–850. doi:10.2307/2111797.
Putnam, R. D. 1988. "Diplomacy and Domestic Politics: The Logic of Two-Level Games." *International Organization* 42 (3): 427–460. doi:10.1017/S0020818300027697.
Reif, K., and H. Schmitt. 1980. "Nine Second-Order National Elections: A Conceptual Framework for the Analysis of European Election Results." *European Journal of Political Research* 8 (1): 3–44. doi:10.1111/j.1475-6765.1980.tb00737.x.
Schain, M. 2006. "The Extreme-Right and Immigration Policy-Making: Measuring Direct and Indirect Effects." *West European Politics* 29 (2): 270–289. doi:10.1080/01402380500512619.
Schimmelfennig, F. 2014. "European Integration in the Euro Crisis: The Limits of Postfunctionalism." *Journal of European Integration* 36 (3): 321–337. doi:10.1080/07036337.2014.886399.
Seyd, P., and P. Whiteley. 1996. "Conservative Grassroots: An Overview." In *Contemporary British Conservatism*, edited by S. Ludlam and M. J. Smith, 63–85. Basingstoke: Macmillan.
Swales, K. 2016. "Understanding the Leave Vote." *Natcen Social Research*.
Taggart, P. 2000. "Populism." Buckingham: Open University Press. Accessed 1 June 2019. https://whatukthinks.org/eu/wp-content/uploads/2016/12/NatCen_Brexplanations-report-FINAL-WEB2.pdf
Taggart, P., and A. Szczerbiak. 2004. "Contemporary Euroscepticism in the Party Systems of the EU Candidates States of Central and Eastern Europe." *European Journal of Political Research* 43 (1): 1–27. doi:10.1111/j.1475-6765.2004.00143.x.
Tilley, J., and G. Evans. 2017. "The New Politics of Class after the 2017 General Election." *The Political Quarterly* 88 (4): 710–715. doi:10.1111/1467-923X.12434.
Tournier-Sol, K. 2015a. "Reworking the Eurosceptic and Conservative Traditions into a Populist Narrative: UKIP's Winning Formula?" *Journal of Common Market Studies* 53 (1): 140–156. doi:10.1111/jcms.12208.
Tournier-Sol, K. 2015b. "The UKIP Challenge." In *The UK Challenge to Europeanization: The Persistence of British Euroscepticism*, edited by K. Tournier-Sol and C. Gifford, 134–147. Basingstoke: Palgrave Macmillan.
Tsebelis, G. 1990. *Nested Games: Rational Choice in Comparative Politics*. Berkeley: University of California Press.
Usherwood, S. 2008. "The Dilemmas of a Single-issue Party: The UK Independence Party." *Representation* 44 (3): 255–264. doi:10.1080/00344890802237023.
Usherwood, S. 2019. "Shooting the Fox? UKIP's Populism in the post-Brexit Era." *West-European Politics* 42 (6): 1209–1229. doi:10.1080/01402382.2019.1596692.
Usherwood, S., and N. Startin. 2013. "Euroscepticism as a Persistent Phenomenon." *Journal of Common Market Studies* 51 (1): 1–16. doi:10.1111/j.1468-5965.2012.02297.x.
Vasilopoulou, S. 2013. "Continuity and Change in the Study of Euroscepticism: Plus Ça Change?" *Journal of Common Market Studies* 51 (1): 153–168. doi:10.1111/j.1468-5965.2012.02306.x.
Whiteley, P. 2019. "Nigel Farage Triumphs: Survey Reveals What Drove Voters to the Brexit Party in the European Elections." *The Conversation*, May 27. https://theconversation.com/nigel-farage-triumphs-survey-reveals-what-drove-voters-to-the-brexit-party-in-the-european-elections-117865

The post-referendum reconfigurations of conservative cleavages around black and Asian minority ethnic MPs

Agnès Alexandre-Collier

ABSTRACT

At the level of the Conservative parliamentary party, one of the main effects of Brexit has been a realignment of party cleavages. While the old cleavage between Europhiles and Eurosceptics is no longer relevant and a new cleavage has appeared between soft and hard Brexiteers, this political upheaval has thus restructured Conservative ideological pluralism in the parliamentary party. Following a study of the 2015 intake of MPs who were supposedly 'less stale, male and pale' and their attitudes to the 2016 British referendum on the EU, this article will take a specific interest in all Conservative Black and Asian Minority Ethnic (BAME) MPs who turned out to be more active on the 'leave' side of the referendum campaign. They arguably embody a new feature of Conservative pluralism by operating a synthesis between inclusive modernisation and hard Brexit. Although the party should capitalise on this group of MPs to rid itself of its persistent image of a 'nasty' party pervaded with anti-immigration sentiment and hard Eurosceptic populism – an expression used by Theresa May in 2002 -, the strategy of 'detoxifying' the Brexit brand did not seem to have ever been part of her priorities as Prime Minister.

Introduction

Following a study of the 2015 intake of MPs who were supposedly 'less stale, male and pale' and their attitudes to the British referendum on the EU (Alexandre-Collier 2018b), this article will take a specific interest in Conservative Black and Asian Minority Ethnic (BAME) MPs elected at the general elections of 2015 and 2017 and who turned out to be overwhelmingly more active on the 'leave' side of the referendum campaign (Wallace 2016). As was noted in the previous survey, 75% (6 out of 8) of newly elected BAME MPs in the Conservative Party supported the leave campaign in the June 2016 referendum (Alexandre-Collier 2018b). Altogether, 11 out of all the 19 BAME MPS now sitting on the Conservative benches declared that they had voted for leave. This represents approximately 58% of the total of BAME Conservative MPs currently elected, a figure which is at odds with three other data: only 40% of Conservative MPs were said to have voted for leave (Bale, Cowley, and Menon 2016); only a quarter of BAME voters presumably did so too (Begum 2018); no BAME Labour MP supported leave (out of a total of only 11 leavers in the party). It is therefore worth understanding the motivations of this specific, albeit small, group of MPs with respect to both EU membership and immigration and extensively their positioning on the ideological map of the party. This article is thus intended to reach two objectives.

On the one hand, it will seek to clarify the apparent paradox, which can be first observed between the social background of a category which, at some stage, had been confronted with immigration, especially from the Commonwealth immigration, either directly or through their ascendants, and a Brexit narrative which has been essentially centered on the need to restrict immigration as a side-effect of freedom of movement. In addition, the xenophobic and anti-immigration tone of the referendum campaign would have been expected to produce an antagonising effect on the BAME community (Begum 2018). As contributions to this volume are expected to demonstrate, political actors are involved in nested games, which are located in multiple arenas and deliver variable payoffs. This article will show that this is particularly the case of BAME Conservative MPs who find themselves engaged in different arenas, as standard-bearers of their community, representatives of their party and supporters of the leave or remain camps in the referendum campaign. This apparent paradox stems from what can be interpreted as conflicting interests. But what seems to appear as a paradox or an irrational act to the observer is also based on disagreements between the observer and the actor. As Tsebelis noted, 'sometimes the observer thinks a priori that exactly the opposite course of action was appropriate, so the actor appears to make a choice totally against his [sic] own interests' (Tsebelis 1990, 8), an observation which applies to the BAME Conservative MPs' decision to side with the pro-Brexit anti-immigration leave campaign. This may appear to run counter to their own interests as expected representatives of their immigrant communities, even though this representative role is disavowed by MPs themselves. It should indeed be noted that the disagreement between the observer and the actor, pointed out by Tsebelis, may also originate from the observer's prejudice and preconceived perception that BAME MPs should represent their ethnic communities.

On the other hand, this study is important because its implications reach out far beyond the simple category of BAME MPs. By exploring and analysing the complex combination between these MPs' motivations and their social backgrounds, this article is thus expected to make a significant contribution to the academic debate about the social and ideological composition of the Parliamentary Conservative Party (PCP) and its prospective evolution in the post-Brexit context. The variety of views can be observed in the multitude of factions, not only in the party, but in the whole House, which gives the impression of a patchwork of attitudes to the question of Britain's role in the world. Therefore, beyond the case of the Conservative Party, this article will also seek to disentangle the intricacies of the various geopolitical scenarios of Britain's future place in the world after Brexit, as a country being still torn between Churchill's three historical circles, i.e. Europe, the Commonwealth countries and the English speaking countries now sometimes identified as the Anglosphere (see Wellings's article in this special issue).

Our study will be methodologically based on a combination of data about the socio-demographic and ideological composition of the parliamentary Conservative Party, data about the group of BAME Conservative MPs and their constituencies, as well as quotations from parliamentary speeches and press articles. Given the small number of MPs concerned, this study is not expected to be quantitative but a consideration of the numbers is essential to understand the importance of the correlation between them and their attitudes to Brexit.

Conservative party cleavages since David Cameron's leadership

Since the 1980s, the ideological pluralism of the Conservative Party has radically evolved. Attempts at mapping Conservative attitudes to various issues were more frequent in the 1980s and 1990s when Thatcherism openly divided the party along the following lines: the role of the State (wets/dries) and the European issue (Eurosceptics/Europhiles) (Alexandre-Collier 2015). But in the 1990s and 2000s moral policy appeared as a new variable while European integration, at the time of the ratification of the Maastricht Treaty, became the sharpest bone of contention (Baker, Gamble, and Ludlam 1993, 1994). After 2010, the agenda of modernisation promoted by Conservative Prime Minister David Cameron included concern for new issues like gay marriage and the protection of the environment which had long been at odds with Conservative creed. Cameron's agenda, which focused on homosexual rights, austerity measures and self-proclaimed 'pragmatism' when it came to EU membership, offered a novel combination of moral and economic liberalism, associated with Euroscepticism. It thus seemed to engrave new and lasting dividing lines in the party along the three ideological variables identified by Garry in the mid-1990s: moral policy; economic policy and European policy (Garry 1995). More recently Heppell et al. were able to map Conservative MPs' attitudes as being predominantly socially liberal (148 out of 330 MPs having voted for Same-Sex marriage) and Eurosceptic even though only 144 of them declared that they had voted for 'leave' in June 2016 (Heppell, Crines, and Jeffery 2017).

Yet earlier research had demonstrated that Cameron's modernisation agenda did not fit well into existing cleavages. Heppell's survey conducted on the 2010 intake of Conservative MPs actually revealed that Cameron's agenda was not fully shared (with Cameron being in the minority on moral matters as only 29% of the PCP identified as social liberals) although the newly elected MPs more clearly reflected their leader's positions (Heppell 2013). The modernisation agenda was also justified by the need to make the party more representative. Since 2010, more and more ethnic minorities and women have been selected in the Conservative Party as the result of reforms to diversify MPs' socio-demographic profiles and enhance their representativeness. Organisational reforms in general and candidate selection in particular were presented as the first part of Cameron's modernisation agenda, what Dommett defines as modernisation at the meso-level of party procedures and structure (Dommett 2015).

The identification of BAME Conservative MPs as a distinctive group in the party has therefore to do with the recent changes in candidate selection. In general terms, the selection of more ethnic minority candidates responds to a dual need: on the supply side, growing diversification and multiculturalism of societies explain the demand for better representation while on the demand side, parties have called for more openness and inclusiveness as an effective response to party dealignment (Dalton and Wattenberg 2002). In the British Conservative Party, the A-list promoted by David Cameron immediately after his election as party leader in December 2005 was an approved list of 100 to 150 priority candidates which was meant to radically transform the face of the party from being primarily white and male to including more women and ethnic minorities (McIlveen 2009; Hill 2013). The party was expected to progressively become less 'pale, stale and male' at each future general election, which turned out to be effectively the case (Bright Future 2015; Criddle 2016). The party had long struggled with the reputation of relying on a narrow core of white middle-class male support reflected by the average profile of its MPs (Kulich, Ryan, and Haslam 2014; Lamprinakou et al. 2017) while there turned out to be an increasing pool of supporters and voters among ethnic minority groups (Heath et al. 2013). Theresa May's description of the Conservatives as a 'nasty party' in her speech to the party conference in 2002 identified this problem as being one the party's main electoral weaknesses during its period of opposition (May 2002). In addition, Lord Ashcroft blamed the poor representation of women and ethnic minorities as one of the main reasons for the party's 2005 electoral defeat (Ashcroft 2005). The image of a 'nasty party' was actually complex: it not only encompassed the idea of a shortage of minority MPs and a lack of diversity and representation but it also referred to ideological cleavages on moral issues like the decriminalisation of drugs or homosexuality which came to the fore in the early 2000s after revelations by former Minister Michael Portillo that he had had homosexual relations when he was younger. The tension between modernisers and traditionalists came to be identified as an enduring opposition between 'mods' and 'rockers' in addition to other existing cleavages (Alexandre-Collier 2010).

Therefore, the new leader's strategy to 'detoxify' the Tory brand (Hayton 2010; see also Dommett 2015) by recruiting more women and ethnic minorities (A-list) was not simply meant to diversify the profile of MPs but also to change the distribution of ideological forces within the party (Hayton 2017). In this context, the idea was not only to select more modernisers but MPs who could symbolise an image of modernity that the party was keen to display under Cameron's leadership. Thus, the recruitment of minority candidates was meant to respond to public demand for better representation and to project this image of modernity, with the A-list being defined as 'better reflecting the make-up of modern Britain' (Cameron 2019, 94). This claim of modernisation was further made by David Cameron in his autobiography when he wrote: 'Our party was more reflective of modern Britain, as well. In 2005 we had just two BME MPs; now we had seventeen. Then, they were just seventeen women MPs; now they were sixty-eight. The stories of our new MPs were the story of modern Britain. On our benches we now had people like Seema Kennedy, who was four when she and her family were forced to flee revolutionary Iran' (578). Yet this assumed image of modernity contradicts the reality of BAME MPs' ideological positioning. As already noted, this contradiction between appearance and reality is also reflected in the disagreement between the observer and the actor. According to Tsebelis (1990), this explains why BAME leavers, who are involved in nested games, do not choose the *apparently* optimal alternative i.e. a pro-immigration anti-Brexit agenda which would have seemed, to the (presumably non-BAME) observer, more consistent with the party's modernising and 'decontaminating' agenda (Hayton 2010). The reality is different. As will be seen later, BAME MPs are no modernisers. Moreover, some ethnic communities are even identified as more culturally conservative than others. Back in 1998, Saggar, for example, had demonstrated that the Conservative campaign to target voters of Indian origins was based on the fact that they represent the most economically successful but also culturally conservative ethnic group (Saggar 1998). Begum's research (2018) confirms this trend by noting that Indian-origin voters were the most likely of all BAME groups to vote leave.

The representation and ideological positioning of BAME MPs

The correlation between the selection of BAME candidates and the profile of their constituencies provides information about the actual representation of these MPs, once elected. The question of representation is usually analysed in two ways: either as substantive or descriptive representation. Since Hanna Pitkin's seminal work (1967) on representation, both notions have been essentially investigated by specialists in gender and politics (Celis 2008; Childs and Lovenduski 2013, among others). As Allen clearly explains, 'descriptive representation refers to the presence of certain types of people in given places or institutions' while 'substantive representation refers to the representation of the political interests, broadly defined, of different groups of society' (Allen 2018, 7). In other words, descriptive representation presupposes that BAME MPs can/should only represent ethnic minority voters while substantive representation is based on the sole representation of views, ideas and political interests. That being said, literature is ambivalent about whether the increasing descriptive representation matters for the substantive representation of minority ethnic interests, while showing that in the UK there are strong electoral incentives for substantive representation (Saalfeld and Bischof 2013).

The process of candidate selection is therefore essential to this aspect. The supply-demand framework provides interesting explanations about the two sides of the process by highlighting the motivations of the party selectors (demand) and the minorities selected (supply) (Norris and Lovenduski 1995). On the demand-side, descriptive representation was not a priority and the need to change the image of the party prevailed. Unlike the Labour Party, literature about the recruitment of BAME candidates in the Conservative Party shows that the procedure does not follow the expected pattern of ethnic minority MPs being selected in 'non-white' seats and elected by ethnic minority voters. More than half were said to have been selected in unwinnable seats (Sobolewska 2013). On the supply side, the motivations of ethnic minority candidates are diverse and fall into the three categories usually identified by specialists: shared experience, motivation to represent and electoral incentives (Sobolewska, McKee, and Campbell 2018), as will be analysed later.

But if BAME MPs are not representative of their ethnic communities, their EU views are more radical than the rest of MPs'. The EU referendum of June 2016 exposed a discrepancy between the result of the popular vote (48.1% for remain and 51.9% for leave) and parliamentary attitudes (40% for leave and 60% for remain) (Bale, Cowley, and Menon 2016; Heppell, Crines, and Jeffery 2017). Previous research indicates that the new generation of Conservative MPs elected in 2015 was however more favourable to 'leave' than their elders, most particularly Black and Asian Minority Ethnic Minority MPs, as 6 out of 8 BAME MPs elected in 2015 and 2017 supported leave. Although the relatively small sample size is admittedly problematic, from a methodological point of view (especially as there are fewer BAME MPs in the party, i.e. 6%, than there are ethnic minorities in the population, i.e. 13.6% according to the 2016 UK Census), this revealed an interesting trend about the ideological and social evolution of the party in the coming years. While the question of the motivations of this new generation of BAME MPs was raised, some of the answers resided in the fact that they had just been elected and were part of a new generation of more independent MPs who were no longer ashamed of expressing uninhibited Euroscepticism. Yet the case of BAME MPs was only partially explored (Alexandre-Collier 2018b).

If we now extend this research to the whole group of Conservative BAME MPs, the findings are equally significant. After the 2017 General Election, the PCP gathered 19 BAME MPs. Eight of them openly declared that they had voted for remain and 11 (58%) voted for leave. The list with precise data is provided in table 5. Despite the very small sample, this indicates a clear majority in favour of Brexit within this group of MPs – compared with the estimated 40% of Conservative MPs who supported Brexit – while previous research also indicated that MPs' Euroscepticism had radicalised and become uninhibited (Alexandre-Collier 2018b; Lynch and Whitaker 2017; Moore 2018).

More specifically, Heppell's survey of parliamentary attitudes in the Conservative Party carried out among the MPs elected in 2010 introduced a two-dimensional map, arguing that the moral and sexual divide (around homosexual rights and gay marriage) and the European divide had become the most significant ideological battlegrounds in the Conservative Party under Cameron's leadership (Hayton 2010, 492–3; Heppell 2013, 343). Heppell's survey included the list of MPs which also showed that Conservative BAME MPs elected in 2010 and before were much more moderate than those elected recently: 6 of them voted for 'remain' and 4 for 'leave' which was in line with the general findings showing that there were 50.3% of soft Eurosceptics, 20.9% Euroagnostics and 26.5% hard Eurosceptics (Heppell 2013). Among the BAME MPs elected in 2010 and before, 4 (40%) were soft Eurosceptics, 5 (50%) agnostics and 1 Hard Eurosceptic (10%). On the moral dimension, BAME Conservatives were positioned similarly as the whole PCP, although the very small number of BAME MPs then elected makes the comparison between both groups more difficult to draw. The survey indicated that there were 91 social liberals (29.7%), 62 morally neutrals (20.3%) and 153 socially conservatives (50%) (346). Among them there were 2 social liberal BAME MPs (20%), 4 neutrals (40%) and 4 conservatives (40%). Taking the key vote of 2013 on Same Sex Couples vote as a crucial bone of contention, with 117 Conservative MPs voting in favour and 127 against, BAME Conservative MPs were divided along similar lines with 6 against and 4 for. On the whole, BAME Conservative MPs followed the same trend on moral and European issues at least until 2013 when Heppell's survey was published. Then there seemed to be no discrepancy between BAME MPs and the whole PCP. So the crucial question is: what can explain that such radicalisation is exclusively related to the European agenda? Even though the whole PCP has clearly radicalised after the Brexit referendum (Lynch and Whitaker 2017), it seems that for BAME MPs, this process of radicalisation was much more acute. An analysis of BAME MPs' voting records since the referendum shows that BAME MPs were keener to find themselves on the rebellious side towards Prime Minister Theresa May's successive draft withdrawal agreements. However, they were not regular rebels. All of them display a very low percentage of rebellions, according to publicwhip.org, that is between 0% (for Kemi Badenoch, James Cleverly – the Deputy Chairman of the party -, Rishi Sunak and Nadhim Zahawi) and 1.2%, with the exception of Sam Gyimah (4.7% of rebellions) who had resigned from the government, then left the party to join the Liberal-Democrats and was a Remainer supporting a second referendum. 6 BAME MPs (out of 19 MPs, that is approximately 32%) only rebelled twice on the two draft agreements presented by the government (i.e. 'meaningful votes'). But while there was a total of 37.3% (118 out of 316) Conservative MPs who voted against the first draft agreement on 15 January 2019, which more or less corresponded with the 32% of BAME MPs, this percentage was reduced to 24.2% for the whole party when it came to vote on the second draft agreement introduced by Theresa May on 12 March, that is 75 MPs out of 310 MPs who took part in the vote. But all BAME MPs maintained their positions and the 6 rebels persisted to vote against the second draft deal, while many Conservative MPs had changed their minds in the meantime. In the series of indicative votes tabled by the government on 27 March 2019, which gave clearer indications about their preferred scenarios, a majority of 11 BAME Conservative MPs voted for either or both of the following options: 'leave the EU without a deal on 12 April' and 'calls for the government to seek to agree preferential agreements with the EU'. But these two options were already the most favoured ones by their party, although all 8 scenarios were eventually rejected by MPs (Holder, Voce, and Clarke 2019).

When we try to understand the motivations behind BAME Conservative MPs' support for Brexit, explanations presumably fall into two categories which have to do with their environment on the one hand, that is their party and constituencies, and their individual motivations on the other hand. This structure and agency outline triggers two main sets of hypotheses which are tightly connected to Norris and Lovenduski (1995) supply and demand framework aforementioned:

H1: Demand-side explanations question the role of the party and the part played by the local (constituency) environment in the Eurosceptic radicalisation of BAME MPs. This set of hypotheses also questions the process of candidate selection to see whether these MPs were selected by the party in specific seats.

H2: Supply-side explanations question BAME Conservative MPs' individual motivations in supporting Brexit. Motivations here appear to be both intrinsic and extrinsic. They include shared experience (intrinsic), motivation to represent (intrinsic) and electoral incentives (extrinsic) (Sobolewska, McKee, and Campbell 2018, 1238, 1244). They will be examined, not in general terms but in relation to these MPs' decision to support Brexit and represent their constituents on this particular issue.

Demand-side explanations of support for Brexit among BAME MPs: candidate selection

Since the election of David Cameron as party leader in December 2005, the party has promoted inclusiveness and more diversity through candidate selection. As already said, following Theresa May's denunciation of a 'nasty party' in 2002, Lord Ashcroft had identified low levels of representation of women and ethnic minorities (Ashcroft 2005; Childs and Webb 2012). The introduction of the A-list and open primaries in 26 constituencies to open the procedure to registered voters were envisaged as the best solution to enhance representation (Alexandre-Collier 2016). Since the Labour party was well known to recruit BAME candidates essentially in non-white seats (Bale 2016, 408), the Conservative Party had to devise a different strategy by selecting more ethnic minority candidates in white seats. This strategy was meant to maximise the symbolic impact of diversifying a party's candidates and result in real changes in representation (Durose et al. 2013). It was even a survival strategy for the party. As Sobolewska argued, 'the only way for the Conservatives and Liberal-Democrats to increase minority representation was to put up minority candidates in mainly "white" areas and persuade white electors to vote for them' (Sobolewska 2013, 623). In this context, at the level of individual MPs, pro-Brexit support in predominantly white areas can be understood as a mechanism of persuasion which assumes that the best way to convince white voters in white areas to vote for ethnic minority candidates is to show them, sometimes overinsistently, that their political views are shared and well represented. Substantive representation was thus prioritised and arguably based on a pro-Brexit bias in predominantly white constituencies. The IPSOS poll published on 5 September 2016 which studies 'How Britain voted in the 2016 EU referendum' found out that among white respondents 46% voted for remain and 54% for leave (while among ethnic minorities 69% supported remain and 31% leave). This could also explain these MPs' decision to outbid potential voters on their nationalistic flank. In any case, at the party level, this indicates a clear departure from the traditional pattern of descriptive representation (Sobolewska 2013).

The process of candidate selection plays an essential part in this set of motivations. Research suggests that half were selected in unwinnable seats, which they were sure to lose (Sobolewska 2013, 624). In addition, Table 1 shows that the few current BAME Conservative MPs were elected with very large majorities in safe seats, with no MP in seats with a majority under 5,000 votes and only 2 elected in 2015 with a majority between 5,000 and 10,000 and 3 in 2017, as shown in Table 1. Taken together, it can be inferred from both data that current Conservative BAME MPs were the few candidates who were selected in safe seats, which seems to suggest that this was part of the leadership's modernising agenda to have more visible minorities in Parliament.

While more than half of BAME candidates had been selected in unwinnable seats, it would tend to suggest that fighting safe seats is the only way for BAME MPs to be elected (Sobolewska 2013). In this context, the notion that support for Brexit among BAME MPs is explained by the need to represent supposedly pro-Brexit white constituents, is confirmed. Yet, for the happy few concerned, being elected in safe seats gave them more leeway to promote their personal stances and not be dependent on constituents' views. Indeed, Table 2 shows that, although there is a clear pro-Brexit predominance in all the constituencies considered (with 16 out of the 19 constituencies with over 51% of votes for 'leave'), there is no consistency between the MPs' Brexit positions and that of their constituencies'.

At the constituency level, explanations of the Brexit vote often noted the influence of anti-immigration views and UKIP's agenda setting (Goodwin and Milazzo 2015; Evans and Mellon 2016). Works about the rise of UKIP (Ford and Goodwin 2014) and its impact on the Conservative Party's Eurosceptic radicalisation (Lynch and Whitaker 2013; Bale and Webb 2014; Tournier-Sol 2015) in the run-up to the Brexit referendum sustain the presumption that many Conservative MPs supported Brexit because of this threat. Indeed, BAME MPs were elected in a majority (16) of constituencies which supported Brexit (> 51% of the votes for leave) compared with only 3 in constituencies supporting remain (<51% of leave votes) (Holder, Voce, and Clarke 2019). Yet, as previous research already demonstrated (Alexandre-Collier 2018a), this potential local threat actually did not weigh much in MP's attitudes to Brexit. This lack of consistency is confirmed here again: BAME MPs who supported remain were much more numerous in constituencies which were more favourable to Brexit (7 in constituencies with leave votes over 51% compared with 1 in constituencies with leave votes under 51%). As for leavers, the local environment did not seem to make much difference either, since there was an overwhelming majority of pro-Brexit constituencies: there were 9 leavers in constituencies with leave votes over 51% and 2 in constituencies with leave votes under 51%.

As already said, immigration was often presented as the primary argument of the June 2016 referendum campaign (although the Ashcroft poll of 24 June 2016 actually identified it as second – 33% – after immigration). Table 3 reveals that a majority of these BAME Conservative MPs (63%) sit in constituencies with poor opinion on immigration and turn out to be as responsive to their constituents on this issue as on Brexit. Following a survey by Hanretty and Vivyan which was however conducted two years before the referendum campaign, constituency opinion on immigration, on

Table 1. Safe/marginal seats in the PCP and BAME MPs.

Marginality (majority)	2015 GE	2017 GE
<5000	0	0
5001–10,000	2 (11.7%)	3 (15.8%)
10,001–20,000	9 (53%)	7 (36.8%)
20,001+	6 (35.3%)	9 (47.4%)
Total	17 (100%)	19 (100%)

Table 2. Constituency Brexit votes and BAME MPs.

Constituency leave votes	Conservative BAME Remainers	Conservative BAME Leavers	Total constituencies
<51%	1	2	3 (15.8%)
>51%	7	9	16 (84.2%)
Total MPs	8 (42%)	11 (58%)	19 (100%)

Source: Holder, Voce, and Clarke (2019).

Table 3. Constituency immigration estimate and BAME MPs.

Constituency opinion on immigration	Conservative BAME Remainers	Conservative BAME Leavers	Total
<3.21	5	7	12 (63%)
>3.21	3	4	7 (37%)

Source: Hanretty and Vivyan (2014)

a scale ranging from bad (0) to good (7), appeared to be less positive in the constituencies held by these BAME MPs (Hanretty and Vivyan 2014). The average opinion on immigration for these constituencies was rather low (3.21) and 63% of these constituencies had even poorer opinion on immigration (less than the average of 3.21) while 37% had slightly more positive opinion (more than the average of 3.21). BAME MPs are more or less evenly distributed between remainers and leavers, which shows that the level of positive/negative opinion on immigration had no real impact on these MPs' attitudes towards Brexit.

The percentage of ethnic minorities in constituencies is often taken into account as a 'motivation to represent' (Sobolewska, McKee, and Campbell 2018). In general terms, descriptive representation is viewed as an obvious endpoint, with ethnic minorities having more chances of being elected in constituencies where voters can easily identify with them and know that their specific interests and needs will be better understood and taken into account. The notion of shared experience or rather the '*perception* of commonality of experience' (Sobolewska et al. 2018, 1240) is understandably a core mechanism of representation. Yet most constituencies with high minority populations are represented by Labour BAME MPs (Bale 2016, 408), hence the need for the Conservative Party to devise a new strategy. As already argued, this strategy has been to target white seats in order to maximise the chances of BAME candidates by potentially capturing more voters (both BAME and white). This strategy is confirmed by the data provided in Table 4. While in average there are 12.8% of ethnic minorities in the whole population of the UK, according to the constituency data website of the House of Commons, a large majority of Conservative BAME MPs (79%) were elected in 'white' seats, with approximately 53% of BAME MPs being elected in constituencies with under 5% of ethnic minorities and 26% in constituencies with 5 to 10% of ethnic minorities. Combined with the fact that most of these seats were pro-Brexit (16 seats with more that over 51% of pro-leave votes against just 3), this provides an unexpected picture of the local environment in which these BAME MPs are elected. Sitting in white and pro-Brexit constituencies, BAME MPs are understandably more likely to favour substantive representation i.e. representing their party stances at the expense of descriptive representation, i. e. representing ethnic minority voters. Arguably party interest is placed above everything else, as most of these BAME MPs feel Conservative first and foremost (Kwarteng 2016; Gyimah 2018). Leaving aside individual motivations, this can also be explained by the 'colour-blind' approach notably favoured by the Conservative party (Sobolewska 2013), with MPs like Adam Afriyie, MP for Windsor, for example declaring their opposition to positive discrimination (Afriyie 2010; see also Kwarteng 2016).

Supply side explanations of support for Brexit among BAME MPs: substantive representation

As mentioned earlier, on the supply side, motivations of the BAME Conservative MPs to support Brexit are to be analysed as falling into three categories: shared experience, motivation to represent,

Table 4. Percentage of ethnic minorities in constituencies/BAME MPs.

Ethnic minorities census	Conservative BAME Remainers	Conservative BAME Leavers	Total
<5%	3 (37.5%)	7 (64%)	10 (52.7%)
5–10%	4 (50%)	1 (9%)	5 (26.3%)
10–13%	0 (0%)	2 (18%)	2 (10.5%)
>13%	1 (12.5%)	1 (9%)	2 (10.5%)
Total	8 (100%)	11 (100%)	19 (100%)

Source House of Commons Library, Constituency data website.

Table 5. Data by BAME MPs.

Conservative MP	Constituency	MP's ref vote	Constit' ref votes	Majority 2017	Immigration opinion	Ethnic pop
AFOLAMI Bim	Hitchin & Harpenden	**L**	60% R	12,031	3.62	9.6%
AFRIYIE Adam	Windsor	**L**	54% R	22,384	3.44	13.9%
BADENOCH Kemi	Saffron Walden	**L**	**51% L**	24,966	3.26	3.6%
CHISTI Rehman	Gillingham and Renham	**L**	**64% L**	9430	2.94	10.4%
CLEVERLY James	Braintree	**L**	**61% L**	18,422	2.98	3.3%
FERNANDES Suella	Fareham	**L**	**55% L**	21,555	3.18	3.4%
GHANI Nusrat	Wealden	**L**	**53% L**	23,628	3.11	2.7%
GYIMAH Sam	Surrey East	R	**54% L**	23,914	3.28	6.5%
GRANT Helen	Maidstone and The Weald	R	**56% L**	17,704	3.18	6.9%
JAVID Sajid	Bromsgrove	R	**55% L**	16,573	3.16	4.2%
JAYAWARDENA Ranil	North East Hampshire	**L**	54% R	27,772	3.43	9.3%
KENNEDY Seema	South Ribble	R	**57% L**	7421	3.00	9.8%
KWARTENG Kwasi	Spelthorne	**L**	**60% L**	13,425	3.12	12.7%
MAK Alan	Havant	R	**62% L**	15,956	3.20	2.9%
PATEL Priti	Witham	**L**	**61% L**	18,646	3.00	3.0%
SHARMA Alok	Reading West	R	**53% L**	2876	3.54	19.1%
SUNAK Rishi	Richmond Yorks	**L**	**55% L**	23,108	3.16	3.1%
VARA Shailesh	Cambridgeshire North West	R	**57% L**	18,008	3.13	4.3%
ZAHAWI Nadhim	Stratford-on-Avon	**L**	**51% L**	20,958	3.25	2.9%

electoral incentives (Sobolewska, McKee, and Campbell 2018), to which can be added ideational alternatives framed via political traditions.

The notion of shared experience is problematic (Celis 2012). It has to be understood not as a reality but a subjective impression, a 'perception', as already mentioned (Burden 2007). Yet, when applied to the case of BAME Conservative MPs, the notion of shared experience relevantly highlights their relation to British past and history and their aversion or at least their indifference to the European project with which the group of MPs feels no cultural and historical affinities (Say Mitchell 2016). As Ehsan notes about South Asian voters, 'first-generation migrants from India, Pakistan and Bangladesh were encouraged to integrate under a social policy based on the adoption of "British values"' (Ehsan 2017). This is also true for other communities. In her maiden speech, Kemi Badenoch, MP for Saffron Walden, mentions her experience of the 'British dream': 'Growing up in Nigeria my view was rather different, she declared. The UK was a beacon, a shining light, a promise of a better life' (Badenoch 2017).

BAME MPs, just like BAME voters, are not particularly sensitive to the European project which they see as a 'white fortress permitting white immigration while obstructing the entry of non whites' (Begum 2018). This is line with the findings of the Runnymede Report on race and immigration which underlined ethnic minority people's ambivalence about the benefits of Europe which they view 'in explicitly ethnic and racial terms, identifying "fortress Europe" as a way of keeping out non-white immigrants while allowing significant levels of European migration' (Khan and Weekes-Bernard 2015, 3). They are worried about Eastern European immigration and the preferential treatment that they believe is applied to this category thanks to freedom of movement. This view echoes the worries of BAME voters who believe Eastern European immigration increases pressures on public services and access to the labour market (Begum 2018). They are also receptive to the view that Brexit would increase trade between the UK and the Commonwealth, especially Asia (Sharma 2016) and ultimately favour the future geopolitical scenario of a hyperglobal post-imperial role for the UK (Baker, Gamble, and Seawright 2002; Gifford 2014). According to Ehsan, 'the pro-Commonwealth rhetoric from the Leave camp (...) would have pulled on the heartstrings of many South Asian voters' (Ehsan 2017). In addition, Conservative BAME MPs promote Conservative values of hard work and individual initiative which they believe they share with BAME voters. Priti Patel alluded to this work ethos when she declared 'After Brexit, the Government will take back control by introducing a new, fairer immigration system that prioritises skills and what people can contribute to the UK, rather than where they come from' (Patel 2019).

On the question of the motivation to represent, we have seen that substantive representation, not descriptive representation, is a primary driver. BAME MPs consider themselves as representatives of their constituents, not their communities, and advocates of the party's views and interests. Kwasi Kwarteng, MP for Spelthorne, is very critical of descriptive representation which he even equals with racism. 'To expect all Chinese people to have the same views on political economy, ethics, religion would rightly be thought as racist', he declared arguing that representing all constituents, regardless of race, creed or social background 'is what an advanced democracy looks like' (Kwarteng 2016). Most BAME Conservative MPs also feel Conservative first and foremost. For them substantive representation is about putting party interests to the fore (Gyimah 2018).

In terms of electoral incentives, which are connected to the motivation to represent, the preference for substantive representation is also a strategy to broaden their electoral base by appealing to BAME and white voters altogether. Research has highlighted the importance of electoral incentives in the UK to confirm the fact that all UK MPs (irrespective of ethnicity) are more likely to articulate issues concerning the rights and problems of ethnic minorities and to avoid the polarising issue of immigration if they represent marginal seats with a large share of minority residents (Saalfeld and Bischof 2013). As we have seen in Tables 1 and 4, data about constituencies showed that BAME MPs were elected in safe seats mostly dominated by white voters. BAME MPs' support for Brexit and anti-EU immigration views can be related to the electoral incentives of representing safe and white seats, while at the same time the Brexit and, to a lesser extent, immigration estimated views of their constituents are not necessarily taken into account, as suggested by Tables 2 and 3. Therefore, while most MPs seem to rank substantive representation above descriptive representation, the importance of the former should also be qualified. It is therefore fair to suggest that BAME MPs, while taking into account a clear pro-Brexit anti-immigration bias in their constituencies, finally display relatively poor responsiveness to their constituents' views on these specific issues.

One of the conundrums of BAME MPs' pro-Brexit motivations, which no data can easily clarify, is also how to handle the question of racism. As mentioned earlier, the xenophobic tone of the EU referendum campaign incited many BAME voters to support 'remain' not necessarily out of enthusiasm for the EU project but as a reaction against the 'leave' campaign. While some BAME MPs acknowledged that they had been already exposed to racism, like for example Suella Fernandes, now Braverman, MP for Fareham and a former Chair of the pro-Brexit European Research Group (Cecil 2014), this was treated as a marginal issue which did not matter in their decision to support 'leave'. Their skin colour was even sometimes an effective argument to justify their preference and demonstrate that the 'leave' campaign should be dissociated from accusations of racism. Furthermore, it even serves as a strategy to speak out loudly and unashamedly on Brexit and immigration, without being accused of promoting narrow-minded xenophobic populist nationalism. As Nus Ghani, MP for Wealden, argued, 'I am no Little Englander, I am the product of immigration and proud of it' (Ghani 2016). In this respect, the association of BAME Conservative MPs with the 'leave' campaign can be seen as contributing to detoxifying the Brexit brand altogether and accusations of racism and xenophobia could therefore be more easily dismissed by Brexiteers themselves.

Conclusion

The case of BAME Conservative leavers is particularly illustrative of the sometimes apparently illogical decisions made by actors who are involved in a network of games in multiple (and sometimes contradictory) arenas, i.e. their ethnic community, the Conservative Party, the EU Referendum campaign. As Tsebelis clearly demonstrated, it may pay off to act 'irrationally' to lose in one game in order to win another (Tsebelis 1990). With only 25% of BAME voters supporting leave (Begum 2018), it may indeed have seemed illogical that so many Conservative BAME MPs made the suboptimal decision to support the 'leave' campaign and run the risk of losing supporters within their community. But since their community was not directly in their constituencies, this potential loss was anyway limited. Furthermore, as actors are involved in nested games, this decision makes sense when one understands that BAME Conservative MPs have actually favoured other arenas (their party, their constituency), which, they believed, would deliver higher electoral payoffs. In that sense, it can be argued that BAME Conservative actors seem to have been ranking political arenas depending on the importance they were ready to grant them, with the EU Referendum campaign being deemed to deliver higher payoffs than the party arena which itself was considered more rewarding than the immigrant community arena.

As we have seen, the recruitment of more ethnic minorities and women was meant to change the image of the Conservative Party by detoxifying the brand to make it more inclusive, more modern and less 'nasty'. Yet the assumption that these new MPs would better represent female and ethnic minority voters and help them feel better represented can be easily dismissed because descriptive representation fails to apply. Moreover, although being branded as the face of the party's modernity, these BAME MPs do not share the moral views which are promoted by the modernisers. This points out a discrepancy between appearance and reality which blurred Cameron's message of modernisation. Their views on moral issues are not different whatsoever from the other MPs', therefore this image of modernity can be interpreted as purely cosmetic. As a consequence, even though they are showcased by the party as symbols of party modernisation (demand-side explanation), it is because of what the party projects on them since they, on the supply-side, are no modernisers. Today, while cleavages along the economy, moral issues and EU membership (Garry 1995; Heppell 2013) are still acute, it would be more accurate to say that the lines along which groups are distributed have been shifting (Jeffery et al. 2018).

It is a truism to conclude that the earthquake of Brexit has had a massive impact on the British Conservative party, where party divisions and leadership issues have entirely blurred the broader picture of if/when/how Brexit will be implemented. Yet the relative realignment of party cleavages, along the same lines but with a different distribution of forces, is the effect of party management of the EU referendum result as much as the long-term impact of David Cameron's agenda of modernisation. Showcasing minority MPs has been part of the marketing strategy of renewing the party brand. To some extent, the case of pro-Brexit Conservative BAME MPs symbolises the former Prime Minister's odd strategy of associating social liberalism and Euroscepticism, while both stances tend to represent the two extremes of a continuum between modernity and tradition. They also symbolise the adverse effects of the bold initiatives taken by Cameron to leave a lasting imprint on British politics. While we argued elsewhere that the decision to hold a referendum on EU membership (and two other ones on the voting system in 2011 and on Scottish independence in 2014) together with party organisational reforms which were meant to open the party to citizen participation (open primaries), could be interpreted as a populist temptation (Alexandre-Collier 2015), the paradoxical impact of Conservative BAME MPs is a striking illustration of the unexpected effects of this phenomenon. While these MPs symbolise the modern 'non-nasty' brand marketed under Cameron's leadership, not only are they no modernisers themselves but they have found themselves on the side of the traditionalist and nationalistic underpinning components of the Brexiteer faction. This reality tends to confuse the map of ideological cleavages.

In any case, BAME MPs represent a rupture in two ways: first, by the colour of their skin, they mark a clear departure from the average white middle-class male MP tainted by the suspicion of a narrow-minded little-England nationalistic agenda. BAME MPs do contribute to broadening the geopolitical vision of the party in a more positive way than the average profile of the Conservative Brexiteer. They project an image of a hyperglobal post-imperial Britain which feels no cultural affinities with the

European continent but shares a sense of belonging to a national community that is shaped by the same British history, values and traditions. This would tend to suggest that if alternative political traditions are available to Eurosceptics, they are more likely to adopt non-EU options involving the Commonwealth or an even more global role for Britain.

Secondly, they illustrate the different strategy of the Conservative Party which departs from the traditional pattern of descriptive representation. BAME MPs do not represent non-white seats which would be culturally diverse and open to immigration. Quite the opposite, since they are usually selected in safe seats. Therefore, their aspiration to represent can be clearly understood as exclusively substantive and dominated by the Conservative agenda. In this context, ethnicity and gender parity were only strategically highlighted under Cameron's modernisation agenda, as if they were only meant to symbolise the party's new direction. BAME Conservative MPs expose the underlying party communication strategy of spotlighting new party cleavages around moral issues, although, since the Cameron years and even more so since the Brexit referendum, party cleavages have actually realigned around hyperglobalism. In addition, their specific stances on immigration contribute to displacing the issue of immigration from the immigrant-friendly agenda that could be stereotypically expected of BAME candidates (descriptive representation) to a global post-imperial and pro-Brexit agenda, therefore justifying an anti-EU immigration and extensively a tougher approach to immigration in general (substantive representation). While serving to decontaminate the Conservative brand, BAME Conservative MPs might also have served to decontaminate the 'Brexit' brand from the white little-England xenophobic prejudice which often tainted the Leave campaign. Unfortunately for the party, since the beginning of her Brexit negotiations with the EU, decontaminating the Brexit had not been part of Prime Minister Theresa May's priorities but rather one of the many missed opportunities which could characterise this painful and critical period. While Boris Johnson's government was then presented as ethnically diverse, with 4 BAME ministers out of 23 appointed on 25 July 2019, the parliamentary party failed to be massively renewed at the general election on 12 December 2019. While the new Parliament did welcome much more women and BAME MPs, the Conservatives were proportionally less concerned by this renewal than Labour. They did increase the number of BAME MPs from 19 to 22 but due to the increase in the number of seats (365), the proportion of MPs from ethnic backgrounds has actually remained the same.

Disclosure statement

No potential conflict of interest was reported by the author.

References

Afriyie, A. 2010. "Adam Afriyie MP: Positive Discrimination Has No Place in the Selection of Candidates for Roles in Politics, Business or Eve, the Pulpit." *Conservative Home*, July 1. Accessed 25 November 2019. https://www.conservativehome.com/platform/2010/07/adam-afriyie-mp-positive-discrimination-has-no-place-in-the-selection-of-candidates-for-roles-in-pol.html

Alexandre-Collier, A. 2010. *Les habits neufs de David Cameron. Les conservateurs britanniques (1990-2010)*. Paris: Presses de Sciences Po.

Alexandre-Collier, A. 2015. "Reassessing British Conservative Euroscepticism as a Case of Party (Mis)management." In *The UK Challenge to Europeanization: The Persistence of British Euroscepticism*, edited by G. Gifford and K. Tournier-Sol, 99–116. Basingstoke: Palgrave Macmillan.

Alexandre-Collier, A. 2016. "The Open Garden of Politics? The Impact of Open Primaries for Candidate Selection in the British Conservative Party." *British Journal of Politics and International Relations* 18 (3): 706–723. doi:10.1177/1369148116636518.

Alexandre-Collier, A. 2018a. "From Soft to Hard Brexit: UKIP's Not so Invisible Influence on the Eurosceptic Radicalisation of the Conservative Party since 2015." In *Trumping the Mainstream. The Conquest of Democratic Politics by the Populist Radical Right*, edited by L. E. Herman and J. Muldoon, 204–221. London: Routledge

Alexandre-Collier, A. 2018b. ""Less Stale, Only Slightly Less Male, but Overwhelmingly Less Pale": The 2015 New Conservative Brexiters in the House of Commons." *Parliamentary Affairs* 72 (3): 588–615. doi:10.1093/pa/gsy023.
Allen, P. 2018. *The Political Class. Why It Matters Who Our Politicians Are*. Oxford: Oxford University Press.
Ashcroft, M. 2005. *Smell the Coffee. A Wake-UP Call for the Conservative Party*. https://www.lordashcroft.com/pdf/GeneralElectionReport.pdf
Badenoch, K. 2017. "Maiden Speech." *Hansard Parliamentary Debates*, vol. 627, col. 930-3, July 19.
Baker, D., A. Gamble, and D. Seawright. 2002. "Sovereign Nations and Global Markets: Modern British Conservatism and Hyperglobalism." *The British Journal of Politics and International Relations* 4 (3): 399–428. doi:10.1111/1467-856X.t01-1-00086.
Baker, D., A. Gamble, and S. Ludlam. 1993. "Whips or Scorpions? The Maastricht Vote and the Conservative Party." *Parliamentary Affairs* 46 (2): 151–166. doi:10.1093/oxfordjournals.pa.a052409.
Baker, D., A. Gamble, and S. Ludlam. 1994. "The Parliamentary Siege of Maastricht 1993: Conservative Divisions and British Ratification." *Parliamentary Affairs* 47 (1): 37–60.
Bale, T. 2016. *The Conservative Party. From Thatcher to Cameron*. 2nd ed. Cambridge: Polity.
Bale, T., P. Cowley, and A. Menon. 2016. "EU Referendum: A Third of MPs Could Still Back Brexit." *The Spectator*. Accessed 3 April 2019. http://blogs.spectator.co.uk/2016/02/eu-referendum-a-third-of-mps-could-still-back-brexit/on
Bale, T., and P. Webb. 2014. "Why Do Tories Defect to UKIP? Conservative Party Members and the Temptations of the Populist Radical Right." *Political Studies* 62 (4): 961–970. doi:10.1111/1467-9248.12130.
Begum, N. 2018. "Minority Ethnic Attitudes and the 2016 EU Referendum." *UK in a Changing Europe*, February 6. Accessed 25 November 2019. https://ukandeu.ac.uk/minority-ethnic-attitudes-and-the-2016-eu-referendum/on
British Future. 2015 "The Class of 2015 Enter Britain's Most Diverse Ever Parliament." Accessed 25 November 2019. http://www.britishfuture.org/articles/class-of-2015-most-diverse-parliament/on
Burden, B. 2007. *Personal Roots of Representation*. Princeton: Princeton University Press.
Cameron, D. 2019. *For the Record*. London: William Collins.
Cecil, N. 2014. "Tories Snub Would-be MP as "Brown and Woman"." *Evening Standard*, December 11.
Celis, K. 2008. "Gendering Representation." In *Politics, Gender and Concepts: Theory & Methods*, edited by G. Goertz and A. Mazur, 71–93. Cambridge: Cambridge University Press.
Celis, K. 2012. "On Substantive Representation, Diversity and Responsiveness." *Politics & Gender* 8 (4): 524–529. doi:10.1017/S1743923X12000542.
Childs, S., and J. Lovenduski. 2013. "Political Representation." In *The Oxford Handbook of Gender and Politics*, edited by G. Waylen, K. Celis, J. Kantola, and S. L. Weldon, 489–513. Oxford: Oxford University Press.
Childs, S., and P. Webb. 2012. *Sex, Gender and the Conservative Party*. Basingstoke: Palgrave Macmillan.
Criddle, B. 2016. "Variable Diversity: MPs and Candidates." In *The British General Election of 2015*, edited by P. Cowley and D. Kavanagh, 336–360. Basingstoke: Palgrave Macmillan.
Dalton, R., and M. Wattenberg. 2002. *Parties without Partisans. Political Change in Advanced Industrial Democracies*. Oxford: Oxford University Press.
Dommett, K. 2015. "The Theory and Practice of Party Modernisation: The Conservative Party under David Cameron, 2005-2015." *British Politics* 10 (2): 249–266. doi:10.1057/bp.2015.21.
Durose, C., R. Combs, C. Eason, F. Gains, and L. Richardson. 2013. ""Acceptable Difference": Diversity, Representation and Pathways to UK Politics." *Parliamentary Affairs* 66 (2): 246–267. doi:10.1093/pa/gss085.
Ehsan, R. 2017. "The British Asian Vote for Brexit Contains a Few Surprises." *LSE Blogs*, February 20. Accessed 25 November 2019. https://blogs.lse.ac.uk/brexit/2017/02/20/the-british-asian-vote-for-brexit-contains-a-few-surprises/on
Evans, G., and J. Mellon. 2016. "Are Leave Voters Mainly UKIP?" *The British Election Study*, July. Accessed 25 November 2019. http://www.britishelectionstudy.com/bes-impact/are-leave-voters-mainly-ukip-by-jonathan-mellon-and-geoffrey-evans/#.WaqoA9FpyUI
Ford, R., and M. Goodwin. 2014. *Revolt on the Right. Explaining Support for the Radical Right in Britain*. London: Routledge.
Garry, J. 1995. "The British Conservative Party: Divisions over European Policy." *West European Politics* 18 (2): 170–189. doi:10.1080/01402389508425112.
Ghani, N. 2016. "To Brexit or Not to Brexit." February 22. Accessed 3 April 2019. https://www.nusghani.org.uk/news/brexit-or-not-brexit
Gifford, C. 2014. *The Making of Eurosceptic Britain*. 2nd ed. Farnham: Ashgate.
Goodwin, M., and M. Milazzo. 2015. *UKIP: Inside the Campaign to Redraw the Map of British Politics*. Oxford: Oxford University Press.
Gyimah, S. 2018. "Sam Gyimah: I'm a Conservative MP – But People Can't Place Me." *The Times*, June 25.
Hanretty, C., and N. Vivyan. 2014. "Opinion Estimates for 632 Constituencies." Accessed 2018. http://constituencyopinion.org.uk/wp-content/uploads/2014/11/estimates-longtab-neat.pdf
Hayton, R. 2010. "Conservative Party Modernisation and David Cameron's Politics of the Family." *Political Quarterly* 81 (4): 492–500. doi:10.1111/j.1467-923X.2010.02126.x.
Hayton, R. 2017. "British Conservatism after the Brexit Vote: The Ideological Legacy of David Cameron." *The British Journal of Politics and International Relations* 20 (1): 223–238. doi:10.1177/1369148117737278.

Heath, A., S. Fisher, G. Rosenblatt, D. Sanders, and M. Sobolewska. 2013. *The Political Integration of Ethnic Minorities in Britain*. Oxford: Oxford University Press.

Heppell, T. 2013. "Cameron and Liberal Conservatism: Attitudes within the Parliamentary Conservative Party and Conservative Ministers." *The British Journal of Politics and International Relations* 15 (3): 340–361. doi:10.1111/j.1467-856X.2012.00546.x.

Heppell, T., A. Crines, and D. Jeffery. 2017. "The United Kingdom Referendum on EU Membership: The Voting of Conservative Parliamentarians." *The Journal of Common Market Studies* 55 (4): 762–778. doi:10.1111/jcms.12529.

Hill, M. 2013. "Arrogant Posh Boys? The Social Composition of the Parliamentary Conservative Party and the Effects of Cameron's A-list." *The Political Quarterly* 84 (1): 80–89. doi:10.1111/j.1467-923X.2013.02430.x.

Holder, J., A. Voce, and S. Clarke. 2019. "How Did Your MP Vote in the Indicative Votes?" *The Guardian*, March 27. Accessed 25 November 2019. https://www.theguardian.com/uk-news/ng-interactive/2019/mar/27/how-did-your-mp-vote-in-the-indicative-votes#top

Jeffery, D., R. Hayton, T. Heppell, and A. Crines. 2018. "The Conservative Party Leadership of 2016: An Analysis of the Voting Motivations of Conservative Parliamentarians." *Parliamentary Affairs* 71 (2): 262–282. doi:10.1093/pa/gsx027.

Khan, O., and D. Weekes-Bernard 2015. "This Is Still about Us. Why Ethnic Minorities See Immigration Differently." *The Runnymede Report on Race and Immigration*, 41. London: Runnymede.

Kulich, C., M. K. Ryan, and A. Haslam. 2014. "The Political Glass Cliff: Understanding How Seat Selection Contributes to the Underperformance of Ethnic Minority Candidates." *Political Research Quarterly* 67 (1): 84–95. doi:10.1177/1065912913495740.

Kwarteng, K. 2016. "Kwasi Kwarteng on Why He Doesn't Need to Represent "Black" Issues." *True Africa*, September 9. Accessed 3 February 2019. https://trueafrica.co/article/british-politician-kwasi-kwarteng-on-why-identity-politics-are-undemocratic/on

Lamprinakou, C., M. Morucci, R. Campbell, and J. Van Heerde-Hudson. 2017. "All Change in the House? The Profile of Candidates and MPs in the 2015 British General Election." *Parliamentary Affairs* 70 (2): 207–232.

Lynch, P., and R. Whitaker. 2013. "Rivalry on the Right: The Conservatives, the UK Independence Party (UKIP) and the EU Issue." *British Politics* 8 (3): 285–312. doi:10.1057/bp.2012.29.

Lynch, P., and R. Whitaker. 2017. "All Brexiteers Now? Brexit, the Conservatives and Party Change." *British Politics* 13 (1): 31–47. doi:10.1057/s41293-017-0064-6.

May, T. 2002. "Full Text: Theresa May's Conference Speech." *The Guardian*, October 7. Accessed 3 April 2019. https://www.theguardian.com/politics/2002/oct/07/conservatives2002.conservatives1

McIlveen, R. 2009. "Ladies of the Right: An Interim Analysis of the A-List." *Journal of Elections, Public Opinion and Parties* 19 (2): 147–157. doi:10.1080/17457280902798974.

Moore, L. 2018. "Policy, Office and Votes: Conservative MPs and the Brexit Referendum." *Parliamentary Affairs* 71,1 (1): 1–27. doi:10.1093/pa/gsx010.

Norris, P., and J. Lovenduski. 1995. *Political Recruitment: Gender, Class and Race in the British Parliament*. Cambridge: Harvard University Press.

Patel, P. 2019. *Hansard Parliamentary Debates*, Col. cWS, September 4.

Pitkin, H. 1967. *The Concept of Representation*. Berkeley: University of California Press.

Saalfeld, T., and D. Bischof. 2013. "Minority-ethnic MPs and the Substantive Representation of Minority Interests in the House of Commons, 2005-2011." *Parliamentary Affairs* 66 (2): 305–328. doi:10.1093/pa/gss084.

Saggar, S. 1998. "A Late, though Not Lost, Opportunity: Ethnic Minority Electors, Party Strategy and the Conservative Party." *The Political Quarterly* 69 (2): 148–159. doi:10.1111/poqu.1998.69.issue-2.

Say Mitchell, D. 2016. "So What if I'm Black and Thinking about Voting for Brexit." *The Guardian*, March 22. Accessed 25 November 2019. https://www.theguardian.com/commentisfree/2016/mar/22/black-voting-brexit-out-campaign

Sharma, A. 2016. "The Future of UK Trade after Brexit." *Speech*, November 24. Accessed 25 November 2019. https://www.gov.uk/government/speeches/alok-sharma-the-future-of-uk-trade-after-brexit

Sobolewska, M. 2013. "Party Strategies and the Descriptive Representation of Ethnic Minorities: The 2010 British General Election." *West European Politics* 36 (2): 615–633. doi:10.1080/01402382.2013.773729.

Sobolewska, M., R. McKee, and R. Campbell. 2018. "Explaining Motivation to Represent: How Does Descriptive Representation Lead to Substantive Representation of Racial and Ethnic Minorities?" *West European Politics* 41 (6): 1237–1261. doi:10.1080/01402382.2018.1455408.

Tournier-Sol, K. 2015. "Reworking the Eurosceptic and Conservative Traditions into a Populist Narrative: UKIP's Winning Formula?" *Journal of Common Market Studies* 53 (1): 140–156. doi:10.1111/jcms.12208.

Tsebelis, G. 1990. *Nested Games: Rational Choice in Comparative Politics*. Berkeley: University of California Press.

Wallace, M. 2016. "The Majority of Ethnic Minority Conservative MPs are Backing Leave." *ConservativeHome*. http://www.conservativehome.com/parliament/2016/03/the-majority-of-ethnic-minority-conservative-mps-are-backing-leave.html

OPEN ACCESS

Northern Ireland and Brexit: where sovereignty and stability collide?

Mary C. Murphy

ABSTRACT

Having been issues which stimulated little discussion beyond Northern Ireland before the Brexit referendum, the 'Irish issue' dominated and complicated the subsequent EU–UK withdrawal negotiations. The 'taking back control' narrative bears the hallmarks of Prime Minister Boris Johnson's notion of a 'recaptured sovereignty'. This conception of sovereignty, however, clashes with the post-sovereign character and content of the 1998 Belfast/Good Friday Agreement. The institutions created by the Agreement move beyond the old frameworks for political order by creating a series of interlocking territorial, cross-territorial, and cross-national institutions based on shared sovereignty. This prompts critical questions about the resilience and sustainability of the Agreement against the backdrop of a shift in sovereignty which appears incompatible with the key tenets of Northern Ireland's peace agreement. This article examines how Northern Ireland's approach to and experience of the EU referendum differed from the rest of the UK. It queries how the referendum result, subsequent political and electoral developments, and difficulties in agreeing a withdrawal formula and future UK–EU relationship, expose the gap between the UK's commitments to a post-sovereign arrangement for Northern Ireland and the preference for a return to an older conception of sovereignty as implied by the Brexit vote.

Unlike other parts of the UK, Northern Ireland's historic experience has been marked by serious and violent conflict. The movement from conflict to peace over a protracted period of time culminated in the signing of the Belfast/Good Friday Agreement in 1998. The evolving process of peace consolidation which followed was interrupted by the June 2016 referendum on the UK's membership of the European Union (EU). In Northern Ireland, a majority voted in favour of Remain. The referendum campaign, however, was different in tone and content to the rest of the UK (see Murphy 2016). It focused less on migration and 'taking back control', and more on issues, such as the future status of the border between Northern Ireland and the Republic of Ireland, the implications of a Leave vote for the (fragile) peace process and the impact on trade and policies. Having been an issue which stimulated little discussion beyond Northern Ireland before the referendum, issues pertaining to Northern Ireland and the Irish border came to dominate and complicate the subsequent EU-UK withdrawal negotiations. The 'taking back control' narrative which so animated Britain, and particularly England's, referendum narrative and the subsequent UK-EU negotiations bears the hallmarks of Prime Minister Boris Johnson's (2020) notion of a 'recaptured sovereignty'. This conception of sovereignty, however, clashes with the post-sovereign character and content of the 1998 Belfast/Good Friday Agreement. The principles and institutions established by the Agreement move beyond the old frameworks for political order by creating a series of novel and interlocking territorial, cross-territorial and cross-national institutions.

Moreover, the status of Northern Ireland as a part of the UK is underpinned by the principle of consent (linked to popular sovereignty) (see Hadfield 1998). The EU framework of open borders and shared sovereignty within which these innovations were situated was an important facilitating context. In contrast, Brexit clashes with an understanding of sovereignty which appears incompatible with the key tenets of Northern Ireland's peace agreement. This prompts critical questions about the resilience and sustainability of the Agreement's institutions and principles, and the long-term prospects for stability in Northern Ireland.

This article examines how Northern Ireland's approach to and experience of the EU referendum differed from the rest of the UK. It explores how the referendum result, subsequent political and electoral developments, and the pronounced difficulties in agreeing a withdrawal formula and future UK–EU trade relationship, expose a gulf between the UK's commitments to a post-sovereign arrangement for Northern Ireland and the return to an older conception of national sovereignty implied by the pro-Brexit rhetoric and narrative. This reconfiguration of the British order which Brexit entails intersects clumsily with Northern Ireland's post-sovereign political settlement and has propelled previously latent debates and discussions in Northern Ireland about the long-term viability of the 1998 Agreement and the prospects for future constitutional change.

The Northern Ireland context

The UK's 2016 EU referendum campaign coincided with a period when Northern Ireland's historically contested politics had settled into a cycle of somewhat mundane normality. The violent campaign of paramilitary violence which began in the late 1960s and had its roots in 'the social, economic, cultural and geographical structure of Northern Ireland' (Darby 1976, 196) had given way to a delicate political equilibrium underpinned by the provisions of the 1998 Belfast/Good Friday Agreement. The fundamental division in Northern Ireland between unionists and nationalists was not eliminated by the peace process. Political and electoral contestation in Northern Ireland continues to be based on a deep and profound constitutional cleavage where unionists support the constitutional link between Northern Ireland and the rest of the UK, while nationalists aspire to the creation of a united Ireland (see Matthews and Pow 2020). The potency of Northern Ireland's communal and political division, however, has been challenged and the UK's devolution settlement has been instrumental in that respect.

Northern Ireland's form of devolution allowed former political foes to share power, and to exercise executive and legislative functions in devolved areas. Tensions between the parties continued to exist after 1998, and were particularly evident in relation to equality issues, language rights, and conflict legacy matters (see Armstrong, Herbert, and Mustad 2019). Differences were also apparent in relation to a lack of progress on key issues, such as integrated education, welfare entitlements and shared housing (see Gray et al. 2019). Local politicians in Northern Ireland have encountered particular difficulties in confronting and reforming these highly sensitive policy domains. The challenges in discussing and agreeing progress, hinges on deeper problems related to the weaknesses inherent in the consociational settlement (see, for example, Hall 2018; Taylor 2008) and a lingering lack of trust between the unionist and nationalist blocs (Teague 2019). At the time of the calling of the EU referendum, Murphy (2018) identified the existence of a 'negative peace' in Northern Ireland epitomised by the ongoing polarisation of politics. Although a 'negative peace' environment is not unexpected for a region in transition from conflict to peace, it is nevertheless a precarious and tenuous moment for any conflict transformation process. The calling of the 2016 EU referendum coincided with such a period in Northern Ireland.

The EU referendum in Northern Ireland

The EU referendum campaign across the UK differed depending on territory. For much of the rest of the UK (and most notably in England), the key referendum themes were immigration and the rather vague notion of 'taking back control'. It included a narrative which reflected not just on UK sovereignty vis-à-vis the EU, but revealed underlying ambiguities and tensions in relation to the exercise of sovereignty vis-à-vis the UK's constituent units (see Sandford and Gormley-Heenan 2020).

In Northern Ireland, the referendum campaign was markedly different and the emphasis was less fixated on calls to recapture British sovereignty and more focused on localised political and economic concerns. These concerns included the impact of a Leave vote on the status of the border between Northern Ireland and the Republic of Ireland; the implications for Northern Ireland trade; the future of EU structural/Peace funding to Northern Ireland; the impact on the agriculture sector; and the consequences for the Northern Ireland peace process (see Murphy 2016). Nationalists, in particular, were concerned about the impact of Brexit on political stability in Northern Ireland. A key achievement of the peace process was that it took the border (between north and south) out of Irish politics (see Gormley-Heenan and Aughey 2017). This facilitated the opening up of the border and the creation of cross-border institutions; and allowed for the removal of border infrastructure and check-points. It was an especially important component of the peace process for nationalists because it legitimised their identification with the rest of Ireland and enabled institutional mechanisms which gave expression to that identity. In this context, a key success of the Belfast/Good Friday Agreement was its ability to neutralise the toxicity which had previously attached to border politics in Ireland. The Agreement, therefore, largely settled the contestedness of the border and both unionists and nationalists were at peace with its existence, its operation and its meaning. Crucially, the open border between north and south was facilitated by UK and Irish membership of the EU, and specifically by membership of the EU's single market. The single market is based on open borders and free movement of people and trade, so there was an easy and almost fortuitous way in which it enabled key aspects of the Belfast/Good Friday Agreement (see Hayward 2018).

The Northern Ireland EU referendum campaign re-opened discussions about how a Leave vote might impact on the settled status of the Irish border. Nationalists, and the Irish government, were vocal during the referendum campaign about the potential for a vote in favour of Leave to lead to the erection of a reinforced physical and metaphorical border between north and south (Aughey and Gormley-Heenan 2017). The economic ramifications of such a development were viewed as being potentially detrimental to the Northern Ireland economy (see, for example, ESRI 2015; Open University 2015; Oxford Economics 2016). Politically, the re-erection of the border was viewed by nationalists as a threat to the viability and stability of arrangements and institutions created by the Belfast/Good Friday Agreement. In contrast, unionists did not share this interpretation of how a Leave vote might impact on Northern Ireland. Given their lesser affinity with the Republic of Ireland, Unionists have traditionally been less wedded to the cross-border element of the Agreement than their nationalist counterparts (see Smithey 2011). Of Northern Ireland's political parties, the largest and pro-Brexit Democratic Unionist Party (DUP) was particularly dismissive of claims that Brexit might challenge Northern Ireland's hard-won peace.

Like all political polls in Northern Ireland, the EU referendum divided nationalists and unionists, although the division was not a clean one. All of the nationalist parties (the SDLP and Sinn Féin) and centrist parties (Alliance Party and Green Party) supported the Remain position. Among unionists, there was less consistency. The DUP and the small Traditional Unionist Voice (TUV) party both advocated for the Leave position. In contrast, the more moderate Ulster Unionist Party was 'on balance' supportive of the UK remaining in the EU. Despite the magnitude and seriousness of the issues confronting Northern Ireland however, the referendum campaign was muted. Political parties tended to shy away from discussing issues which touched on contested issues of sovereignty and which exposed tensions between nationalism and unionism (see Murphy 2016).

The UK-wide referendum result revealed different territorial preferences. Where the UK, as a whole, supported Leave, Northern Ireland (like Scotland) voted in favour of remaining in the EU (see McCann and Hainsworth 2017). The breakdown of the referendum result in Northern Ireland demonstrates how the vote divided unionists and nationalists. Research by Garry (2017, 2) notes that voter choice was largely driven by 'the deep underlying ethno-national divide in Northern Ireland politics'. In other words, 66% of self-described 'unionists' voted to exit the EU while almost 90% of self-described 'nationalists' voted Remain. Although this does not demonstrate a clear-cut unionist-nationalist divide, it hints at a degree of latent division in Northern Ireland on the issue of Brexit. The depth of this division, however, crystallised and intensified during the ensuing UK-EU withdrawal negotiations. That divide between unionists and nationalists was influenced by the immense difficulties in agreeing a withdrawal formula which facilitated the maintenance of an open border between Northern Ireland and the Republic of Ireland.

The UK-EU referendum and the absence of an Irish narrative

Issues related to the Irish border, trade, and the peace process which animated the referendum campaign in Northern Ireland did not enjoy any sort of airing outside Northern Ireland. The broader UK-EU referendum campaign was essentially an Ireland free zone. As Hayward and Murphy (2018, 282) note: 'the 2016 UK referendum on EU membership highlighted ... the low priority of Northern Ireland for the UK government's campaign and the British electorate'. There was no serious or significant attention paid to how Brexit might impact on Northern Ireland's tenuous and delicate political situation (see Burke Wood and Gilmartin 2020). There was no sense that the timing, even the very fact of the referendum, might prove challenging for a region in transition from conflict to peace. Glencross (2016, 9–10) observes that a lack of attention by Prime Minister David Cameron to the wider dynamics of the referendum beyond Britain 'illustrates how far this vote was essentially a domestic party political matter'. This obliviousness to Northern Ireland's particular situation was evident across both Remain and Leave campaign groups while few within either the Conservative Party or Labour Party broached the subject during the referendum period. And this was despite the acute concerns expressed by the Irish government[1] and nationalists in Northern Ireland about the referendum outcome and its potential implications for Ireland, north and south.

This lack of awareness of Northern Ireland's particular situation resulted in a marked lack of consideration, preparation, or contingency planning for the fallout from the Leave vote for Northern Ireland. More tellingly, it also overtly revealed an evident disconnect between Britain and Northern Ireland: a lack of basic awareness at elite (and public) level as to the potential for the Irish border issue to be problematic. This hinged not just on day-to-day detachment and disconnection of peoples, it also underlined the limited appreciation, and in some cases, the dissatisfaction with the kind of constitutional and political construct the UK had become after 1998. The EU referendum campaign, which was dominated by largely English discontents, also revealed an element of English dissatisfaction with 'the perceived unfair advantages Scotland gets from devolution, [and] the absence of an institutionalised political voice for England' (Henderson et al. 2017, 638). These tensions and misunderstandings, though evident during the EU referendum campaign, played out much more emphatically during the UK-EU Brexit negotiations which followed.

Northern Ireland and the Brexit Negotiations

Having been little more than a footnote during the wider UK referendum campaign, issues pertaining to Northern Ireland moved front and centre during the ensuing EU-UK negotiation process (see O'Rourke 2019). The withdrawal negotiations were structured around three key priorities: citizens' rights for EU-27 citizens in the UK and UK citizens in the EU-27; the settlement of the UK's financial obligations; and ensuring the Northern Ireland peace process is not compromised. Specifically, the *Negotiating Directives for Article 50 Negotiations* (22 May 2017) resolved that: 'Negotiations should in particular aim to avoid the creation of a hard border on the island of Ireland, while respecting the integrity of the Union legal order' (Paragraph 14).

Given that the Republic of Ireland shared a land border with Northern Ireland and was acutely attuned to the potential pitfalls of Brexit for economic and political stability on the island of Ireland, the Irish government fought hard for issues concerning the island of Ireland to be high on the EU's negotiating agenda. The threats and challenges which Brexit posed for Ireland – north and south –

were immense (see for example, Economic and Social Research Institute (ESRI) 2015). Indeed, the Republic of Ireland stood to be more impacted by Brexit than any other EU member state. With a view to protecting Irish interests: 'Ireland's objective from the outset was to transform Irish interests into those of the EU' (Laffan 2018, 571). The Irish government deployed an extensive and sustained programme of meetings and briefings with key figures across the EU institutions and all EU capitals. This exercise aimed to communicate the implications of Brexit for Ireland, and in particular to explain the complexities of the Irish border issue for Ireland and its relationship with the UK.

The EU was receptive to Irish concerns. This was not solely due to the diplomatic persuasiveness of the Irish government, but linked to the EU's prolonged interest in Northern Ireland. The EU had long been supportive of the Northern Ireland peace process. Following the calling of paramilitary cease-fires in 1994, the European Commission (1995) moved quickly to create the *Special Support Programme for Peace and Reconciliation in Northern Ireland and the Republic of Ireland* worth €400 million for the period 1995–1999. The programme aimed to bolster moves towards peace by supporting economic development and peace-building projects (see Racioppi and O'Sullivan See 2007), and has been continuously renewed since 1995. The programme has also been supplemented by other supporting and networking initiatives in the intervening period (see Hayward and Murphy 2012).

Like the EU, the UK was also sensitive to specific Irish concerns. A number of these concerns were raised in a letter to Prime Minister Theresa May in August 2016 from the First Minister and Deputy First Minister of Northern Ireland (Northern Ireland Executive 2016). The DUP First Minister and Sinn Féin Deputy First Minister had taken different positions on the EU referendum, but they demonstrated some shared awareness in highlighting Brexit issues of specific concern to Northern Ireland. These included the potentially negative impact of Brexit on the Irish border, the energy sector, agriculture, EU peace funding and trade. In her letter of withdrawal, forwarded to the EU in March 2017, the Prime Minister acknowledged that Brexit posed particular challenges for Ireland. Her letter noted 'the UK's unique relationship with the Republic of Ireland and the importance of the peace process in Northern Ireland' and expressed a desire that there not be a return to a hard border on the island of Ireland (10 Downing Street 2017).

In the early period of withdrawal negotiations, British, Irish and EU protagonists evidently shared similar objectives in relation to preventing the imposition of a hard border on the island of Ireland. However, although all sides agreed on *what* the negotiations should achieve, there was little consensus about *how* to realise the outcome of a frictionless and seamless border between north and south. The situation was complicated in the period following the referendum as the Brexit debate in the UK became increasingly characterised by calls to patriotism, marked disagreement over what form Brexit should take, and pernicious discord between pro- and anti-Brexit camps. Westminster party politics became 'caught in a catastrophic equilibrium' with 'the two major party leaders ... unable to offer clear, consistent and compelling plans for Brexit' (Wincott 2018, 15). As the negotiations progressed, the gulf between EU and UK negotiators, particularly on the Irish border issue, became mired in political dispute and disagreement. This hostile atmosphere did little to quell the anxiety and divisiveness which Brexit was stoking in Northern Ireland, and as the issue became increasingly politicised, so Brexit produced a polarising effect on Northern Ireland politics (see Murphy 2018).

The progress of the withdrawal negotiation process was also impacted by a series of unanticipated developments. In January 2017, a financial scandal in Northern Ireland (the so-called Cash for Ash scandal) resulted in a serious breakdown in relations between the DUP and Sinn Féin and effectively collapsed the devolved institutions and produced a political vacuum there (see Birrell and Heenan 2017). The fragility of Northern Ireland's political situation was complicated further by Prime Minister Theresa May's position on what form Brexit should take. In an attempt to satisfy pro-Brexit Conservative Party MPs, and as a means to secure support for a UK-EU withdrawal deal, the Prime Minister's Lancaster Speech (17 January 2017) signalled her support for a harder form of Brexit which would see the UK leaving the single market and customs union. In the absence of special arrangements for Northern Ireland, the UK being outside the single market and customs union would necessitate a border on the island of Ireland. The Prime Minister's ability to negotiate and agree special arrangements for Northern Ireland was derailed by her decision to call a general election in June 2017. The election produced an extraordinary political arithmetic and unexpectedly propelled the DUP into a Confidence and Supply Agreement supporting a minority Conservative Party government. The terms of the agreement involved approximately £2 billion of financial support for Northern Ireland and a commitment from the DUP to support the British government on all Brexit-related decisions (Tonge 2017). The DUP's political elevation and their king-making position at the heart of British politics angered Irish nationalists who accused the British government of abandoning all impartiality in relation to Northern Ireland (Birrell and Heenan 2020).

Relations between the DUP and Prime Minister May were not harmonious. May's early attempts at fashioning a bespoke arrangement for Northern Ireland by keeping it within the EU customs union and single market, while the rest of the UK remained outside, was roundly rejected by the DUP and their pro-Brexit allies in the Conservative Party (see Connelly 2018). A revised 'backstop', involving the entire UK remaining in the EU customs union (unless and until the UK and EU deem the arrangement no longer necessary), and Northern Ireland continuing to align with some single market rules, would have necessitated some checks on goods entering Northern Ireland from the rest of the UK. Unionists' perception of this arrangement creating an Irish Sea border between Northern Ireland and the rest of the UK, was viewed as undermining the constitutional integrity of the UK. May's formula which acknowledged the specificity of the Northern Ireland situation, and experimented further with post-sovereignist formulations for the region, although acceptable to nationalists, was not considerate of unionist fears and vulnerabilities. Unionists in general, and the DUP in particular, viewed the 'backstop' as anathema to unionist principles and as an afront to all British unionists for the way in which it treated Northern Ireland differently from the rest of the UK (see Murphy and Evershed 2020). Such a prospect would mean not just the application of different rules and regulations in Northern Ireland, it also meant that Northern Ireland would not be part of the return to a traditional form of British sovereignty as implied by Brexit.

This series of developments and decisions which materialised after the EU referendum demonstrates the immensely challenging political sensitivities which Brexit awoke in Northern Ireland. It also lays bare the sheer complexity of fashioning a Brexit withdrawal process which attends to the wider agenda of retrieving some semblance of Britain's traditional sovereignty character, but simultaneously respects and accommodates the special circumstances which pertain in Northern Ireland.

The clash of sovereignties: Brexit and the Belfast/Good Friday Agreement

The problems and challenges which have beset the UK's Brexit process link to what Gordon (2016, 333) describes as 'a captivation with the concept of sovereignty' which has shaped UK constitutionalism. Discomfort with the consequences of EU membership for British sovereignty has been an enduring and contested feature of the UK's relationship with the EU (see for example, Geddes 2013). The 'Take Back Control' rhetoric espoused by Leave supporters during the referendum alluded to Britain recovering its confiscated sovereignty. Before and after the EU referendum, discussion of Brexit by both Leavers and Remainers touched explicitly and implicitly on both the legal and political dimensions of sovereignty (see Gordon 2016). As Agnew (2020) observes however, the entire Brexit debate (and the subsequent UK-EU negotiation period) was largely oblivious to the meaning, implications and complexities of the sovereignty concept.

A central principle of British constitutionalism is the doctrine of parliamentary sovereignty (see Dicey 1996). This denotes that there is no higher source of authority than parliament and all other branches of the state are subordinate to parliament. In many ways however, this conception of parliamentary sovereignty is both inaccurate and outdated. Elliott (2004) notes that: 'The changing [British] constitutional landscape ... is causing the net around parliamentary sovereignty to tighten'. This refers to developments in British politics including UK accession to the EU in 1973, the introduction of devolved powers for Scotland, Wales and Northern Ireland in 1999, and an increased emphasis on human rights which have (and are) undermining Britain's constitutional landscape in ways that do not sit comfortably with the key tenets of the parliamentary sovereignty doctrine. By way of example, the supremacy of EU law conflicts with the canons of parliamentary sovereignty because when the UK was an EU member state, Westminster was constrained by EU law. The 1998 Human Rights Act also challenges the doctrine of parliamentary supremacy by requiring that Westminster laws must, whenever possible, be compatible with the European Convention on Human Rights (ECHR). The asymmetrical devolution of powers to Northern Ireland, Scotland and Wales occasioned a new constitutional convention which dictates that Westminster, though legally permitted, will not normally legislate with regard to devolved matters as this risks undermining the legitimacy of the devolution scheme. In these instances, the supremacy of the British parliament is severely constrained by EU interdependence, human rights commitments and a programme of domestic political decentralisation.

In many ways, the EU referendum was a response and reaction to the ways in which British parliamentary sovereignty was being diluted by the obligations attached to EU membership. For many voters, leaving the EU was conceived as the only way for the British people and their parliament to regain control of national and parliamentary sovereignty. Such a view, that the means to regain sovereignty was to leave the EU and to recoil from the ECHR; however, failed to acknowledge the other ways in which the doctrine of British parliamentary sovereignty was already challenged by internal domestic developments. Bogdanor (2009) has characterised devolution as 'a very radical constitutional reform', one which transformed Britain 'from a unitary state to a quasi-federal state'. In effect, the UK's devolution of powers to constituent units challenges the extent to which Westminster maintains supremacy. As noted by Bogdanor (1999):

> 'It is in constitutional theory alone that the supremacy of Parliament is preserved. Power devolved, far from being power retained, as implied by constitutional theory, will be power transferred, as dictated by political reality; and it will not be possible to recover that power except under pathological circumstances'.

Devolution, therefore, fundamentally restructured the location and exercise of power in UK politics and undermines the extent to which the Westminster parliament is truly sovereign and supreme. This is particularly apparent in relation to Northern Ireland's devolution settlement which is partly a conventional exercise in territorial decentralisation, but more substantially designed to address a highly contested political situation and so incorporates extra-territorial, popular sovereignty and shared sovereignty concepts.

Before Brexit became a reality, Meehan (2014) noted 'despite continuing attachment to the old language of sovereignty, the UK has adapted how it "does" sovereignty in connection with [the EU and] Ireland/Northern Ireland'. Similarly, Todd (2017) determines that the Belfast/Good Friday Agreement, which contains the terms of Northern Ireland's devolution settlement, 'transcended the traditional state-centred meaning of sovereignty'. In line with a historic attachment to the supremacy of Westminster, the UK traditionally rejected any role for Ireland in addressing the Northern Ireland conflict, construing such involvement as interference in the internal affairs of the UK. However, British attitudes to sovereignty in Ireland and Northern Ireland evolved gradually during the conflict, and from the 1970s onwards, successive UK governments began to accommodate an 'Irish dimension' to attempts at resolving the conflict. This took different forms at different times, but at a basic level, it spoke to the UK government's acknowledgement that cooperation with the Republic of Ireland on the vexed issue of achieving peace in Northern Ireland was merited and justified. This morphed into a more determined role for Ireland which was elucidated in various agreements and joint documents. The 1985 Anglo-Irish Agreement heralded a new approach to sovereignty by placing the problem of Northern Ireland 'within a cooperative Anglo-Irish intergovernmental framework' (Tonge 2002, 127). The 1993 Downing Street Declaration and the 1995 Framework Documents signed by the British and Irish governments signalled some relaxation in British government attitudes to Northern Ireland's territorial autonomy by endorsing roles for the Irish government in cooperation with Northern Ireland, the British government and other parts of the UK (see McCall 1999; Meehan 2014). These developments spoke to a less absolutist notion of sovereignty being considered by the UK government vis-à-vis Northern Ireland (Tannam 2001).

The Belfast/Good Friday Agreement built on the foundations contained in previous British-Irish agreements. The 1998 Agreement engages with creative and innovative post-sovereign principles and institutions. In this context, the Agreement is grounded in the principle of consent and incorporates an element of popular sovereignty. The document recognises 'the legitimacy of whatever choice is freely exercised by a majority of the people of Northern Ireland with regard to its status, whether they prefer to continue to support the Union with Great Britain or a sovereign united Ireland' (p. 3). In other words, it is for the people of Northern Ireland to decide the territory's constitutional future. The principle of consent performs two key functions (see Mac Ginty et al. 2001). Firstly, it serves to reassure those who felt threatened by the peace process (namely unionists) that Northern Ireland's constitutional status as part of the UK would not be undermined unless a majority in Northern Ireland favoured change. Given the historic dominance of unionism and unionist representation in Northern Ireland, the principle of consent relieves concerns about the possibility or likelihood of constitutional change. Secondly, by offering the prospect of constitutional change in the future, should circumstances and preferences shift, the principle of consent entices those on the extremes (namely Republicans) into engagement with the peace process. The 1998 Northern Ireland Act gives legal effect to the Belfast/Good Friday Agreement. There, the principle of consent is practically facilitated by a provision in that Act which loosely outlines the criteria for calling a referendum on Irish unity. The Secretary of State for Northern Ireland is enabled to call such a referendum 'if at any time it appears likely to him that a majority of those voting would express a wish that Northern Ireland should cease to be part of the United Kingdom and form part of a united Ireland' (Schedule 1).

Notwithstanding the principle of consent, Hadfield (1998) argues that, in theory, Westminster retains ultimate authority. It would, however, be egregious (in the extreme), following a majority decision in favour of Irish unity, endorsed by referendums in Northern Ireland and Ireland, if the Westminster parliament chose to override and deny the popular wishes of the electorate on the island of Ireland. The exercise of the doctrine of parliamentary sovereignty in such a purist form would pose immense political difficulties and would entail considerable risks in terms of peace and stability. Therefore, although theoretically supreme, in reality, Westminster is, in fact, constrained by the constitutional wishes of the electorate on the island of Ireland. Westminster's sovereignty is therefore qualified and must be exercised in accordance with the 1998 Agreement and its institutions (see O'Leary 2018, 233).

In addition to creating a Northern Ireland Assembly and Executive which operates according to power-sharing principles, the Belfast/Good Friday Agreement also contains a novel set of cross-border and cross-national institutions which bear the hallmarks of a post-sovereign settlement. A North-South Ministerial Council and set of cross-border bodies ostensibly recognise and acknowledge nationalist identification with Ireland by providing executive opportunities for cross-border cooperation on issues of mutual interest. The East-West institutional dimension of the Agreement formalises contact between Ireland, the UK and its constituent units on policy areas of shared concern through the British-Irish Council (although this body does not have executive powers).

Crucially, the Agreement's blurring of sovereign boundaries happened against the backdrop of joint UK and Irish membership of the EU. Although the Agreement makes only minimal explicit reference to the EU, there is an assumption of Irish and UK membership of the Union forming the framework within which the Agreement is situated. By facilitating an open border, cross-border movement and North-South institutions, the EU was supporting the redefinition of relationships across the island of Ireland and between Ireland and the UK which were set out in the Agreement. As Hayward (2020) notes:

> 'the integrative model of sovereignty exemplified in the EU . . . has been fundamental to the Good Friday (Belfast) Agreement of 1998 and, therefore, to the political environment in Northern Ireland. This is why, in the most fundamental terms, a "clean break" Brexit was always impossible when it comes to this small region of the UK'.

By severing the link between the UK and the EU, Brexit removes some of the practical and conceptual framework which supports the invisible border between Northern Ireland and the Republic of Ireland, and so challenges the fundamentals of the UK's existing post-sovereign political architecture in ways which are consequential for Northern Ireland.

The implications for Northern Ireland's constitutional settlement

Attempts to prevent a hard border on the island of Ireland were the key stumbling block throughout the entirety of the UK-EU withdrawal process. Prime Minister Theresa May's failure to win Westminster support for a withdrawal agreement (on three separate occasions) effectively ended her premiership. Her successor Boris Johnson faced similar challenges, but with a larger and more solid parliamentary majority which was not dependent on DUP support following the December 2019 general election, the Prime Minister was able to agree a formula which prevented a hard border on the island of Ireland, but created a *de facto* border between Northern Ireland and the rest of the UK. The Northern Ireland Protocol, agreed between the UK and the EU in October 2019, is a complex arrangement which allows Northern Ireland to remain formally part of the UK's customs territory, but required to apply EU customs rules and align with EU single market provisions (see European Commission, 17 October 2019). This effectively places a customs and regulatory border in the Irish Sea. Moreover, it is a permanent arrangement and not one which is superseded by the UK-EU trading relationship. It means that Northern Ireland will have a different trading relationship with the EU than that which applies for the rest of the UK. Inbuilt to the Protocol arrangement is a 'consent mechanism' which allows the Northern Ireland Assembly the opportunity to vote to either continue or suspend the trade and regulation provisions applicable to Northern Ireland. If the Assembly refuses consent, the possibility of a physical border between Northern Ireland and the Republic of Ireland is reopened.

The terms of the Protocol are deemed by unionism to be constitutionally and economically detrimental to Northern Ireland. Nationalists are also unenthusiastic about the arrangements, although their reservations are linked to their opposition to Brexit outright. Vociferous cross-party objections, and a Northern Ireland Assembly vote (on 20 January 2020), which enjoyed the support of Northern Ireland's five main political parties, withheld consent for the Withdrawal Agreement Bill, but did not prevent its passage through Westminster. The terms of the withdrawal bill, the manner of its achievement and the support it won at the centre was achieved on the back of a complicated relationship between Northern Ireland, the UK and Ireland, and typified by differing interpretations of Brexit and its meaning for UK sovereignty. This is evident in three key ways outlined below. Firstly, Brexit exposes a limited understanding of Northern Ireland in general, and the post-sovereign character of the Belfast/Good Friday Agreement in particular, among the British political elite and more widely. Secondly, the British government's approach to Brexit challenges key features of the UK's devolution settlement by undermining some devolved powers and by exposing the consequences of weak arrangements for intergovernmental cooperation. And thirdly, Brexit has disrupted a key plank of Northern Ireland's peace settlement, the bilateral British-Irish relationship.

British ambivalence

The long and tortuous road to agreement on a Brexit formula which maintains an open border in Ireland demonstrated the extent to which Northern Ireland political interests and concerns were either unknown (in the early phase of withdrawal negotiations) or readily overlooked and side-lined by the UK government (during the final phase). Prime Minister Theresa May's goals for Brexit and the Irish border were based on the UK leaving the single market and customs union, but without the need for infrastructure or checks at the border between Northern Ireland and the Republic of Ireland, or barriers to trade between Northern Ireland and rest of the UK. These goals were essentially incompatible with each other and ultimately unachievable in the absence of special provisions for Northern Ireland. British prescriptions for using technology to maintain an open border on the island of Ireland revealed the limited understanding in British government circles in relation to the political contestedness of the Irish border. As McCall (2018) notes, the use of technology at the border would not mean an invisible border, while border technology itself would likely be vulnerable to destruction for being a regressive marker of division and for being perceived (predominantly by nationalists) as undermining a key achievement of the Belfast/Good Friday Agreement. These British prescriptions for dealing with Northern Ireland's Brexit challenge illustrated a lack of appreciation for the immense sensitivities which attach to the border issue in Ireland. It reflects what Hayward (2020) describes as 'the simplistic [British] understanding of territorial sovereignty behind the Brexitian quest' which limits the space wherein complex understandings and applications of sovereignty, identity and multi-level governance as they pertain to Northern Ireland can be accommodated.

A further example of British ambivalence was demonstrated by Prime Minister Boris Johnson following his signing up to the Protocol in October 2019. Less than one year previously, in a speech to the DUP Annual Conference in Northern Ireland (in November 2018), Johnson promised unionists that he would never contemplate a border in the Irish Sea when he stated: 'no British Conservative government could or should sign up to any such arrangement [which places checks at the Irish Sea border]' (Channel 4 News, 17 October 2019). Within a year however, the depth of his commitment proved malleable when set against mounting pressure from the pro-Brexit wing within the Conservative Party. His political u-turn was widely viewed as 'a betrayal of unionism' (Lowry 2019). This ambivalence intensified further following the publication of the Internal Market Bill on 9 September 2020. The bill included provisions detailing how trade between Great Britain and Northern Ireland would remain barrier-free after the Brexit transition period ended on 31 December 2020. Part 5 of the bill empowered UK ministers 'to prevent the application of, and unilaterally re-interpret and disapply parts of the Protocol, as well as ignore their legal obligations under both domestic and international law to enact the Protocol'. In other words, the bill included express provisions to override the UK's international treaty obligations by not complying with provisions of the Northern Ireland Protocol. According to a spokesperson for the UK Attorney General's Office: 'the Bill is designed to create a legal safety net and is in accordance with principles of parliamentary sovereignty' (Venis 2020). The British government's explicit prioritisation of parliamentary sovereignty clashed not just with the UK's international legal obligations, but also with the assumptions which underpin devolved power in the UK by restricting the legislative powers of the devolved regions in regulating economic activity (see Dougan et al. 2020). Although offending clauses related to the Northern Ireland Protocol were eventually dropped from the bill, the UK Internal Market Act – which came into force on 1 January 2021 – maintains provisions which undermine devolved powers.

The difficulties facing Northern Ireland during the Brexit period are complicated further by apparent British public apathy in relation to Northern Ireland. The complexity of the Irish border issue and the (perceived) intransigence of Northern Ireland political parties frustrated and exasperated many (pro-Brexit) British voters. This translated into weakening support for Northern Ireland's place in the UK. A YouGov (2019) poll illustrates the extent of the disconnect between Northern Ireland and the rest of the UK: 'Given the choice between having their preferred outcome on Brexit and Northern Ireland staying in the Union, a majority of 58% chose the former and only 18% the latter'. A 2020 YouGov poll notes that many British people feel distant from Northern Ireland and 54% would not care if Northern Ireland left the UK.

A desire to reclaim sovereignty subsequent to Brexit has shed light on the existence and extent of British ambivalence towards Northern Ireland at the level of both elite and the general public. The meaning of UK sovereignty in the era of Brexit is based on an apparently narrowing and simplistic conception of the territorial limits of the British state and increasingly ambivalent attitudes in relation to the very parameters of that same state.

Intergovernmental inadequacies

Northern Ireland's ability to influence the withdrawal process was severely constrained by the collapse of Northern Ireland's devolved institutions in January 2017. In the absence of a functioning Northern Ireland Assembly, Northern Ireland lost a forum wherein discussion of Brexit might have taken place between the various political parties. Northern Ireland, however, was not alone in being unable to influence the UK's withdrawal negotiations. The Scottish and Welsh devolved units expressed serious frustration with the lack of opportunities and gateways for inputting to the UK negotiation process and for limiting the hollowing out of devolved powers which materialised in the Internal Market Act (2020). In these ways, Brexit brought the weaknesses of the UK's devolution settlement into sharp focus and 'created new tensions between the UK government and the devolved administrations' (Greer 2018, 136). Despite the use of the Joint Ministerial Committee (JMC) mechanism, which brought together representatives from central government and the devolved units, the UK's asymmetrical devolution arrangement never fully accommodated voices and input from the UK's constituent units. Although this was particularly problematic for Northern Ireland which – owing to the collapse of devolved institutions there – was unable to participate (or even agree a detailed shared position on how to prevent a border on the island of Ireland), it was also challenging for the Scottish and Welsh devolved units who perceived that their voices and perspectives were not being adequately heard. In effect, the more coherent national positions developed by the Scottish and Welsh were stymied by the underdevelopment of the UK's arrangements for intergovernmental relations (see McEwen et al. 2020).

The weaknesses of the intergovernmental system pre-dated Brexit, but its inadequacies and flimsiness were illuminated by the EU referendum result. Territorially different referendum outcomes and emerging differences as to what form Brexit should take produced deepening tensions between central government and the devolved units. Devolved units are effectively caught in a clash between Brexit and the more traditional conception of national sovereignty which characterises it, and the reality of the devolved system which inherently challenges (and diminishes) those older sovereignty doctrines.

Bilateral tensions

The Northern Ireland peace process was built on the back of close British-Irish cooperation (see Tannam 2001). The provisions set out in the 1998 Belfast/Good Friday Agreement accommodate formal cooperation between the two states on issues related to Northern Ireland. This provision departs from the UK's historic adherence to the traditional tenets of national sovereignty by institutionalising an approach to Northern Ireland which encompassed elements of shared sovereignty including, for example, North-South institutions. The transformation in British–Irish relations during this period facilitated a progressive deepening of a previously strained political relationship and helped to sustain the peace process during troubled periods after 1998. The sense that historic enmity between the two states had been overcome and replaced with respect was deeply felt (although arguably moreso in Ireland). The strength and depth of that relationship, however, was challenged during the EU referendum campaign, and following the vote, relations between the two neighbouring states were unsettled as both embarked on different future trajectories – one inside the EU, the other outside (see O'Brennan 2019). Marked differences about how to maintain an open border on the island of Ireland created tensions between the two governments to the point where: 'the assumption that there is long-term robust mutual trust between both governments and predictability in the relationship has greatly weakened' (Tannam 2020). The notion of a shared future based on a shared approach to Northern Ireland no longer holds fast following the UK exit from the EU. The disparities between the two governments centred not just on the detail of the Brexit negotiations, but also reflected differences in terms of respective British and Irish interpretations of the Irish border issue, prescriptions for maintaining an open border on the island, and distinct British and Irish perspectives on the exercise of the shared sovereignty provisions contained in the Belfast/Good Friday Agreement.

Brexit begs questions about the nature and depth of altered British-Irish relations and how the relationship can be maintained and nurtured post-Brexit. Keeping the border open between north and south demonstrates some continuing acceptance of a shared sovereignty framework. However, the relationship has been fractured (at least temporarily) not just by the decision and act of the UK leaving the EU, but also by an altered perspective on UK national sovereignty which does not fully accommodate the post-sovereign framework within which Northern Ireland's stability is situated. In the aftermath of Brexit, the Irish government has signalled its support for re-energising and reinvigorating British-Irish relations by engaging more deliberately and effectively with the institutions created by the Belfast/Good Friday Agreement (see Irish Government 2020). The British government, however, appears less enthusiastic than their Irish counterparts in terms of engagement with the British-Irish Council (see Murphy

2018, 107) and is more circumspect in its commitment to British-Irish cooperation. Vocal support for enhanced cooperation post-Brexit, as expressed by Prime Minister Boris Johnson (*Belfast Telegraph*, 13 August 2020), has not been matched by more weighty UK proposals for developing the British-Irish relationship. In effect, Brexit's attempt to recapture British sovereignty jars with a bilateral relationship which challenges the fundamentals of that same sovereignty model.

Conclusion

The rupture which Brexit has occasioned in UK politics has had far-reaching consequences for Northern Ireland including economic upheaval, political instability, and constitutional uncertainty. These developments are taking place within the context of a wider process of dislocation and reconfiguration of the British political order related in substantial part to altered conceptions of British national and parliamentary sovereignty. The Irish dimension and the Irish border dilemma are both the driver and potentially the casualty of this Brexit-related rupture.

Brexit lends new significance to old arguments around borders, identity and sovereignty, and is feeding the forces of contestation and change in Northern Ireland. The EU referendum vote and the tortuous attempts to extract the UK from the EU revealed a pronounced disconnect between Northern Ireland and the rest of the UK where difficulties in acknowledging and accommodating the distinctiveness of Northern Ireland's situation and its peace settlement were encountered. Brexit highlights the limited knowledge and appreciation at the UK centre of highly politicised and contested issues with direct ramifications for different territories within the UK, and indeed for the British state itself. Relatedly, Brexit heralds in a period of political and constitutional instability for the UK polity. This is evident in relation to increased support for Scottish independence and an emerging conversation around Irish unity (see McEwen and Murphy forthcoming 2021). For Northern Ireland, the prospect of Irish unity would be constitutionally transformative and profound and may usher in a period of political instability and volatility.

A harking back to traditional conceptions of sovereignty which are not entirely compatible with a system of asymmetrical devolution, and more particularly with the post sovereign and shared sovereignty dimensions of Northern Ireland's political architecture, has complicated the UK's post-Brexit political situation. The changes and challenges unleashed by Brexit in Northern Ireland touch on some very fundamental considerations about how Northern Ireland is understood as a component and constituent part of the UK, and about how it is simultaneously accommodated by a system of devolution which is vulnerable to altered constructions of sovereignty. The outworking of these dynamics confronts not just Northern Ireland, but the UK as a whole, with fundamental questions about what model of sovereignty accommodates future constitutional stability. For Northern Ireland, Brexit is no longer solely about the UK's future outside the EU, it is also about Northern Ireland's place within a UK whose sovereign and constitutional moorings are being transformed.

Note

1. See for example Irish Ambassador to the UK, Daniel Mulhall's speech 'An Irish perspective on the UK's EU referendum', Liverpool Hope University, 20 April 2016.

Disclosure statement

No potential conflict of interest was reported by the author.

Funding

This work was supported by the Economic and Social Research Council [ES/P009441/1].

References

10 Downing Street. 2017. *Letter from Prime Minister Theresa May to President of the European Council Donald Tusk*, March 29. https://assets.publishing.service.gov.uk/government/uploads/system/uploads/attachment_data/file/604079/Prime_Ministers_letter_to_European_Council_President_Donald_Tusk.pdf

Agnew, J. 2020. "Taking back control: The myth of territorial sovereignty and the Brexit fiasco." Territory, Politics, Governance 8 (2): 259–272

Armstrong, C. I., D. Herbert, and J. E. Mustad, eds. 2019. *The Legacy of the Good Friday Agreement*. Basingstoke: Palgrave.

Aughey, A., and C. Gormley-Heenan. 2017. "Northern Ireland and Brexit: Three Effects on the "The Border in the Mind"." *The British Journal of Politics and International Relations* 19 (3): 497–511.

Birrell, D., and D. Heenan. 2017. "The Continuing Volatility of Devolution in Northern Ireland: The Shadow of Direct Rule." *The Political Quarterly* 88 (3): 473–479.

Birrell, D., and D. Heenan. 2020. "The Confidence and Supply Agreement between the Conservative Party and the Democratic Unionist Party: Implications for the Barnett Formula and Intergovernmental Relations in the UK." *Parliamentary Affairs* 73: 586–602.

Bogdanor, V. 1999. "Devolution: Decentralisation or Disintegration?" *The Political Quarterly* 70 (2): 185–194.

Bogdanor, V. 2009. *The New British Constitution*. Oxford: Hart Publishing.

'Boris Johnson promises to develop Britain's relationship with Ireland'. *Belfast Telegraph*, August 13, 2020. https://www.belfasttelegraph.co.uk/news/northern-ireland/boris-johnson-promises-to-develop-britains-relationship-with-ireland-39447284.html

Burke Wood, P., and M. Gilmartin. 2020. "Irish Enough: Changing Narratives of Citizenship and National Identity in the Context of Brexit." In *Brexit Geographies*, edited by M. Boyle, R. Paddison, and P. Shirlow. London: Routledge.

Channel 4 News. 2019. 'Boris Johnson Speaks at the DUP Conference in 2018."https://www.facebook.com/Channel4News/videos/boris-johnson-speaks-at-the-dup-conference-in-2018/2490329994585799/

Connelly, T. 2018. Brexit and Ireland: The dangers, the opportunities and the inside story of the Irish response. London: Penguin

Darby, J. 1976. "Conflict in Northern Ireland: A Background Essay." In *Facets of the Conflict in Northern Ireland*, edited by S. Dunn. Basingstoke: Macmillan Press Limited.

Dicey, A.V. 1996. An introduction to the study of the law of the constitution (8th edition) Basingstoke: Macmillan

Dougan, M. 2020. *UK Internal Market Bill: Devolution and the Union*. Edinburgh: Centre on Constitutional Change https://www.centreonconstitutionalchange.ac.uk/sites/default/files/2020-10/UK%20INTERNAL%20MARKET%20BILL%2C%20DEVOLUTION%20AND%20THE%20UNION%20%282%29_0.pdf

Economic and Social Research Institute (ESRI). 2015. *Scoping the Possible Economic implications of Brexit on Ireland*, November. https://www.esri.ie/pubs/RS48.pdf

Elliott, M. 2004. "United Kingdom: Parliamentary Sovereignty under Pressure." *International Journal of Constitutional Law* 2 (3): 545–554.

European Commission. 2019. *Protocol on Ireland/Northern Ireland*, TF50 (2019) 64, October 17. https://ec.europa.eu/commission/sites/beta-political/files/revised_withdrawal_agreement_including_protocol_on_ireland_and_nothern_ireland.pdf

Garry, J. 2017. "'The EU Referendum Vote in Northern Ireland: Implications for Our Understanding of Citizens' Political Views and Behaviour'." *Northern Ireland Assembly Knowledge Exchange Seminar Series*.https://www.qub.ac.uk/brexit/Brexitfilestore/Filetoupload,728121,en.pdf

Geddes, A. 2013. *Britain and the European Union*. Basingstoke: Palgrave.

Glencross, A. 2016. *Why the UK Voted for Brexit: David Cameron's Great Miscalculation*. Basingstoke: Palgrave.

Gordon, M. 2016. "The UK's Sovereignty Situation: Brexit, Bewilderment and beyond . . . ." *King's Law Journal* 27 (3): 333–343.

Gray, A.-M., J. Hamilton, G. Kelly, B. Lynn, M. Melaugh, and G. Robinson 2019. *Northern Ireland Peace Monitoring Report* (No. 5). Belfast: Community Relations Council. https://www.community-relations.org.uk/sites/crc/files/media-files/NIPMR%205%20%282%29%20new%20version.pdf

Greer, A. 2018. "Brexit and devolution." The Political Quarterly 89 (1): 134–138

Hadfield, B. 1998. "The Belfast Agreement, Sovereignty and the State of the Union." *Public Law* Winter: 599–616.

Hall, A. 2018. "Incomplete Peace and Social Stagnation: Shortcomings of the Good Friday Agreement." *Open Library of the Humanities* 4 (2): 1–31. doi:10.16995/olh.251.

Hayward, K. 2018. "The Pivotal Position of the Irish Border in the UK's Withdrawal from the European Union." *Space and Polity* 22 (2): 238–254.

Hayward, K. 2020. "Why It Is Impossible for Brexit Britain to "Take Back Control" in Northern Ireland." *Territory, Politics, Governance* 8 (2): 273–278.

Hayward, K., and M. C. Murphy. 2012. "The (Soft) Power of Commitment: The EU and Conflict Resolution in Northern Ireland." *Ethnopolitics* 11 (4): 439–452.

Hayward, K., and M. C. Murphy. 2018. "The EU's Influence on the Peace Process and Agreement in Northern Ireland in Light of Brexit." *Ethnopolitics* 17 (3): 276–291.

Henderson, A., C. Jeffery, D. Wincott, and R. Wyn Jones. 2017. "How Brexit Was Made in England." *The British Journal of Politics and International Relations* 19 (4): 631–646.

Irish Government. 2020. *Programme for Government: Our Shared Future*. Dublin: Irish Government.

Lowry, B. 2019. "As DUP Meets Today, the Full Scale of Boris Johnson's Betrayal of Unionism Is Still Only Sinking In." *Belfast Newsletter*, October 26. https://www.newsletter.co.uk/news/opinion/ben-lowry-dup-meets-today-full-scale-boris-johnsons-betrayal-unionism-still-only-sinking-928973.

Mac Ginty, R., R. Wilford, L. Dowds and G. Robinson. 2001. "Consenting adults: The principle of consent and Northern Ireland's constitutional future." Government and Opposition 36 (4): 472–492

Matthews, N., and J. Pow. 2020. "The Politics of Northern Ireland." In *The Routledge Handbook of British Politics and Society*, edited by M. Garnett. London: Routledge.

May, T. 2017. "The Government's Negotiating Objectives for Exiting the EU: PM Speech' [Lancaster House Speech]". https://www.gov.uk/government/speeches/the-governments-negotiating-objectives-for-exiting-the-eu-pm-speech

McCain, G., and P. Hainsworth. 2017. "Brexit and Northern Ireland: The 2016 Referendum on the United Kingdom's Membership of the European Union." *Irish Political Studies* 32 (2): 327–342.

McCall, C. 1999. *Identity in Northern Ireland: Communities, Politics and Change*. Basingstoke: Macmillan.

McCall, C. 2018. "Brexit, Bordering and Bodies on the Island of Ireland." *Ethnopolitics* 17 (3): 292–305.

McEwen, N., M. Kenny, J. Sheldon, and C. Brown Swan 2020. "Intergovernmental Relations in the UK: Time for a Radical Overhaul?" *The Political Quarterly*. (early access).

McEwen, N., and M. C. Murphy. 2021. "Brexit and the Union: Territorial Voice, Exit and Re-entry Strategies in Scotland and Northern Ireland after EU Exit." *International Political Science Review*. forthcoming.

Meehan, E. 2014. "The Changing British–Irish Relationship: The Sovereignty Dimension." *Irish Political Studies* 29 (1): 58–75.

Mulhall, D. 2016. *'An Irish perspective on the UK's EU referendum'*, April 20. Speech at Liverpool Hope University. https://www.dfa.ie/irish-embassy/great-britain/news-and-events/2016/an-irish-perspective-on-the-uks-eu-referendum/

Murphy, M. C. 2016. "The EU Referendum in Northern Ireland: Closing Borders, Re-Opening Border Debates." *Journal of Contemporary European Research* 12 (4): 844–853.

Murphy, M. C. 2018. *Europe and Northern Ireland's Future: Negotiating Brexit's Unique Case*. Newcastle-upon-Tyne: Agenda Publishing.

Murphy, M. C., and J. Evershed. 2020. "Between the Devil and the DUP: The Democratic Unionist Party and the Politics of Brexit." *British Politics* 15 (4): 456–477. c.

Northern Ireland Executive. 2016. *Letter to Prime Minister Theresa May*, August 10. https://www.executiveoffice-ni.gov.uk/sites/default/files/publications/execoffice/Letter%20to%20PM%20from%20FM%20%26%20dFM.pdf

O'Brennan, J. 2019. "Requiem for a Shared Interdependent Past: Brexit and the Deterioration in UK-Irish Relations." *Capital and Class* 43 (1): 157–171.

O'Leary, B. 2018. "The Twilight of the United Kingdom & Tiocfaidh Ár Lá: Twenty Years after the Good Friday Agreement." *Ethnopolitics* 17 (3): 223–242.

O'Rourke, K. 2019. *A Short History of Brexit: From Brentry to Backstop*. London: Pelican.

Open University Business School and Northern Ireland Assembly. 2015. *The Consequences for the Northern Ireland Economy from a United Kingdom Exit from the European Union*, Briefing Note: CETI/OU, 2/15, March.

Oxford Economics. 2016. *Assessing the Economic Implications of Brexit: Executive Summary*. Oxford: Oxford Economics Limited.

Racioppi, L., and K. O'Sullivan See. 2007. "Grassroots Peace-building and Third-party Intervention: The European Union's Special Support Programme for Peace and Reconciliation in Northern Ireland'." *Peace and Change* 32 (3): 361–390.

Sandford, M., and C. Gormley-Heenan. 2020. ""Taking Back Control", the UK's Constitutional Narrative and Schrodinger's Devolution." *Parliamentary Affairs* 73 (1): 108–126.

Smithey, L. 2011. *Unionists, Loyalists and Conflict Transformation in Northern Ireland*. Oxford: Oxford University Press.

Tannam, E. 2001. "Explaining the Good Friday Agreement: A Learning Process." *Government and Opposition* 36 (4): 493–518.

Tannam, E. 2020 "From Anglo-Irish to British-Irish Relations: What's Next?" LSE Blog, February 6. https://blogs.lse.ac.uk/brexit/2020/02/26/long-read-from-anglo-irish-to-british-irish-relations-whats-next/

Taylor, R. 2008. "The Belfast Agreement and the Limits of Consociationalism." In *Global Change, Civil Society and the Northern Ireland Peace Process: Implementing the Political Sentiment*, edited by C. Farrington, 183–198. London: Palgrave Macmillan.

Todd, J. 2017. "'Contested Constitutionalism: Northern Ireland and the British-Irish Relationship since 2010'." *Parliamentary Affairs* 70 (2): 301–321.

Tonge, J. 2002. *Northern Ireland: Conflict and Change*. 2nd ed. Essex: Pearson.

Tonge, J. 2017. "Supplying Confidence or Trouble? the Deal between the Democratic Unionist Party and the Conservative Party." *The Political Quarterly* 88 (3): 412–416.

Venis, J. 2020. *'Internal Market Bill prompts questions on UK's commitment to rule of law'* October1. International Bar Association. https://www.ibanet.org/Article/NewDetail.aspx?ArticleUid=9BAF06E8-251F-4DFF-B6D5-504D9555CAD8

Wincott, D. 2018. "Brexit and the State of the United Kingdom." In *The Routledge Handbook of the Politics of Brexit*, edited by P. Diamond, P. Nedergaard and B. Rosamond, 15–26. London: Routledge.

YouGov. 2019. "Four in Ten Mainland Britons Don't Care about Northern Ireland." November 11. https://yougov.co.uk/topics/politics/articles-reports/2019/11/11/four-ten-mainland-britons-dont-care-about-northern

Disintegration reversed: Brexit and the cohesiveness of the EU27

Thierry Chopin and Christian Lequesne

ABSTRACT

This contribution analyses the political impact of Brexit on the EU27. The main argument is that Brexit is not just about disintegration. The UK policy proposals on Brexit have reinforced among the governments, public opinions and even Eurosceptic parties of the EU27 the cohesiveness in favour of the preservation of European integration. The article is divided into four parts. First, it presents a critical review of the theoretical literature on EU disintegration and defines the concept of cohesiveness. In the second section, it analyses why the EU27 member states remained cohesive during the Brexit negotiation talks on major policy issues such as the Single Market, free movement of persons and budgetary contribution. In the third section, the article explains why Brexit did not succeed to convince the public opinions of the EU27 that leaving the EU was a relevant issue. In the fourth section, it analyses the reasons why Eurosceptic parties (especially right wing ones) within the EU27 started using Brexit as a strategic argument against EU integration but quickly abandoned it in favour of the request that EU must be changed from inside.

Introduction

Until the coming into force of the Treaty of Lisbon on 1 December 2009, there was no procedure in the EU treaties allowing a member state to leave the EU and renationalize entirely its policies. Demands for exit never concretely happened, even if Algeria in 1962 and Greenland in 1985 quit the European Communities as the first left France and the second became more detached from Denmark (Patel 2018). The Treaty of Lisbon introduced article 50 in the Treaty on the European Union. It states that 'any member state may decide to withdraw from the Union in accordance with its own constitutional requirements'. There are reasons why such a provision on exit was introduced so lately in the EU treaties. For five decades, national politicians considered the EU as a polity that evolves through crises (sometimes severe ones) and requires differentiation to accommodate diversity among the member states, but never abandoned the teleological goal of having more 'integration' (Saurugger 2013). It is with the rise of Eurosceptic parties in the 2000s (Lecomte 2010) that some national politicians, at the edge of the political spectrum, started contemplating the possibility for a Member State to give up its membership and renationalize entirely its policymaking. Such a scenario became a reality with the UK referendum on Brexit on 23 June 2016, in which 51.9% of the British citizens supported exit from the EU (Evans and Menon 2019). With Brexit, national politicians started seeing the EU not from the sole perspective of 'integration' between the member states, but also with the perspective of 'disintegration'.

If Brexit can effectively be considered as a form of disintegration, this article shows that looking at the EU27 member states shows a paradoxical effect of Brexit, which is a movement towards cohesiveness to preserve integration. To demonstrate this thesis, the article proceeds in four parts. First, it presents a critical review of the theoretical literature on EU disintegration and defines the concept of cohesiveness. Second, it demonstrates empirically how the EU27 governments remained cohesive during the Brexit negotiation talks on major issues such as the Single Market, free movement of people and EU budgetary arrangements. Third, the article explains why Brexit did not contribute to a rise of Euroscepticism among the public opinions of the EU27 member states. Finally, it analyses the reasons for which Eurosceptic parties (especially right-wing ones) in the EU27, considering the serious difficulties to decide on Brexit in the UK, abandoned in their programmes the proposal to leave the EU. The article concludes by taking the view that Brexit does not necessarily imply disintegration and break-up of the EU but also the preservation of integration.

Brexit, disintegration and cohesiveness

Scholarly research has followed a similar path than political debate regarding the study of the EU. From the 1950s to the 2010s, the theoretical literature, both in international relations and comparative politics, focused on the concept of European 'integration', postulating that the EU was a process of convergence between the policies, politics and polities of its member states (Bulmer and Lequesne 2013). Differentiation between the member states was taken more seriously into account from the 1990s onwards (Leuffen, Rittberger, and Schimmelfennig 2013), but without upsetting the concept of 'integration', with only a few exceptions (Vollaard 2014; Webber 2014). While the British referendum on Brexit opened the concrete possibility for a member state to leave the EU, scholars activated the new concept of 'disintegration' and questioned more in-depth the relevance of the existing EU theories to understand such a perspective (Webber 2019a, 2019b).

In his book, Douglas Webber identifies three forms of political disintegration in the EU (Webber 2019a, 2019b). Sectoral disintegration equates to the reduction of issue areas in which the EU exercises policy-making competences. Vertical political disintegration concerns the reduction of the formal (i.e. treaty-based) competences and effective authority of the EU's supranational political organs vis-à-vis the intergovernmental institutions and/or those of the member states. Finally, horizontal political disintegration corresponds to a decrease of membership with one or several member state(s) leaving the EU (Webber 2019a, 14). If Webber's multidimensional definition of political disintegration of the EU is inspiring, it also provides a certain risk of confusion with preexisting concepts. For instance, sectoral political disintegration in Webber's terms is close to the definition of differentiation, except that scholars of differentiated integration often discuss the effects of differentiation on the continuity of European integration and do not really deal with disintegration (Leuffen, Rittberger, and Schimmelfennig 2013). In Webber's terms, vertical political disintegration can also be confused with intergovernmental cooperation, even if the definition also captures situations where the member states pursue their own, unilateral policies. In this article, disintegration will be defined in the restrictive sense of the retreat of a member state from the EU and, as a consequence, the re-nationalization of its policies and polity. We consider disintegration as the result of a process where a state exits completely from the EU and assumes that it will not be submitted anymore to the power of the EU institutions and EU policies. In this situation, the classic distinction made by Tanja Börzel between 'scope' and 'level' in political integration becomes a non-issue (Börzel 2005).

Our analysis will also demonstrate that the withdrawal of the UK from the EU has reinforced cohesiveness among the 27 remaining member states to preserve the political *acquis* of European integration. Cohesiveness is a common concept in the psychology literature, where it is defined as 'the resultant forces, which are acting on the members to stay as a group' (Festinger 1950, 274). In the EU context, it has been mostly used to capture the effectiveness of the EU on the external scene by being united internally. In their introduction to a special issue on the EU in global governance, Eugenia Conceição-Heidt and Sophie Meunier define cohesiveness as a concept to measure 'the resistance of the members to leave the group, their willingness to coordinate their efforts, and their overall level of team spirit' (Conceição-Heidt and Meunier 2014, 964). It is this meaning that we are retaining to show the resistance of the EU27 vis-à-vis a number of British policy proposals which could alter the functioning of EU integration during the Brexit negotiation talks.

The theoretical argument to explain the cohesiveness of EU 27 is grounded in Hans Vollaard's work (Vollaard 2014, 2018). This work reminds us that European integration is first of all 'a process of boundary re-definition: state boundaries are transcended, while the boundaries of the EU are constructed'. Disintegration can 'subsequently be described in opposite terms. A polity is disintegrating when there is a weakening in boundary control' (Vollaard 2014, 8). According to Vollaard, the three main challenges which can lead to disintegration are: first, European integration would face continued dissatisfaction, in particular, because of the growing gap between the citizens who access the benefits of European integration and those who consider themselves to be the losers; second, an unsufficient political democratization and institutionalization undermine a strong political structure at European level in the absence of post-national politicization; and third, the EU defense and foreign policy remains weak to cope with external challenges.

In such a context, the decision to leave the EU was possible in the UK only because a majority of British citizens expressed in a referendum their belief in credible national alternatives to EU membership. We can mention three of these alternatives: all Brexiteers desired a return to a full control of the national parliament on policies; neoliberal Brexiteers wanted a move towards a Global Britain and a Singapore-upon-Thames economic model; left-wing Brexiteers wished a return to a Welfare State based on an increased national budget (Evans and Menon 2019). But there is a British idiosyncrasy regarding the belief in national alternatives to EU boundaries. In all EU 27, no government is prepared to accept a reorganization of the polity, policies and politics around purely national boundaries. For this reason, Brexit has been a cohesive incentive in the 27 member states to preserve the existing EU and, accordingly, European integration.

Governmental cohesiveness in Brexit negotiation talks

The Brexit negotiations between the UK and the EU27, under the provisions of article 50 TEU, took place from June 2017 to November 2018. This section focuses on this 18 month-period of negotiations while the 27-member states were represented by a plenipotentiary negotiator, Michel Barnier, a former French minister and EU commissioner, who got his mandate approved by the 27 member states on 22 May 2017 (Toute l'Europe 2019). If Michel Barnier worked with an ad hoc team composed of Commission staff, his negotiating positions were supervised during the whole process by the governments of the 27 member states to which he was accountable. Michel Barnier, who had to deal with three different UK chief negotiators during a period of 18 months, did not define his positions in total autonomy. He was constrained by the positions expressed on a regular basis in the European Council, the 'General Affairs' Council of Ministers, and the Committee of Permanent Representatives (COREPER) (Jacobs 2018).

The preferences of the 27 member states during the negotiations can be identified through positions, declarations and speeches made by national ministers and officials. There is only a small body of academic literature on these member states' preferences to Brexit (Kassim and Usherwood 2018; Martill and Staiger 2018). This section will mostly refer to the documented country case studies published in Kassim and Usherwood's research on the EU27 reactions to Brexit.

If all 27 member states expressed regrets after the UK government's decision in March 2017 to activate article 50 TEU, more concerns could be expected from some member states than others, because they were politically close to the UK on EU issues. We focus on these member states to demonstrate that political closeness with the UK did not impact the cohesiveness of member states' preferences regarding Brexit. Political closeness is defined by means of two criteria: (i) interest and (ii) ideology. Interest closeness refers to the high degree of economic exchanges and/or public policies that a member state shares with the UK. Ideological closeness refers to a shared macroview on the future of EU polity and/or the process of European integration.

On the interest side, Ireland, Denmark, the Netherlands and Poland, but also Germany, had an history of political closeness with the UK inside the EU. The UK is Ireland's third partner for export sales (Laffan 2018), the Netherlands' third biggest trade partner (UK Government 2018) and the second-trade partner of Poland after Germany, absorbing 7% of the Polish sales in 2017 (Styczynska 2018). In Denmark, experts consider that Brexit could represent a loss of 0.5 to 2% of the GDP due to the dynamic economic exchanges (Dagnis Jensen and Dahl Kelstrup 2018), while in Germany, Brexit is mostly perceived by the CDU-CSU/SPD coalition government as the loss of a close partner in EU negotiations dealing with internal market and trade policy issues (Heidbreder 2018).

On the ideological side, Central European member states such as the Czech Republic, Poland and Hungary, since they joined the EU in 2004, have seen in the UK a political guarantor to balance the power of the Franco-German tandem in the EU (Turner and Green 2017; Kaniok 2018; Krotz and Schild 2018). The balancing function of the UK has been perceived in the same way in Denmark and Sweden, which remain outside the Eurozone (Dagnis Jensen and Dahl Kelstrup 2018; Braun 2018). In Poland and Hungary, the minimal engagement of the UK regarding European integration has also been considered by the right-wing conservative leaders, such as Kaczynski and Orban, as a useful limit to the evolution of the EU towards more supranational decision-making procedures (Styczynska 2018; Csehi 2018).

These two forms of political closeness – interests-based and ideology-based- with the UK could have led these member states to accept generous concessions during the Brexit negotiation talks. But it is not at all what happened. The EU27 member states remained cohesive on setting red lines to UK demands, making Michel Barnier's task easier than the British negotiators first expected. Three issues on which the preferences of the EU27 showed cohesiveness vis-à-vis the British demands are: (i) the internal market and customs union, including the management of the Irish border; (ii) the free movement of persons; (iii) the British budgetary contribution.

On the internal market and customs union issues, it appeared after Theresa May's speech at Lancaster House in January 2017 that the UK government did not want to stay in both frameworks. The Norwegian or Swiss models consisting in implementing the Single Market rules without being an EU member state were ruled out by the British Prime Minister (May 2017). A major problem happened immediately regarding the relationship of Northern Ireland to the Republic of Ireland in the absence of a hard border. In her Lancaster House speech, Prime Minister May said that 'the United Kindgom will share a land border with the EU, and maintaining that Common Travel Area with the Republic of Ireland will be an important priority for the UK in the talks ahead' (May 2017). For the EU27 governments, a logical question ensued from the British Prime Minister's proposal: how to have border-free traffic between Northern Ireland and the Republic of Ireland if the former (a constitutive unit of the UK) leaves the EU Single Market and the Customs Union? The Irish border soon became the hot potato of the Brexit talks. During the negotiation rounds, the British delegation tried to downplay the problem by proposing various technological means of control – most of them to be invented – to avoid the re-establishment of a hard border. But the EU27 governments considered that there was no alternative to the reestablishment of a hard border, because accepting derogation would immediately open a breach in the integrity of the Single Market. Whatever their previous political closeness to the UK, the EU27 governments showed cohesiveness on the question of the Irish border, which contributed to the so-called 'Irish backstop' solution. As Michel Barnier's proposals to keep Northern Ireland entirely in the Single Market or to establish customs border controls between the two islands were first not acceptable for the British government, it was decided in the November 2018 Withdrawal Agreement that the UK as a whole would stay in the EU customs union until a new decision has been taken, forming with the EU a single customs territory (Withdrawal Agreement and Political Declaration 2018). This compromise, which avoided a need for tariffs, quotas and checks on rules of origin between the EU and the UK, became a controversial reason for the hard-line Brexiteers in the Conservative Party (notably the European Reform Group) to reject the EU-UK deal at the House of Commons. But it also showed that the EU27 governments preferred remaining cohesive on the functioning of the EU internal market and the customs union than accepting the break-up proposed by the UK.

Free movement of persons was the second element of the Brexit negotiation talks on which the EU27 governments showed cohesiveness. According to the United Nations and UK National Office of Statistics, 1.3 million British citizens lived and worked in the EU27 member states (mostly in Spain, France and Germany), while 3.8 million EU27 citizens (mostly from Poland and Ireland, but also Italy and France) lived and worked in the UK (*Financial Times* 4 November, 2018; Full Fact 2019). As the issue of reducing migration in general, and intra-EU migration in particular, were presented as priorities by the Brexiteers during the referendum campaign, EU27 governments worried about the future of their citizens in the UK. In Poland, the main issue of Brexit discussed in bilateral exchanges between the Polish Prime ministers and the UK Prime Minister during the Brexit talks was the rights of the Polish citizens (estimated between 700,000 and 900,000 in 2017) to stay and work in the UK (Styczynska 2018). In Czech Republic, the government rejected during the negotiation 'any attempt to limit free movement of people' (Kaniok 2018, 43). In Italy, 'the preservation of the rights for Italian citizens living in the UK' was also essential (Brunazzo and Dela Salla 2018, 35). All governments, whatever their previous political closeness with the UK supported a strong protection of the rights of the 3.8 million EU citizens living in the UK and a strict reciprocity of treatment between their citizens in the UK and the UK citizens in their countries. On this issue as well, the EU27 governments showed cohesiveness based on preserving the *acquis* of free movement of persons. There was no breach consisting in accepting flexible demands from the UK during the negotiation talks.

Regarding British budgetary contribution, the 27 member-states agreed that the UK must pay a budgetary compensation to the EU in order to respect its previous commitments to the EU policies. This issue was particularly controversial on the British domestic scene, especially among hard Brexiteers from the Conservative Party and UKIP. Again, the debates in the member states traditionally close to the UK are relevant to analyse. In the Netherlands, the UK's possible refusal to pay opened a debate about refusing the increase in the Dutch contribution to the EU budget, as the country was already an important net contributor (DutchNews.nl 2018). The same concerns emerged in France, Germany and Sweden, while in Poland and Lithuania–net beneficiaries to the EU budget- safeguarding a generous funding from the EU was the issue at stake (Styczynska 2018; Vilpisauskas 2018).

Three conclusions can be drawn from the preferences of the EU27 governments in the Brexit negotiations, in particular, if we look at the member states which had been close to the UK inside the EU. First, ideology was never a sufficient criterion among the EU27 governments to grant concessions to the UK. The British government was not able to use Brexit as an ideological argument to obtain concessions in the negotiations, including from Eurosceptic governments such as in Poland and Hungary. Past relations with the UK did not influence the preferences of the EU27 governments on the Single-market rules, free movement of persons and budgetary contribution. The rhetorical game consisting in linking Brexit to a strong critic of the EU (as Orban or Kaczynski are used to do) did not fit with the game consisting in preserving the economic interests provided by the EU. Second, and as a consequence of the first conclusion, rational economic interest matter for the EU27 governments and explain their cohesiveness to preserve the Single Market rules, free movement of persons and budgetary arrangements. Third, if Brexit corresponds to disintegration according to our definition, the EU27 governments reaffirmed their commitment to integration through their cohesiveness in the negotiation talks. They demonstrated that they did not agree with a reverse movement of their political boundaries from the EU to the exclusive nation-state.

The counter-incentive of Brexit on EU27 public opinions

This section focuses on the impact that Brexit had on the public opinions of EU27. In *Exit, Voice and Loyalty*, Albert Hirschman distinguishes between two alternative modes for citizens to express dissatisfaction with organizations: 'exit' which consists in leaving the organization, and 'voice' which consists in claiming dissatisfaction with the aim of influencing and changing the organisation. 'Loyalty' may delay the expression of dissatisfaction and affect the choice between 'exit' and 'voice' (Hirschmann 1970). In the late 2000s, academic literature introduced a typology distinguishing between 'soft' Euroscepticism and 'hard' Euroscepticism in order to differentiate protest from outright rejection taking the form of Europhobia (Szczerbiak and Taggart 2008). In the first case, Euroscepticism consists in accepting the principle of European integration, while criticising EU policies; in the second case, Euroscepticism consists in rejecting membership to the EU and supporting leave.

In the literature, three approaches explain the attitude of public opinions towards Euroscepticism. First, a utilitarian and economic approach (cost/benefit calculation) shows that citizens with low human capital, such as education and income, tend to reject European economic integration and the Single Market (Gabel 1998). Second, studies on identity stress that citizens with an exclusive attachment to their nation-state are more likely to be Eurosceptic (Mc Laren 2002). Third, the 'cue theory' focusses on the importance of political mediation (Hooghe and Marks 2005); it considers the EU as an integral part of national policies and assumes that political attitudes towards the EU are influenced by national political institutions. In other words, elites and political parties at the national level mediate the way public opinion perceives the EU. In this perspective, while the mainstream parties provide positive cues towards the EU, the far-left and far-right parties generally show a Eurosceptic attitude (De Vries and Edwards 2009).

These different approaches are useful to understand public attitudes towards the EU and Euroscepticism. However, they do not provide a full analysis of how the outcome of the referendum on Brexit has impacted public opinions in the EU27. As De Vries wrote, 'public opinion towards the EU is best understood with reference to benchmarks' and the 'benchmarck theory suggests that people's attitudes towards Europe are ultimately rooted in a comparison, namely in a comparison between the benefits of the current status quo of membership with those associated with an alternative state of one's country being outside the EU (…) When we understand support and scepticism as a comparison between the benefits of the current status quo of membership and those associated with an alternative state, the Brexit vote and its immediate aftermath become crucially important' (De Vries 2017, 40–42). Opinion polls conducted after the British referendum suggest that public opinions have become more favourable to EU membership in all EU member states including the UK (Bertelsmann Stiftung 2016; Pew Research Center 2017). Other survey data (European Parliament 2018; Eurobarometer 2018; Friedrich-Ebert-Stiftung 2018) show in the same way that support for EU membership has increased significantly since the Brexit referendum (Figure 1).

Moreover, as shown in Figure 2, there is no majority in favour of leaving the European Union ('exit') in any public opinion of the EU27 member states – including Hungary, Poland and Italy – although there are strong criticisms of EU policy-making ('voice').

Research shows that immigration has a strong effect on Euroscepticism among the EU27 public opinions (Krastev 2017). As we will see in the next section, it explains why Eurosceptic political parties seek to promote a discourse focused on the rejection of immigration against the EU. It is considered as a top priority of the political agenda in more than two-thirds of the EU27 member states and it is the main issue that fuels Euroscepticism among public opinions (Figure 3).

But the effect of immigration on the rise of Euroscepticism does not mean that public opinions in the EU27 support an exit from the EU (Jacobs 2018). First, the high tensions among the different components of the UK polity on Brexit have increased the perception of a risk attached to a leave of the EU (De Vries 2017). Second, the fear of the economic and financial consequences has led a majority of public opinions to argue against leaving the EU (Roth, Johnung, and Nowak-Lehmann 2016; Hobolt and Wratil 2015; Hobolt and Leblond 2014). Recent studies (Bergbauer et al. 2019) and opinion surveys show that support for the Eurozone membership stands also very high in the Eurozone, 75% of respondents supporting the single currency, while only 20% being against (Figure 4).

Third, a majority of voters in the EU27 considers that a reduction of migration flows requires European solutions rather than national ones (Clarke, Goodwin, and Whiteley 2017) (Figure 5). One consequence of the refugee crisis of 2015 has been a growing awareness that the problem of border

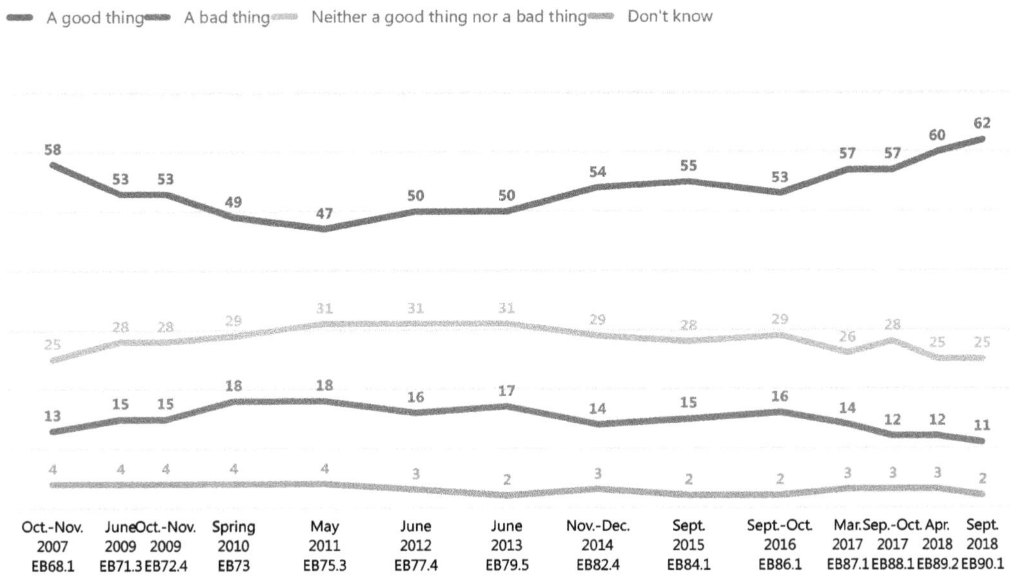

Figure 1. EU28 public opinions and membership to the EU (2007–2018).
Source: Eurobarometer Survey 90, European Parliament, October 2018

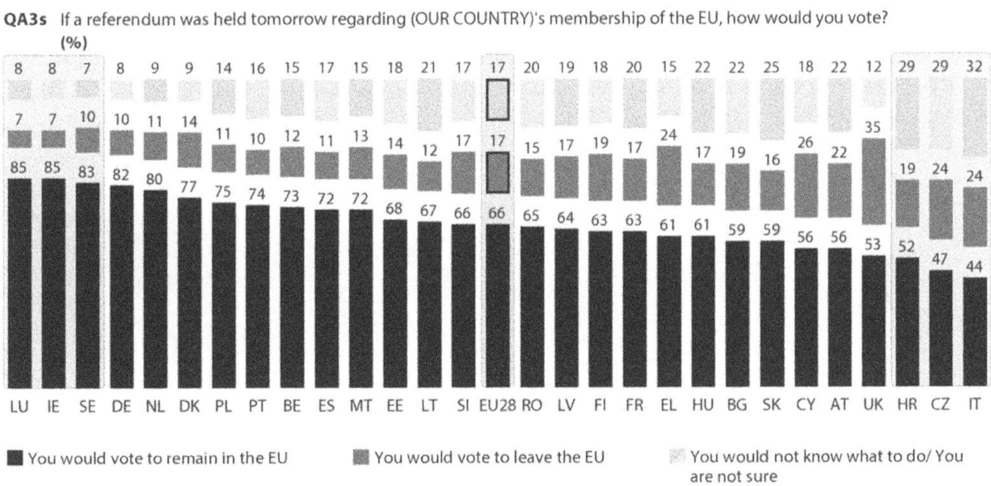

Figure 2. Attitudes towards EU membership at the national level (October 2018).
Source: Eurobarometer Survey 90, European Parliament, October 2018

controls must become a European public good. Figure 5 shows that a majority of Europeans is in favour of a more organised European migration policy.

Three conclusions can be drawn to show that Brexit negotiations favour the cohesiveness of EU27 public opinions towards refusing exit as a legitimate issue and, accordingly, preserving integration. First, public opinions dissociate critics against the EU (especially on immigration), which feeds into Euroscepticism, from any support to exit (Van der Burg et al. 2000). Second, a majority of EU27 public opinions make a rational calculation that they are benefitting more from being inside the EU and the Eurozone than outside. Third, strong domestic tensions about Brexit in the UK have been a counter-incentive for public opinions to support a process of exit in their own country.

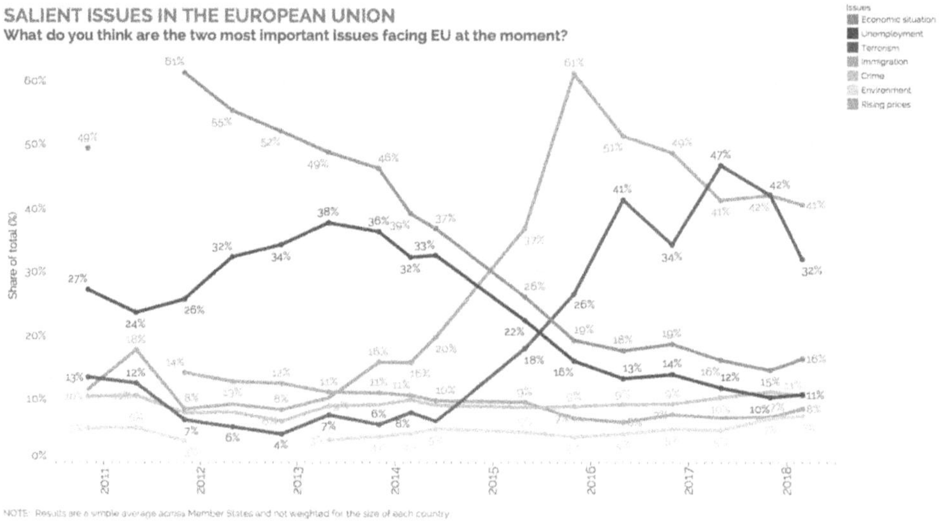

Figure 3. Salient issues at EU level.
Source: Standard Eurobarometer surveys

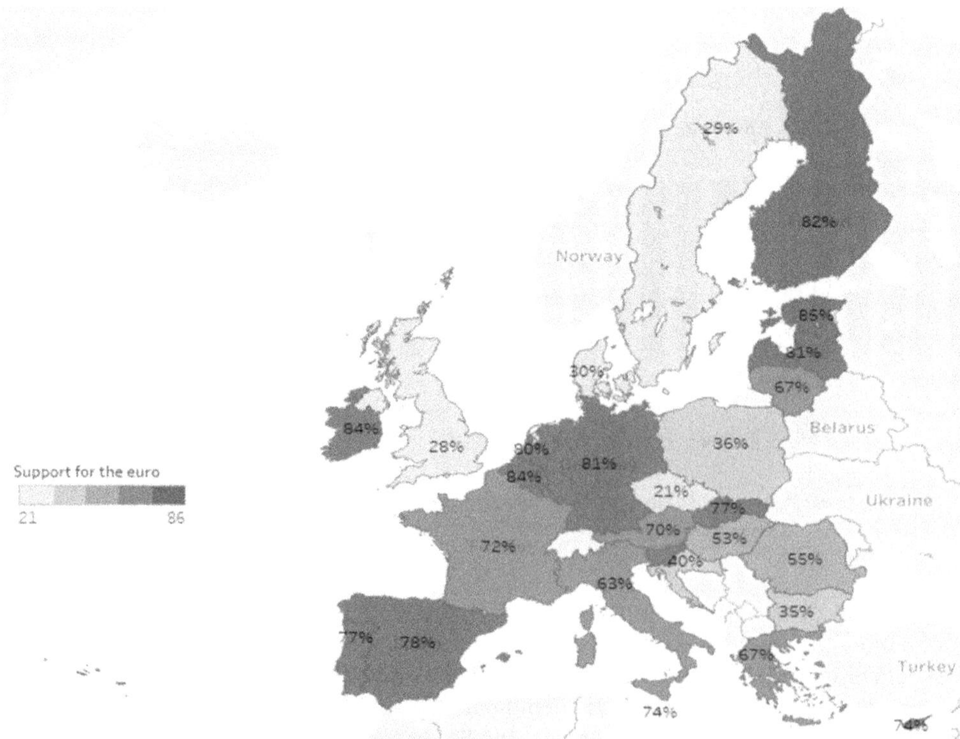

Figure 4. Support for the Economic Monetary Union and the euro in EU Member states (November 2018).
Source: Standard Eurobarometer Survey (EB 90), November 2018

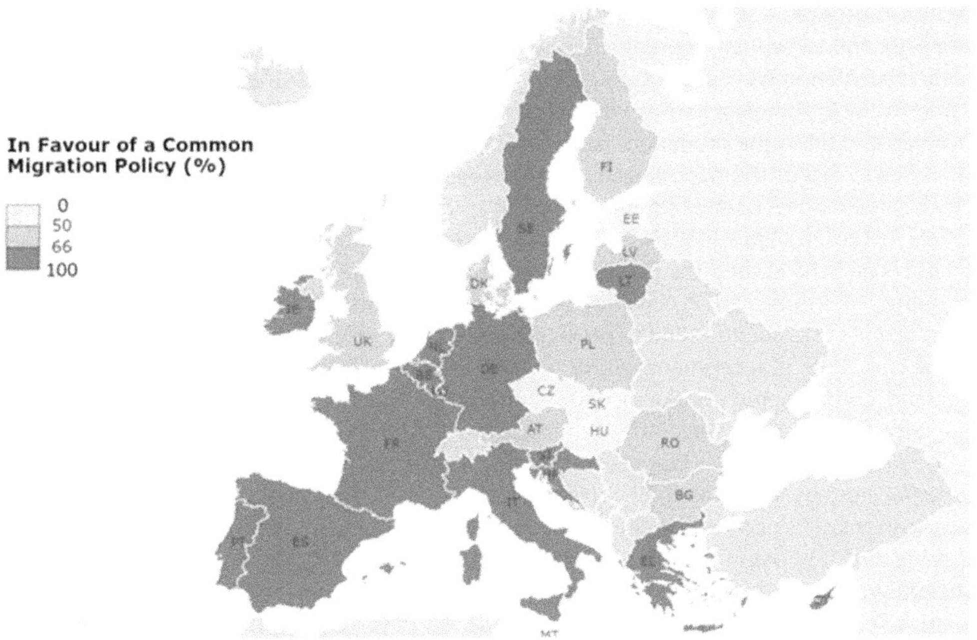

Figure 5. Europeans in favour of a common migration policy.
Source: Eurobarometer Standard 89 Spring 2018

The changing effect of Brexit on Eurosceptic political parties

In this section, we first analyse how Eurosceptic political parties in the EU27 were tempted to use Brexit as an instrumental strategy to claim for drastic changes in the EU policy agenda. Second, we identify the reasons why Eurosceptic parties rapidly changed their strategy in abandoning the use of Brexit in their political programmes.

The analysis starts with Brexit as an instrumental strategy for Eurosceptic parties (Kitchelt 2018). In several EU27 member states, such as the Netherlands and Czech Republic, new neologisms like 'Nexit' and 'Czexit' appeared in the aftermath of the British referendum of June 2016. During the 2017 campaign for the presidential election in France, far-right leader Marine Le Pen mentioned Brexit to 'regain France's national sovereignty in a Europe of independent nations at the service of its peoples' (Le Pen 2017). It directly echoed the slogan of Brexiteers in the UK to 'take back control'. Two reasons explain the initial temptation of Eurosceptic parties to use Brexit as an instrumental strategy. First, the success of the Brexiteers in the referendum convinced Eurosceptic parties that EU integration was not an irreversible process and that it was possible to stop it (Webber 2019a). Imitating Nigel Farage's neo-sovereignist narrative was perceived as a means to break the 'rhetoric of impossibilism' (Krastev, quoted in Dujin 2019). Second, the British referendum appeared in a context where several crises had succeeded in the EU. The financial and economic crisis had shown how vulnerable the Eurozone was and the refugee crisis had highlighted the weaknesses of the EU in controlling its external borders. In such a context, Eurosceptic parties tried to exploit Brexit discursively to stress more generally the vulnerabilities of the EU and maximize their electoral benefits (Chopin 2017).

Eurosceptic parties in the EU27 also used Brexit as an instrumental strategy to make EU membership conditional on substantial reforms of the EU agenda. Such a strategy was developed during the 2017 presidential campaign by the French left-wing Eurosceptic party La France Insoumise. The party leader, Jean-Luc Mélenchon, denounced the 'submissiveness' of France to the EU and asked for a radical reform of the European treaties in order to 'free' the European peoples from the 'austerity' policies imposed by the Economic and Monetary Union. In case such a strategy failed, Jean-Luc

Mélenchon suggested a 'B Plan' for France consisting in withdrawing from the European treaties (Drake 2018). The same instrumental strategy was used by other Eurosceptic political parties in the EU27, such as Alternative für Deutschland in Germany (Conrad, Brunet-Jailly, and Hallgrimsdottir 2019) and Fidesz in Hungary, in their claim for a radical change in the EU policymaking (Orbàn 2018).

However, and this is the prominent factor of our analysis, Eurosceptic parties in the EU27 changed the reference to exit as the negotiation talks between the EU and UK progressed. The U-turn in the strategy of the French Rassemblement National is an enlightening illustration of this evolution. After her failure at the 2017 presidential election, party leader Marine Le Pen no longer defended the project of leaving the EU and the Eurozone, and refocussed her criticisms about the EU on the issue of immigration (Perrineau 2017). Similarly, Alternative für Deutschland, created in 2013 as a response to the Eurozone crisis, abandoned the project that Germany should leave the Eurozone and return to the Deutsche Mark (Bertelsmann Stiftung 2017; Paterson 2018). Henceforth, Alternative für Deutschland concentrated its Eurosceptic strategy on the negative consequences of the 2015 refugee crisis for Germany (Lees 2018; Grimm 2015).

Three reasons explain that Eurosceptic parties in the EU27 decided to stop using Brexit as an instrumental strategy. First, the difficulties resulting from the negotiations between the EU and the 27 but also in the UK's domestic politics convinced Eurosceptic parties, in parallel to public opinions, that leaving the EU implies too high political costs (Schnapper 2019). Second, Brexit negotiation talks convinced Eurosceptic parties that the Single Market has been on the long term in the interest of their voters. In the EU27 Eurosceptic parties, there has never been a majority ready to accept the economic risks of leaving the EU's internal market or the Euro (UK in a Changing Europe, 2018). Third, the immigration issue constituted – more than Brexit – the core of the political supply of the Eurosceptic parties, insofar as this issue supports political discourses that differentiate and divide (Chopin et al. 2019).

For the three reasons, Eurosceptic parties in the EU27 accepted that it was better to criticize the EU from inside rather than outside. Brexit reinforced the cohesiveness of European integration in the sense that it paradoxically helped Eurosceptic parties among the EU27 to accept EU membership as an unavoidable component of national economy and politics.

Conclusion

As an unprecedented phenomenon, Brexit pushes EU studies to look more in-depth into the new debate on disintegration appearing in the scholarly literature of the 2010s under the effects of several crises. The main conclusion of this article is that Brexit has contributed to a reinforcement of the cohesiveness of the EU27 to preserve EU integration. Brexit has opened not just one game between states but several games in parallel, equivalent to what George Tsebelis identified as 'nested games' (Tsebelis 1991). In focusing on the situation of the EU27 member states, we draw three leading conclusions from the effects of Brexit on governments, public opinions and Eurosceptic parties. First, mainstream neofunctionalist theory of the EU, which assumes that crises are a crucial vector to stimulate integration, remains valid when we look at the effects of Brexit on EU27 member states (Saurugger 2013). Brexit has not called into question the interdependencies that exist and have developed over the years between the various EU member states. In particular, trade and monetary interdependencies act as a guarantee against EU disintegration. They create common interests on issues such as the single market, the free movement of people and the EU budget that go against the extension of Brexit. Second, government cohesiveness and popular cohesiveness follow a similar path in the preservation of EU integration, as they could have been asymmetric. Governments, public opinions and Eurosceptic parties, although tempted to echo the scenario of Brexit, all chose cohesiveness consisting in preserving integration. Third, the contextual variable of the negotiation talks, highly uncertain between the UK and the EU but more again inside the UK institutions, catalyses the cohesiveness of the EU27. Causes are therefore multiple and must not be mixed up.

Brexit confirms that disintegration can be considered as a relevant concept to describe the loss of a member state from the EU. Disintegration is defined as a full re-nationalization for a member state of its polity, politics and policies. But this article shows that the UK preference for such a re-nationalization has favoured a reverse effect on the EU27 member states. Through their reactions to Brexit negotiation talks, governments, public opinions but also Eurosceptic parties of the EU27 showed their commitment to preserve EU memberstateness and EU integration despite strong critics and even strong trends towards Euroscepticism.

Acknowledgments

The authors would like to thank Agnès Collier-Alexandre, Pauline Schnapper, Douglas Webber and two anonymous referees for their useful comments

Disclosure statement

No potential conflict of interest was reported by the authors.

References

Bergbauer, S., J. F. Jamet, E. Persson, and N. H. Eric 2019. "The Reputation of the Euro and the ECB: Interlinked Od Disconnected?" Paper presented to the 2019 EUSA conference in Denver.

Bertelsmann Stiftung. 2016. "Brexit Has Raised Support for the European Union." November 21.

Bertelsmann Stiftung. 2017. "A Source of Stability? German and European Public Opinion in Times of Political Polarisation." 2017/3.

Börzel, T. A. 2005. "Mind the Gap! European Integration between Level and Scope." *Journal of European Public Policy* 12 (2): 217–236. doi:10.1080/13501760500043860.

Braun, M. 2018. "A Swedish View on Brexit. An Ally Lost." Kassim and Usherwood, 56–58.

Brunazzo, M., and V. Dela Salla. 2018. "Brexit: The Perspective from Italy." Kassim and Usherwood, 35–37.

Bulmer, S., and C. Lequesne, eds. 2013. *The Member States of the European Union*. Oxford: Oxford University Press.

Chopin, T. 2017. "Defending Europe to Defend Real Sovereignty." *Policy Paper* 194, Jacques Delors Institute/Robert Schuman Foundation, April 25.

Chopin, T., N. Fraccaroli, N. Hernborg, and J. F. Jamet. 2019. "The Battle for Europe's Future." *LSE Blog Brexit*, May 21.

Clarke, H. D., M. Goodwin, and P. Whiteley. 2017. *Brexit! Why Britain Voted to Leave the European Union*. Cambridge: Cambridge University Press.

Conceição-Heidt, E., and S. Meunier. 2014. "Speaking with a Single Voice: Internal Cohesiveness and External Effectiveness of the EU in Global Governance." *Journal of European Public Policy* 21 (7): 961–979. doi:10.1080/13501763.2014.913219.

Conrad, M., E. Brunet-Jailly, and H. Hallgrimsdottir. 2019. "Reclaiming the Idea of Europe? Brexit, Soft Euroscepticism and EU Constestation in Germany." Paper presented for the panel "Pro-European backlash? Responses to Euroscepticism and Right-Wing Populism in Europe" at the 2019 EUSA Conference in Denver.

Csehi, R. L. 2018. "Brexit and Hungary: Advancing the Orban Government's Euro-Realist and Anti-Immigration Political Agenda." Kassim and Usherwood, 47–49.

Dagnis Jensen, M., and J. Dahl Kelstrup. 2018. "Denmark's Developing Position on Brexit." Kassim and Usherwood, 53–55.

De Vries, C. E. 2017. "Benchmarking Brexit: How the Bristish Decision to Leave Shapes EU Public Opinion." *Journal of Common Market Studies* 55: 38–53. Annual Review. doi:10.1111/jcms.12579.

De Vries, C. E., and E. E. Edwards. 2009. "Taking Europe to Its Extremes: Extremist Parties and Public Euroscepticism." *Party Politics* 15 (1): 5–28. doi:10.1177/1354068808097889.

Drake, H. 2018. "France, Britain and Brexit." In *Brexit and Beyond. Rethinking the Futures of Europe'*, edited by B. Martill and U. Staiger, 97–104. London: UCL Press.

Dujin, A. 2019. "L'Europe face au spectre de la guerre culturelle." *Le Monde*, January 18.

DutchNews.nl. 2018. "Hard Brexit Would Cost the Dutch Government €2.3 Bn over Two Years." December 10.

Eurobarometer Survey 90. 2018. "European Parliament." October.

European Parliament. 2018. "Brexit Effect: Public Opinion Survey Shows that EU Is More Appreciated than Ever." (EP press release on Eurobarometer data).

Evans, G., and A. Menon. 2019. *Brexit and British Politics*. Cambridge: Polity.

Festinger, L. 1950. "Informal Social Communication." *Psychological Review* 57 (5): 271–282. doi:10.1037/h0056932.

Financial Times. 2018. "Britons Living in EU Urged to Act to Guarantee Brexit Rights." November 4.
Friedrich-Ebert-Stiftung. 2018. "What Holds Europe Together? the EU in the Wake of Brexit."
Full Fact. 2019. "EU Immigration to the UK." Accessed 26 June 2019. https://fullfact.org/immigration/eu-migration-and-uk/
Gabel, M. J. 1998. *Interests and Integration: Market Liberalization, Public Opinion and European Union*. Ann Arbor: University of Michigan Press.
Grimm, R. 2015. "The Rise of the German Eurosceptic Party Alternative Für Deutschland, between Ordoliberal Critique and Popular Anxiety." *International Political Science Review* 36 (3): 265–278. doi:10.1177/0192512115575384.
Heidbreder, E. G. 2018. "Negotiating Brexit: The View from Germany." Kassim and Usherwood, 13–16.
Hirschmann, A. 1970. *Exit, Voice and Loyalty. Responses to Decline in Firms, Organizations and States*. Cambridge: Harvard University Press.
Hobolt, S. B., and P. Leblond. 2014. "Economic Insecurity and Public Support for the Euro: Before and during the Financial Crisis." In *Mass Politics in Tough Times: Opinions, Votes and Protest in the Great Recession*, edited by N. Bermeo and L. M. Bartels, 128–147. Oxford/New York: Oxford University Press.
Hobolt, S. B., and C. Wratil. 2015. "Public Opinion and the Crisis: The Dynamics Support for the Euro." *Journal of European Public Policy* 22 (2): 238–256. doi:10.1080/13501763.2014.994022.
Hooghe, L., and G. Marks. 2005. "Calculation, Community and Cues: Public Opinion on European Integration." *European Union Politics* 6 (4): 419–443. doi:10.1177/1465116505057816.
Jacobs, F. B. 2018. *The EU after Brexit. Institutional and Policy Implications*. Basingstoke: Palgrave Macmillan.
Kaniok, P. 2018. "Brexit as a Way Out from the Problematic Past." Kassim and Usherwood. 44–46.
Kassim, H., and S. Usherwood, eds. 2018. *Negotiating Brexit. What Do the UK's Negotiating Partners Want?* London: UK in a Changing Europe Programme.
Kitschelt, H. P. (in collaboration with A.J. McGann) 2016. "The Contemporary Radical Right: An Interpretative and Explanatory Framework." In *The Populist Radical Right: A Reader*, edited by C. Mudde, 352–385. London: Routledge.
Krastev, I. 2017. *After Europe*. Philadelphia: Penn Press.
Krotz, U., and J. Schild. 2018. "Back to the Future? Franco-German Bilateralism in Europe's Post-Brexit Union." *Journal of European Public Policy* 25 (8): 1174–1193. doi:10.1080/13501763.2018.1467951.
Laffan, B. 2018. "Negotiating Brexit. Irish Approaches and Dynamics."
Le Pen, M. 2017. "Engagements présidentiels Marine 2017." http://www.marine2017.fr/programme/
Lecomte, C. 2010. *Understanding Euroscepticism*. Basingstoke: Palgrave Macmillan.
Lees, C. 2018. "The 'Alternative for Germany: The Rise of Right-Wing Populism at the Heart of Europe." *Politics* 38 (3): 295–310. doi:10.1177/0263395718777718.
Leuffen, D., B. Rittberger, and F. Schimmelfennig. 2013. *Differentiated Integration. Explaining Variation in the European Union*. Basingstoke: Palgrave Macmillan.
Martill, B., and U. Staiger, eds. 2018. *Brexit and Beyond. Rethinking the Futures of Europe*. London: UCL.
May, T. 2017. "Lancaster House Speech." January 17. Accessed 26 June 2019. https://www.independent.ie/business/brexit/theresa-mays-brexit-speech-in-full-35374214.html
Mc Laren, L. M. 2002. "Public Support for the European Union: Cost/Benefit Analysis or Perceived Cultural Threat?" *Journal of Politics* 64 (2): 551–566. doi:10.1111/1468-2508.00139.
Orbàn, V. 2018. "Speech." June 16.
Patel, K. K. 2018. "Something New under the Sun? the Lessons of Algeria and Greenland." In *Brexit and Beyond. Rethinking the Futures of Europe*, edited by B. Martill and U. Staiger, 114–120. London: UCL Press.
Paterson, W. E. 2018. "Germany and the Brexit Crisis." In *Brexit and Beyond. Rethinking the Futures of Europe*, edited by B. Martill and U. Staiger, 88–96. London: UCL Press.
Perrineau, P., ed. 2017. *Le vote disruptif. Les élections présidentielle et législatives de 2017*. Paris: Presses de Sciences Po.
Pew Research Center. 2017. "Post-Brexit, Europeans More Favorable Towards EU." June.
Roth, F., L. Johnung, and D. F. Nowak-Lehmann. 2016. "Crisis and Public Support for the Euro, 1990–2014." *Journal of Common Market Studies* 54 (4): 944–960. doi:10.1111/jcms.12338.
Saurugger, S. 2013. *Theoretical Approaches to European Integration*. Basingstoke: Palgrave Macmillan.
Schnapper, P. 2019. "Le Brexit. Chaos politique au Royaume-Uni." *Commentaire*, 166.
Styczynska, N. 2018. "The Polish Perception of Brexit." Kassim and Usherwood, 41–43.
Szczerbiak, A., and P. Taggart, eds. 2008. *Opposing Europe? the Comparative Party Politics of Euroscepticism*. Oxford: Oxford University Press.
The UK in a Changing Europe. 2018. "Cost of No Deal Revisited." September 3.
Toute l'Europe. 2019. "Tous les évènements depuis le référendum." June 20.
Tsebelis, G. 1991. *Nested Games. Rational Choice in Comparative Politics*. Berkeley: University of California Press.
Turner, E., and S. Green. 2017. *Priorities, Sensitivities, Anxieties: German and Central European Perceptions of Brexit*. Birmingham: Aston Centre for Europe.
UK Government. 2018. "UK-Dutch Trade Relationships Goes from Strength to Strength." November 24.
Van der Brug, W., M. Fennema, and J. Tillie. 2000. "Anti-immigrant Parties in Europe: Ideological or Protest Vote?." *In European Journal of Political Research* 37 (1): 77–102. doi:10.1111/ejpr.2000.37.issue-1.

Vilpisauskas, R. 2018. "Lithuania and Brexit: Security, Money and Citizens." Kassim and Usherwood, 50–52.

Vollaard, H. 2014. "Explaining European Disintegration." *Journal of Common Market Studies* 52 (5): 1142–1159. doi:10.1111/jcms.12132.

Vollaard, H. 2018. *European Disintegration. A Search for Explanations*. Basingstoke: Palgrave Macmillan.

Webber, D. 2014. "How Likely Is It that the European Union Will Disintegrate? A Critical Analysis of Competing Theoretical Perspectives." *European Journal of International Relations* 20 (2): 341–365. doi:10.1177/1354066112461286.

Webber, D. 2019a. *European Disintegration? the Politics of Crisis in the European Union*. Basingstoke: Palgrave Macmillan.

Webber, D. 2019b. "Trends in European Political (Dis)integration. An Analysis of Postfunctionalist and Other Explanations." *Journal of European Public Policy* 26 (8): 1134–1152. doi:10.1080/13501763.2019.1576760.

Withdrawal Agreement and Political Declaration on the Future of EU – UK relations. 2018. Accessed 26 June 2019. https://www.gov.uk/government/publications/withdrawal-agreement-and-political-declaration

Index

Note: Figures are indicated by *italics*. Tables are indicated by **bold**. Endnotes are indicated by the page number followed by 'n' and the endnote number e.g., 20n1 refers to endnote 1 on page 20.

Abbott, Diane 41, 46
Agnew, J. 110
Alexandre-Collier, Agnès 5
Algeria 119
al Gharbi, M. 15
Allen, D. 15
Anglo-British nationalism 55
Anglosphere 3, 6, 54, 92
anti-austerity project 38
anti-EU MPs 40
Anti-Federalist League 80
anti-immigration 18, 92
antimigrant cultural nationalism 52
Antonucci, L. 12, 14
Ashcroft, M. 12
Atlantic 10, 12
Attlee, Clement 60
austerity 127
Austro-Hungarian Empire 25
authenticity 45
Avril, Emmanuelle 5

BAME MPs: candidate selection 96–8; Constituency Brexit votes **97**; Constituency immigration **98**; data **99**; ethnic minorities **98**; representation and ideological positioning 94–6; safe/marginal seats **97**; substantive representation 98–100
Barnett, Anthony 61
Barnier, Michel 68, 75
Bartolini, Stefano 3
Begum, N. 94
Behr, Rafael 41
Belfast/Good Friday Agreement, 1998 42, 62, 105, 107, 110–13, 115
Bell, Emma 6
Benn, Tony 60
'bespoke' agreement 70, 72
Bhambra, G. K. 14
bilateral tensions 115–16
Black and Asian Minority Ethnic (BAME) 5, 37, 91; *see also* BAME MPs
Blacks for Trump 17
Blair, Tony 60
Blühdorn, I. 11
Bogdanor, V. 111
Bornschier, S. 11
The Break-Up of Britain (Nairn) 4
Brexit: Battle for Britain 36
Brexit debate 35, 38, 39, 43–7, 109, 110
Brexit fiasco 71
Brexit party 85–7; anti-Brexit parties 46–7; EU 17; European elections 45; Nigel Farage 77, 85; political game 85–7; UKIP 16, 43, 59, 87–8
Brexit referendum 2, 4, 9, 11, 14, 23, 26–9, 31, 44, 52, 55, 95, 97, 102, 124
Britain Stronger in Europe campaign 40
British ambivalence 113–14
British disintegration 23, 25, 27–32
British Election Study 37–8
British-Irish Council 115–16
British Nationality Act, 1981 17
British National Party (BNP) 85
British Social Attitudes (Harding) 17
Britons: Forging the Nation (Colley) 4
Brubaker, W. R. 15
Brussels 72–3, 75, 77
Butzlaff, F. 11

Cameron, David 4, 39, 82, 84, 88; Conservative party cleavages 92–4
Canada 70, 72, 75
CDU-CSU/SPD coalition government 122
Cerutti, Furio 26
Checkel, Jeffery 26
Chequers plan 75, 76, 85
Chopin, Thierry 6
Churchill, Winston 59
civic nationalism 52, 61–3
cleavage 1, 2, 12, 14, 16, 18, 25, 38, 81–2, 101, 102, 106; contemporary European debates 83; David Cameron's leadership 92–4; formation 10–11; social and political 6, 10; theory 10, 11; in the West 10
'cliff-edge' 70

Cole, G. D. H. 60
Colley, Linda 4
Committee of Permanent Representatives (COREPER) 121
Commonwealth Immigrants Acts, 1962 and 1968 15
communicative discourse 71, 72, 74, 77
Conceição-Heidt, Eugenia 120
Conservative BAME MPs 5, 91–3, 95–102
Conservative–Liberal Democrat coalition government 56
Conservative Party 5, 6, 17, 53–4, 56, 69, 73–4, 81–3, 88; Alexandre-Collier, Agnès 5; BAME MPs 91, 92, 100–1; Brexit party 86–7; Cameron, David 17, 82; DUP 110; Johnson, Boris 6, 38–9; 2017 election 43, 46–7; 2019 election 42; 2016 EU Council 72; Eurosceptic radicalisation 97; MEPs 86; nativism 56–9; parliamentary attitudes 95; Parliamentary Conservative Party 92; parliamentary nationalism 54–6; pro-Brexit Conservative Party MPs 109; risks 62; Scotland 74; service of neoliberalism 53–4; UKIP voters 84
constraining dissensus 80
Constructive ambiguity 42
contested sovereignties 29–32
coordinative discourse 71
Corbyn, Jeremy 5, 35, 36, 38–41, 43, 47
Corn Laws in 1846 53–4
coronavirus 4–5
COVID-19 pandemic 4, 6
critical juncture 1, 4–5, 10, 27, 80

Daily Mail 30
Datapraxis 37
deindustrialisation 61
democracy 11, 30, 37, 38, 52–5, 58, 59, 61–4, 86, 88, 100
Democratic Unionist Party (DUP) 68–9, 107
de-nationalisation 11, 16
Department for Exiting the EU (DexEU) 68
Deutsch, Karl 25, 27
de Wilde, P. 10–11
discursive institutionalism 42
disintegration 1, 3, 4, 6, 23–32, 119–21, 128, 129
Disraeli, Benjamin 59
Dorling, D. 12, 14
Downing Street Declaration, 1993 111
Dunlop, C. A. 71
Dyson, Kenneth 24

Eatwell, R. 14, 19n1
economic globalisation 9, 54
economic protectionism 53
electoral politics 5, 35–6, 38
Elliott, M. 110
English nationalism 16, 31, 63
Englishness 4, 16, 31
ethnicity 14, 15, 18, 57, 100, 102
EU-27 6, 70, 76–8, 119–24, 128; public opinions 123–7
EU-28: public opinions and membership *125*
EU Act, 2011 29
EU integration 121, 127–9
EU level, salient issues *126*
EU membership 41, 55, 82, 87, 91–3, 101, 108, 110, 111, 121, 124, *125*, 127, 128
EU Member States 4, 60, 109, 111, 122, 124, *126*, 128
EU referendum 2–4, 36, 37, 39, 42, 44, 71, 94, 96, 100–1, 110, 111, 115, 116; Northern Ireland 106–8; UK-EU referendum, Irish border issue 108
Euroagnostics 95
European Convention on Human Rights (ECHR) 111
European Court of Justice (ECJ) 70
European disintegration 22–3, 27, 28, 30–2; *see also* disintegration; nationalism and Brexit 23–7
European integration 2, 3, 6, 22–8, 30–2, 80–3, 87, 88, 92, 120–2, 124, 128
Europeanisation 26, 60
Europhiles 92
Euroscepticism 6, 16, 17, 24–6, 31–2, 51, 60, 78, 81, 82, 92–3, 95, 101, 120, 123–5, 128, 129
Eurosceptic political parties 127–8
Eurozone crisis, 2015 23, 24, 128
Evans, G. 13, 61
Exit, Voice and Loyalty (Hirschman) 123

Falklands War 59–60
Farage, Nigel 77, 81, 84–6, 88–9
First-Past-The-Post system 37, 38, 46
FitzGibbon, J. 26
Forte, G. 59
free movement 15, 17, 39–40, 44, 57, 59, 73–5, 81, 107, 120, 123, 128
frictionless trade 70, 72, 75

Galileo satellite project 75
Gänzle, Stefan 3–4, 25
Garry, J. 93, 107
Ghani, Nus 100
Gifford, Chris 6, 29
Glencross, A. 108
globalization 2, 6, 10–14, 18, 22, 27, 52, 60
Goodhart, David 10, 14
Goodwin, M. J. 14, 19n1, 38
Great Recession 14
The Guardian 56–7

Hadfield, B. 112
Hanretty, C. 97
Hayward, K. 108, 112, 114
Heath, O. 38
Henderson, A. 16, 28
Hirschman, Albert 123
Hochschild, A. R. 10, 13, 14
Hooghe, L. 69, 81

hostile environment policy 56, 57
House of Commons 43, 73, 75, 77, 98, 122
Human Rights Act, 1998 111
humiliation 76, 78n16

immigration 16, 81, 100, 102
Immigration and Social Security Co-ordination (EU Withdrawal) Act 57
Inglehart, R. F. 11
intergovernmental inadequacies 114–15
Internal Market Act, 2020 114–15
'Irish backstop' 122
Irish Citizen's Assembly 55, 57

James, S. 71
Johnson, Boris 4, 6, 32, 39, 46, 52, 54, 63, 73, 82, 87, 105, 114, 115–16
Joint Ministerial Committee (JMC) 115

Katzenstein, Peter 26

Labour In For Britain campaign 40
Labour MPs 36, 40, 46, 55, 61, 62, 77, 91
Labour Party 5, 6, 31, 35–6, 38–42, 52, 53, 94, 96, 108; Brexit debate 43–7; nationalism 59–63
Laski, Harold 60
'Latinos for Trump' 17
Leave.EU 82
Lequesne, Christian 6
Leruth, Ben 3–4, 25, 26
Liberal Democrats 37, 38–9, 86
Libertarian-Authoritarian scale 83
Lisbon Treaty, Article 50 1
Lovenduski, J. 96

Maastricht Treaty 2, 80, 81, 92
Machiavellian conceptualisation 4
Mair, P. 11
'managed surrender' 74
Marks, G. 69, 81
Martill, B. 71
May, Theresa 31, 39, 41, 44–5, 54, 70, 73–7, 85, 87, 93, 102, 113, 122
McCall, C. 113
McDonnell, John 37, 40, 41
McGeever, B. 16
Mckenzie, L. 13
Meehan, E. 111
Menon, A. 45
Metzgar, J. 12
Meunier, Sophie 120, 121
Milne, Seamus 41
Moravscik, Andrew 23
multiculturalism 10, 14, 52, 56, 60, 93
municipal socialism 61
Murphy, Karie 37, 41, 105
Murphy, M. C. 108
muscular liberalism 58

Nairn, Tom 4, 26
'nasty party' 93, 96
nationalism 6, 51–4, 59
nationalist neoliberalism 54
nationalist politics 2, 6, 25–7, 31, 83
nativism 56–9, 63
neofunctionalism 23
neoliberalism 53–4, 59, 61, 62
neo-liberal societies 16
nested games 2–5, 25, 35, 36, 47, 70–1, 77, 81, 92, 94, 101, 128
Norris, P. 11, 96
Northern Ireland 116; and Brexit negotiations 108–10; constitutional settlement 113; EU referendum 106–8
Northern Ireland Act, 1998 112
'Norway minus' 75

Obama, Barack 14, 15
Offe, Claus 23

Parliamentary Conservative Party (PCP) 92, 93, 95, **97**
Parsons, Craig 25
Peel, Robert 53–4
permissive consensus 80
placeism 58–9, 63
polarisation 9, 10, 14–18, 42, 45, 47, 106
policy contestation 25
political cleavage 6, 10, 12, 18, 85
political elites 10, 44, 52, 113
political parties 1, 9, 11, 16, 38, 53, 70, 85, 88, 107, 113, 114, 124, 127–8
political polarisation 9, 10, 14–18
politicization 24, 69, 80–3
'politics of place' 61
populism 3, 11, 12, 14, 44, 52, 59, 61, 63, 82
populist parties 11
Portes, J. 59
Powell, Enoch 55, 56
pragmatism 92–3
Putnam, Robert 69, 70, 77, 81

quadruple crisis, 2010 23, 24

'racialised economics' 18
racism 14–18, 57, 100; and political polarisation 14–18
Radaelli, C. M. 71
radicalization 5, 13, 39, 59, 82, 85, 87, 88, 95, 96
recaptured sovereignty 105
Rees-Mogg, Jacob 75
Reif, K. 2, 3
reluctant nationalists 51
Revolutionary Communist party 86
R (Miller) v. Secretary for Exiting the European Union 30, 55
The Road to Somewhere (Goodhart) 10
Robbins, Oliver 68
Rosamond, Ben 3

Salzburg EU summit, 2018 76
Savage, M. 13
Schengen Agreement 24, 78
Schimmelfennig, Frank 25, 70
Schmidt, Vivien 5, 71, 77
Schmitt, H. 2, 3
Schnapper, Pauline 5
Schulz-Forberg, H. 24
Scotland Act, 1998 75, 76
Scotland's Place in Europe 73
Scottish Constitutional Convention 63
Scottish National Party (SNP) 28, 29, 44
Scottish Parliament, 2011 28
Second World War 15, 51
Sides, J. 18
Social Democratic Party 40
social division 9–14
Staiger, U. 71
Standing, G. 13
Starmer, Keir 6
Startin, N. 26
Stråth, B. 24
Suez crisis, 1956 4
Swales, K. 12
Szczerbiak, A. 81

Taggart, P. 81
Take Back Control theme 72
Taylor, Paul 23, 27, 74
technocrat-populist trap 23
Tesler, M. 18
Thornberry, Emily 40, 41
Todd, J. 111
Tomlinson, S. 12, 14
Tory Party 87–8
Traditional Unionist Voice (TUV) party 107
transient terraces 37
Treaty of Lisbon, 2009 119
Trenz, Hans-Jörg 24, 31
triple effacement 28
Trondal, Jarle 3–4, 25
Tsebelis, G. 2, 5, 81, 94, 100–1
two-level game theory 2, 5, 29, 69–71, 73, 77, 81

UK-EU referendum 108
UK General Elections, 2017 and 2019 28
UK Independence party (UKIP) 5, 16, 17, 31, 37–9, 44–5, 52, 59, 80, 81, 86–8, 97, 123; British politics 83–5; first-order game 81–3
UK Internal Market Act 114
unleashing demons 5

Vavreck, L. 18
Virdee, S. 16
Vivyan, N. 97
Vollaard, Hans 3
Vote Leave 82

Wales Act, 2017 29
Walley, C. J. 13
Webber, Douglas 3, 23, 24, 120
Wellings, Ben 6
Westminster model 1–2, 29–32, 44, 52, 54–8, 60, 63, 71, 72, 74, 76, 86–8, 109, 111–13
Whiteley, Paul 86
Williams, Raymond 61
Wilson, Harold 42

xenophobic movement 9, 58–9, 92

YouGov 114

Zielonka, Jan 23
Zürn, M. 10–11

For Product Safety Concerns and Information please contact our EU representative GPSR@taylorandfrancis.com
Taylor & Francis Verlag GmbH, Kaufingerstraße 24, 80331 München, Germany

www.ingramcontent.com/pod-product-compliance
Ingram Content Group UK Ltd.
Pitfield, Milton Keynes, MK11 3LW, UK
UKHW050054200926
475702UK00019B/2839